"—that ye stand fast in one spirit, with one mind *striving together* for the faith of the gospel". Philippians 1:27

"STRIVING TOGETHER"
IN THE
DIVINE TRUTHS
OF
SCRIPTURE

LESSON LECTURES
BY
REV. J. FRAANJE

Translated
by
Marinus Westrate

CONTENTS

FOREWORD BY THE TRANSLATOR

Eva Corenwijck, a young lady about 15 years old, attended the catechism class taught by Rev. J. Fraanje, who was the minister in the congregation of Barneveld, The Netherlands. He taught from the Hellenbroek catechism book, "Specimens of Divine Truths." These truths caused her deep concern. The effect was such upon her that as she returned to her home after catechism she thought, "If only I could retain all that we have been taught today."

Once, while she was reading the preface of her catechism book her attention was drawn strongly to the part which reads, "Endeavor to retain it [the teaching] in heart and memory, even making notes of it, so as to be able to use them when you need them. Pray therefore unto God for His Spirit, to help you retain what was heard and to make you mindful of it."

These words stayed with her continually until it led her to speak to her parents of her wish to write down as much of the lesson as she could remember.

Her intention was only to be able to review in her later life that which she had learned in her youth.

As soon as the opportunity presented itself she took notes of the lessons taught by Rev. Fraanje until they finished the whole book.

Many times she experienced sadness and tears while she was busy writing them out because she could not remember exactly how the minister had said it. She realized that her shortcomings were a result of her depravity and lack of spiritual knowledge.

No one knew, except her parents and a few friends, that she was making notes of the lessons for it was done merely for the interest she had in the teachings. Even in those years the minister did not know about it.

There came a time about 15 years later when her friends encouraged her to arrange for printing them. She never had expected that these writings with her limited grammar education would ever come in print. But, Rev. Fraanje, after reading them consented to have these writings printed. The contents agreed perfectly with what he had taught them.

Since she had written out these notes as she recalled them, it was necessary to rewrite them and in many instances to put them in plainer language.

Fifteen years after the lessons had been taught verbally they were printed to be used as God would bless them.

What is so remarkable is the providential leading of God in using this young lady to preserve the pure truth for the youth of the church and those who are able and who desire to read the book in the Holland language.

It is a wonderful book when we consider that Rev. Fraanje never attended a formal school, yet had deep insight in God's Word. He had the ability to proclaim the doctrines purely and soundly. He holds the teachings of the Triune God as in the twelve Articles of Faith. He could in faith say, "I believe in God the Father, the almighty Maker of heaven and earth." He knew with assurance that God was his Creator, his Judge and Father.

His humble way of speaking to the children in deep concern for their souls is always mingled with the Word of God as he proceeds through the lessons.

It is characteristic of one in whom the faculty of faith has been implanted to search for spiritual knowledge. We hope Rev. Fraanje's teaching may be a blessing to such searchers and strivers for the truth.

This book is the result of a translation of the lessons of his book "Notes out of the catechism classes" from the Holland language into the English language.

God works in mysterious ways His wonders to perform. In the case of this book, He did not choose to use an expert in either the Dutch or English language. The reason for this is best known to Him. Certain events and circumstances in my life and accomplishments performed are irrefutable evidences of God's direction to bring about His purpose. When viewed in perspective they consolidate themselves into one objective, the translation of the book authored by Rev. Fraanje.

It is our ardent desire that all of our youth and adults also *may have the precious experience of reading the explanation of the Hellenbroek Catechism book written by this man of God.*

We trust the purpose for this book's existence will be honor to God alone from those of us who have been blessed and from those who may yet receive a blessing.

I am grateful for the inspiration given by Rev. Lamain, for the editing by Mrs. Abe DeBruyn, for the loan of reference books by Mr. Joe Winters, for the various and sundry assistance given by Mrs. Anthony Westrate and many other friends. I am especially thankful for the patience, encouragment and loving consideration given me during my involvement with this work by my dear wife and true helpmeet, Helen Ruth Westrate.

Marinus Westrate

PREFACE

Everyone living on earth has a certain work he must accomplish. This holds true also in the church militant. The Holy Scripture speaks of marksmen who aim at a target with bow and arrows. So also might this written material center in to its purpose regardless of the circumstances and the persons who put forth effort in this work. (I am speaking now only in regards to man, because God's purposes are never brought about by chance or happenstance. They are accomplished according to His Will.)

I had never in the least ever thought about putting Hellenbroek lessons into writing. Now that it has happened, through Divine Providence, I hope that all human involvement in it be set aside. I do not mean to the extent we are used as means in God's hand, but to the extent that attention is brought to ourselves.

The reader will notice it is not a scholarly undertaking. It is merely some simple explanations made while teaching the catechism to boys and girls.

There are many precious writings authored by our forefathers which we continually recommend to young and old in the churches for profitable reading. Though I recognize my weakness and foolishness, I hope, that God in Christ, through the precious

Holy Spirit, will bestow His blessing on this writing, and, through grace, to be one of those "marksmen with bow and arrow", (being, in this, a secondary cause) having as the object of our intentions that of which we read in Psalm 111:3, "His work is honourable and glorious; His righteousness endureth forever."

The difficulty now is to give honor to the God of that work and praise for His willingness to do it.

I have been taught, through a personal experience, that God, in the solitude of eternity, has the desire to glorify His own work and to save His church; both in and through Christ.

At a certain time in my life God opened my understanding to two matters; His justice, and, my guilt. I had brought about my own guilt; it being justly imputed unto me by my relationship in Adam, and my own sins which brought shame upon His holy justice and virtues.

When I admitted to the guilt of this, God struck such a grievous wound in my heart that nothing could possibly heal it. I had brought His wrath upon me and now my conscience became His holy sword.

At that time I was no longer able to carry my guilt. Furthermore, I did not know Christ. My guilt and the sword of God's justice was descending upon me. I had sinned and now it meant death.

O, the submission under the sword of His justice. Recognizing, approving and being totally convinced of God's excellence! It was at that point, thru God working in me, that I might make Him my choice. God had not to relinquish one virtue and though I had offended them all I had a perfect love for them.

Then, I saw this concerning me; the smoke of Sodom went up as the smoke of a furnace; I lay there consumed. I shall never forget it. My sins had not been mere deficiencies. They were things I had committed.

I had made onslaughts against God's crown and justice. O, it is a terrifying experience to discover one's lost condition, and to lay there in it, having been severed from one's life and existence.

When I had sunken, God did something miraculous. He revealed His Son unto me and gave me life in Christ. Christ had sustained God's virtues and kept His laws holily and perfectly. He took upon Himself my sins and guilt as though they were His own, not in that He had committed them, but He appropriated them as surety, just as though they were His very own. He went on through with His work of Mediator without ceasing. I was aware then that God the Father applied these to my own soul in forgiveness, conciliation, cleansing and obliterating of my sins. Now I stood before Him so clean and undefiled, so holy, white and without stain. Snow could not be whiter. He would remember my sins no more because He had cast them in the sea of eternal forgetfulness.

He gave me a right of existance in His Son; to live and not perish; instead of death, inheritance in eternal life.

It was then that the Holy Spirit came, not only with convincing and uncovering work in my heart but with an assuring and sealing work. He came to live in me as in a temple prepared by God for Him.

O, here I can make a beginning but not bring to an ending. Eternity will enlighten me, who am less than the least of all saints, in the way of communion with a Triune God, amidst the great and holy multitude of angels and redeemed creatures.

Oh, now I am so poor; I know nothing waiting for that precious Jesus. He is with the Father interceding for me, and, will be in me, being what He is and has been for me. This is because He lives not only in me but also for me. Oh, would that I be for Him, what I have become through Him and that eternally!

Alas, how dreadful is the misery in heart and home! Oh, people, young and old, how deeply we have sunken. The way of a believing experience is seldom heard anymore. We contend about various points of doctrine without having the experience of sensing the awful guilt that is upon us. There is much sighing in the world in opposition to one another. Oh, may there be a sighing in behalf of one another.

I must say, though, (I am not ashamed to speak of it) there has been a sighing in my prayers not only for Christians and heathens but especially for the awfully back-slidden Jews. Only a short time ago my soul, filled with tears, was touched in its wrestling, whereupon I called out, "Oh, God, has the last of the elect been removed from amongst the Jews? Have you cast those remaining completely over to themselves? Oh, Lord my King, I implore Thee for Thy Own Sake".

Permit me to say this without seeming

presumptious, I do not mean to imply this to be a prophesy. It had become a daily matter of concern at prayer time and, then, I began to think,"I had better cease praying for those Jews; it is hopeless anyhow."But, then, the Lord spoke saying, "Is anything too hard for the Lord?"

In this my soul laid hold on courage. God knows His time, and how many or how few there shall then be. He knows.

I hope that God will bless these feeble words in His troubled church to its comfort and revival; that He will bestow blessings upon this book bringing about conversion in persons young and old. I still languish upon this earth, but the Most High glorifies Himself in His own work.

This is the wish of your unworthy servant in Christ.

Barneveld, The Netherlands   J. Fraanje
August, 1936

NOTES OUT OF THE CATECHISM CLASSES OF REV. J. FRAANJE

Using The Catechism Book
SPECIMENS OF DIVINE TRUTHS
by
REV. A. HELLENBROEK

Lesson 1   Concerning the Knowledge of God and of the Holy Scripture.

Before answering the questions you have memorized of the first lesson today, I would have you tell me who composed this little book?

Answer: "Rev. Hellenbroek."

Exactly, Rev. Abraham Hellenbroek. And who knows in which place this man served as minister and approximately what year was he born?

Answer: "He was born in 1658 and was a minister in the Rotterdam Congregation".

You remembered that well, but before we begin our lesson, I would ask one more question. Rev. Hellenbroek entitles his question book "A Specimen Of Divine Truths." Where would he have obtained these truths?

You know gold is mined from the ground and some pearls are obtained from the sea. Where would this man have found these Divine Truths? Naturally, not in the sea or in the ground; for only material and perishable things come from such places. From where then? Out of his heart? No,

1

because since our first sin in Paradise, only lies come out of our hearts.

He has, through the guidance of the Holy Ghost taken these Divine Truths out of God's Word and arranged them in the form of questions and answers so that you children will be able to easily understand and learn them by heart, thus remembering them all your life. The lessons that you learn, from which you recite the questions and answers, are based on God's Word and so are as surely the truth as if the Lord had caused them to be written to us. That is why he calls it Divine Truths. For if they were merely ideas of Rev. Hellenbroek that were put in writing, they would have been human truths.

The first question that he has in his little book is:

From what source do we know that there is a God?

Answer: from nature and the Holy Scripture!

Immediately after this answer he asks further: Of how many kinds is the knowledge of God from nature?
Answer: Of two kinds:

(1) An internal or innate.

(2) An external or acquired knowledge.

The knowledge of God from nature is:

Internally innate and externally acquired.

Which knowledge do you think all men have of the two here mentioned? If you had learned your lesson well and attentively read the answers, it would not be necessary to think long about this question. Hellenbroek says it right to the point in the third answer: The internal or innate knowledge is the knowledge that all persons have by nature, inborn in their hearts. He proves this from Romans 1:19 where Paul, in speaking of the heathens who do not know God as the true God, says "Because that which may be known of God is manifest in them, for God hath showed it unto them." By that he means: even though the blind

2

heathen do not know and serve the Lord as the true God, nevertheless, they believe that there is a God and their conscience accuses them when they have done wrong. They serve all sorts of idols because they know there is a God. They will, therefore, be without excuse as he says in verse 21, "Because that, when they knew God, they glorified Him not as God, neither were thankful but became vain in their imaginations, and their foolish heart was darkened".

Now Hellenbroek asks, is it true, that all men have an inborn knowledge that there is a God? There are many fools in the world that say in their heart as well with their mouth, "There is no God". Yes, says he, it still is true. It is rather a desire than an actual belief that there is no God.

All men have a conscience whether they want to know it or not. Their conscience tells them that there is a God.

Conscience actually means man's knowledge or awareness, that is to say, it is man's awareness of the law of God.

We can observe that a conscience can be in various conditions. So we shall distinguish them as follows:

1. A disturbed conscience; this we see in King Herod after he had beheaded John the Baptist.
2. A reconciled conscience. David had this after he repented and had received forgiveness of his great sin.
3. An erring conscience, such (taking our examples from God's Word) the Athenians had in serving all the strange gods.
4. There is also a hardened conscience. Sometimes men call this unconscionable or indifferent to right or wrong. It is then that the conscience does its work no more. Now, it it true, there are many persons who act as if they have no conscience or never had any. There are many parents that never talk to their children about God or the Bible. These children grow up as if there is no God. But even though these people do not want to know that there is a

3

God and they pay no attention to their conscience, is there therefore no God? And do they not still have a conscience that accuses them?

It would be foolish to say there is no God just because some people do not believe it. Isn't that so?

Every person certainly does have a conscience even though they wished they didn't have one. But do you know what is so sad? That many persons have as it were closed their conscience by their sins.

Paul said it in I Timothy 4:2, "Having their conscience seared with a hot iron."

I shall use an example to show you that these people do have a conscience even though it does not accuse them anymore. For example, I have ten fingers on my two hands which I can use to do my work. But I sprain one of my fingers in an accident so badly that I can do nothing with it; this finger remains stiff and numb. Even if I can no longer use that finger, because of the accident, can I therefore say that I never had that finger? Surely, no one would believe that. So it is with the conscience.

All men have, by means of their conscience, a consciousness (inner knowledge) that there is a God. We are informed of this in the records of the oldest pagans (heathens). They worshipped all sorts of heathen gods and were afraid of their punishment. For that reason they sacrificed animals and sometimes people to stay in the good graces of the gods they thought existed.

And have you, even though you are still so young, ever noticed that you have a conscience? I am sure, when you did something evil, your heart beat rapidly and something inside you said you should not have done it. I am right, am I not?

Even though no one had seen it, you feel inside that things are not right. The conscience is the strictest police

4

there is. Do you understand how I mean that? For example: When by and by you leave here to go to your homes and on the way you do no wrong; you don't fight, you don't steal, but you walk in good behavior along the way. If a police officer comes to see your father and mother this evening, would you be afraid? Of course not! You would know definitely that you had done no wrong for which you could be punished.

Consider another case; that you stole something on the way. No one knew it. But if a police officer came this evening what do you think would happen? Wouldn't your heart begin to beat fast when you saw him coming? And why? Nobody saw what you had done. The police did not come to arrest you. Your conscience inside you accused that you had done wrong and you feared for punishment. That's what takes place, doesn't it?

I think not one of you will say he has no conscience. And do you think those creatures who go eternally lost have a silent conscience? They would wish it, for then Hell would still be bearable. But even though they had here a conscience seared shut as with a hot iron to the extent it never accused them of their wrong doings anymore, yet as soon as they are in eternity that same conscience shall be opened and will accuse them of all sinful thoughts, words and deeds. They will never say there is no God. Even though they said it and wished it to their death. But then they will curse and slander Him.

When a person is born and comes to the age of discretion he can, through an inner knowledge, come to know that there is a God. If he dies unconverted, eternally lost, he will surely know it.

What is so dangerous then? It is so dangerous, during our lives, between the time we are born and the time we die, to close our consciences by sin. In this state we shall no more be warned by it. Oh, that is so very terrible because then we are insensible to everything and we go on living as if God does not exist. But one day He will ask of us an account of how we have conducted our lives.

This is, then, something about the first point on the "Knowledge of God from nature," namely, the inner or innate knowledge which every person consciously or unconsciously carries about with him.

Hellenbroek asks in the 5th question, "What is the external or acquired knowledge?" What kind of knowledge is that? It is that knowledge which is derived from the visible creation. Psalm 19:1 The heavens declare the glory of God and the firmament showeth His handywork.

We can conclude from created beings that there must be a God. This is proven in the 6th answer: Because they cannot exist nor continue to be of themselves, but must necessarily be created, and still sustained by God Himself. Job 12:9 Who knoweth not in all these that the hand of the Lord hath wrought this?

You have all learned the answers of our first lesson.

All the creatures that have been created on the earth and in the sea are like clear letters in a large book in which men can read that there is a God. But do you know what men cannot learn from nature and the creation alone?

Men can observe from them that there IS a God but they do not teach us WHO God is.

Where can we learn this?

The Holy Scriptures alone can teach us the pure knowledge of who God is.

Though we can clearly see in creation and in our consciences that God exists, can we from nature learn that God is Triune, one in essence, but three in persons?

No, that is impossible. Therefore, the external knowledge that there is a God is not sufficient to salvation. Men do not learn about Christ in that way. And what does the 9th question ask? "Is the knowledge of Christ absolutely necessary to salvation? Yes; John 17:3, "And this is life eternal, that they might know thee, the only true God, and Jesus Christ whom thou hast sent."

Do you see how Rev. Hellenbroek without hesitation may call his questions and answers "Divine Truths"?

He can prove nearly every answer from Scripture.

That saving knowledge, which every person needs, can be found only in God's Word, which we call the Bible.

Does every person who has a knowledge of God, received through conscience or nature, also have a knowledge of who God is?

No. the illiterate heathen does not have the knowledge of God from Holy Scripture. They know there is a God because most of them have some sort of worship, but they do not have a Bible, and so do not know who God is in His Holy Trinity.

Rev. Hellenbroek asks in another lesson whether there has always been a written word; "No," says he; "before the time of Moses there was no written word."

Maybe you are now thinking, "You just said that we can only know who God is from the Bible and from it receive the necessary knowledge to be saved. What happened before Moses time; before God's Written Word came? Could no one at that time be saved? "Fortunately they could, because the Lord was the same God in Moses' time as He is now, but He then used other means to reveal himself to the people.

How did God then communicate His word?

Answer: By verbal language and revelation to the fathers. Gen. 18:1 "And the Lord appeared unto him in the plains of Mamre; and he sat in the tent door in the heat of the day." God sometimes spoke to Jacob through dreams.

7

Thus they received knowledge of God through God even though there was no written Bible. The fathers related to their children all that the Lord had revealed, and these children later told their children.

God's Word was faithfully preserved from generation to generation. That could be done so much better in those days because people lived longer than they do now. You know from Bible stories that people living before Moses' time became very old.

How old did Adam become?·

"Nine hundred and thirty years old."

And Methuselah?

"Nine hundred and sixty-nine years old."

In that way these old men could relate to three or four generations what the Lord had said unto them.

Now there are perhaps boys or girls in the catechism class today who are thinking, "If the people in those days had no written Word, how could they know whether it was the Lord who spoke to them?"

We know according to 2 Tim. 3:16 that all Scripture is given by inspiration, and that these words were not produced through the will of men, but that the Holy Ghost inspired all things. So, it is truly God's Word.

How do you think the Lord revealed himself before Moses' time?

Abraham, Isaac, Jacob, Moses and all the other faithful believers received by faith the words and revelations through which God spake to them.

We find in Genesis 12: "The Lord said unto Abram, Get out of thy country and from thy kindred and from thy father's house, unto a land that I will show thee." Did Abram reply, "I do not know who or what said this to me. I shall not do it"? No, it only says, "Abram departed, as the Lord had spoken unto him."

Abram believed God's Word, even though it was not written on paper.

It happened that way with Jacob also. He fled before Esau and went to Haran and when he was on his way, according to Genesis 28:11, he lighted upon a certain place and tarried there all night. While he lay sleeping he dreamed that a ladder was set on the earth and that the top of it reached to heaven and he saw the angels of God ascending and descending on it. The Lord stood above the ladder and said, "I am the Lord God of Abraham thy father, and the God of Isaac: The land whereon thou liest, to thee will I give it, and to thy seed."

God promised much more to Jacob. And what did Jacob say? Did he not believe the words God had spoken to him?

Just read in verse 16 whether he actually believed everything even though the Lord spoke directly to him, without the Bible. It says: and Jacob awaked out of his sleep and he said, "Surely the Lord is in this this place": and he called the name of that place, "Bethel" which means "House of God".

Do you understand now, that when the Lord spoke to the church of old they received everything in faith?

After Moses led the children of Israel out of Egypt, the Lord in his sovereign wisdom found it necessary to have His Word written. At that time the people no longer reached such an old age and could not accurately hand down these matters to one another.

We hope to tell next week, if the Lord spares us, what means the Lord used and whom He chose to write His word.

Our class time is nearly gone. You must go to your homes. Most of you still have a father and mother to whom you can go. Some can go to relatives, but all of you, fortunately, have a "home". Boys and girls, have you ever seriously considered that by and by all of us shall go to our eternal home? Every person that has been born in this world must die. Even persons in the early days who reached eight and nine hundred years of age also had to die. You know how that came about, don't you?

Dying was not necessary in Paradise. God created man to live, but because we sinned there, now we are born only to die. The wise Solomon spoke of it in Ecclesiastes 12:5: "Man goeth to his long home."

Will that eternal home be the same for everyone? No, the difference can never be expressed in words.

This is sure: the children of God who have learned to believe in Him and in His Word here, shall, through Christ, go to their blessed home, to be eternally with their Father. The others who have lived here unconverted and died in that condition shall go to their own eternal home with the devils in Hell.

By our disobedience we have brought that fate upon ourselves. The Lord had said, "For in the day that thou eatest thereof thou shalt surely die." And how long will this death last? It will not be for just a short time. No, it will last eternally, without end.

If it lasted a million years, there would sooner or later be an end, and those poor creatures in hell could still have hope, but it is not so. This eternity will have a beginning but never an end. Oh, children, may you in your youth learn to know the Lord before the time of death comes; because, if you do not become reconciled with God here, through Christ, it will be impossible after death. As a result, your place will remain an eternal home of darkness from where it will be impossible to be delivered ever.

Do not mock death! Surely it will not be long before you become old and will have very little time left to be converted.

May the Lord cause you to break away from being at ease in this world while you are young, and may you find in Him the only true rest.

Lesson 2

Continuing the subject of the Holy Scriptures

Last week we considered how the Lord at the beginning of the church under the old testament made known His will to the people by word of mouth and they then received these words by faith as God's word to them. But now, since the time of Moses, we have God's written Word from which we can learn the truths that can make us "wise unto salvation."

Continuing the subject of the Holy Scripture, Hellenbroek asks: Who has ordered the Holy Scriptures to be written?

Answer: God. 2 Tim. 3:16 All scripture is given by inspiration of God.

And by whom did He cause them to be written?

Answer: The Old Testament by prophets and the New Testament by evangelists and apostles.

In Exodus 17:14 The Lord said to Moses: "Write this for a memorial in a book" and in Revelations 1:19 "Write the things which thou hast seen and the things which are and the things which shall be hereafter."

It is pointed out plainly in 2 Peter 1:21 that these persons did not write their own words or thoughts. It states: "For the prophecy came not in old time by the will of man, but holy men of God spake as they were moved by the Holy Ghost."

Do you see, boys and girls, that Rev. Hellenbroek would not teach you things that are not in accordance with God's Word? You can find every answer confirmed in the Bible.

You, too, should always try to speak the same way. Do not believe or say things that are not in accordance to God's Word. We as human beings always make mistakes. That is why the Holy Scripture must always be our guide in faith and life. The persons writing those things could never make mistakes in them because God the Holy Spirit communicated to them and guided them into all the truth.

Because of this they are not human truths but divine truths.

We shall run through the questions as they are written for awhile this afternoon because you must learn the historical aspects of God's Word too.

Of course, you all know that there are two testaments in the Bible. The Old Testament was originally written in the Hebrew language, except a part of the books of Daniel and Ezra which were written in Chaldean.

The New Testament, with exception of some Latin and Hebrew words, was written in the Greek language.

Now our 13th question asks: Is the whole Bible a divine book?

He answers, yes, because it contains such things as can proceed only from God. Which things are they? Mysteries, as the triune God, the creation out of nothing in six days, that Jesus is God and man, the Mediator, and prophecies: which are predictions of future events that were performed on the exact time and place.

In brief, we could say: The Bible, the divine book, is perfect:

1st. In its entirety.
2nd. In its two testaments.
3rd. In its 66 books.

4th. In its chapters.

5th. In every one of its verses.

You must never forget your whole life long that the whole book is perfect, meaning that not even one part can be taken from it. Neither can words be stricken or added because the Lord said in the next to the last verse of the last book, Revelation 22:19, "And if any man shall take away from the words of the book of this prophecy, God shall take away his part out of the book of life." In the 18th verse it states: "If any man shall add unto these things, God shall add unto him the plagues that are written in this book."

Boys and girls, that would be a perilous thing to do; don't you think so, too?

Therefore, never let yourself be brought from the way of truth by those who say that God's word is in the Bible (they mean there are various things in the Bible that are actually of God) but the entire Bible is not God's Word!

The Ethicals, especially, have taken this position. They teach that men may, without fear (or conscience qualms), reject certain parts of the Bible because only God's Word is considered to be the Bible.

They contend they can possess true faith and be saved without accepting the Holy Scriptures as an entirely divine book.

They consider the Bible merely raw material from which they take confidence and in so doing pretend that they also believe God's Word. In reality they deny it, because, when men believe only parts of the Bible to be God's Word, they reject the remaining parts, and as a consequence render any trust they have worthless.

There is nothing to be added or to be taken away.

We shall not take the remaining time this afternoon in discussion of the division of the books or the meaning of

13

their names.

If you want to, you can find these in your Bibles at home. They are listed in the front part of it.

You remember that the first 17 books of the old testament, from Genesis to Esther, are historical. Then follow the 5 poetical or moral books of Job to the Songs of Solomon. Then follow the 17 prophetical books of Isaiah to Malachi.

The New Testament is divided into the 4 gospels, from Matthew to John; the Acts of the Apostles, then, the 21 epistles, of which Paul wrote 14, and ending with the prophetical book, The Revelation of John.

Now, men would logically say: The men that God used to write such divine writings must have had an exceedingly high education and must have been very intelligent.

There too (reverently speaking) the Lord used very expedient means.

It was decided in His Holy council from eternity that Moses would be the first man to write the Divine Words. And now just notice the wisdom of God in making Moses qualified for it.

The Lord promised Abraham the whole land of Canaan. During the famine in Joseph's time, the children of Jacob stayed in Egypt. So also, many generations after them. They lived there more than 400 years.

You know from Bible History that Pharaoh oppressed them. They had to work hard and were not much more than slaves. Of course, in those times, there were not many bright educated men amongst the Israelites because without exception, according to the Bible, they all had to work for Pharaoh.

Moses was born in those terrible times. The child that God had chosen had arrived in time, became old and brought the children of Israel, according to God's promise,

14

name of John Hus who preached the truth and was burned to death for doing so. The name "Hus" means goose in the Bohemian language and before he died he said, as if it were prophecy, "A goose is a bird that cannot fly high but from the ashes of *this* goose there will arise an eagle that will soar high and will attract all other birds to himself."

This prophecy would be fulfilled in Martin Luther.

He was still a strict Roman Catholic. But once, while he was studying, something happened that brought a change to his entire life.

A certain historian wrote that Luther was a great lover of books and spent many solitary hours at the library of the High School. Once while he was looking over the books on the shelves, he found a book that was completely different from all the others. He took it from its place and opened it. To his amazement, he saw that it was a Bible; a complete translation of the entire Bible in the Latin language.

This was the first time he had ever seen a complete Bible. The Roman church chose single passages from the scriptures which they continually read in the church in the Latin language. Luther had never known that more of the Bible existed.

You can understand how amazed he was when he found books and epistles in the Bible of which he had never heard. He read it through completely. It was God's time and Luther felt as if a new life was opened for him. The historian relates, "When He came to the words, 'He raiseth up the poor out of the dust,' he cried out 'O God, these words of comfort are given also to poor students such as I.' "

That was the beginning of the great change in his life.

It would take too long to tell the complete history of Luther now. I hope that all of you are acquainted with it. But, the conclusion was, that Martin, stirred by the word of God, went to seek rest in a monastary. In those days it was the only known means of finding peace. You must understand that this was not at all to the satisfaction of his old father Hans. Instead of earning lots of money, his son now shut himself up inside four walls. He reasoned that that can only be the instigation of the devil.

But the Lord knew very well what He had in store for Martin. His written Word had its power and would have still further effect.

Luther was to be the great reformer of the church in Germany and his earlier education would be of excellent use in his translation of the Latin Bible and his many writings against the Roman church.

Do you see now, boys and girls, the preciousness of the written Word?

Our class time is at an end.

I hope and wish that this Word might be a sharp two-edged sword to your young hearts as it was to Luther's. Because, even if it is not required of you to become reformers, it will be necessary for each one to be arrested by that Word in a personal way.

Do not mock with God's Word nor speak of it in an unholy way. Remember, it is God's Word. Do not neglect to read and search in it while you are still able to do so. There was a time when men were punished with death for reading the Bible. People hid loose pages of it in their shoes and clothes to be able to read parts of that precious Word.

Who knows what fearful times you will have to experience when you become older. And even though it does not become precisely as it was in Luther's time, yet the Word of God could be denied us too. So, read and search it now, while you are in the flower of life. May the Lord bless it. The Lord is calling to you every day saying "Remember now thy creator in the days of thy youth, while the evil days come not", even though you pay no attention to Him.

Now you play and flit about like a butterfly from one flower to another. But children, you have such a precious soul to be saved for eternity.

May the Holy Spirit keep you restless, so that you can find no peace in the world without Christ.

You cannot ever be at peace with God, though, with merely an open conscience nor with just tears and good works.

Luther discovered that too. May you be taught as he was: That only the blood of Jesus Christ, the Son of God cleanses from all sins.

Now boys and girls, I wish that the Lord would apply all this to your heart for a blessing to your young but never dying souls.

Lesson 3

on the Holy Scripture.

Who can remember which are the two great "books" from which we can learn to know that there is a God?

Answer: The "book" of Nature and The Holy Scriptures.

Correct! We shall not repeat that which we spoke in the former lessons, but I do want to know what you remembered about them.

We had said that Nature and the Bible are the two great books from which men can know that there is a God. But, can men receive more knowledge of God from one book than from the other?

Yes. The book of nature can only teach that there is a God, while we find in the Holy Scripture that God is triune and that we must learn to know the Mediator in order to be saved.

Now men could think: If nature merely teaches that there is a God, it is really not in accordance with the Bible which teaches so much more about Him.

Is that true?

No. That is not true. The Bible is superior to nature, but the "book" of nature is not contrary to the Bible.

If you pay attention, you can easily understand this with a couple of examples.

1st. Despite the fact that two boys are equally strong they contend in a fight with one another. They are in opposition to one another.

2nd. Now consider two girls, who both know something of a certain matter. What one knows of that matter, the other knows also. But one girl knows an additional something that the other girl does not know. Now, these girls are not opposed to one another. One is, however, more informed than the other.

It is the same in this matter. Even though God's Word is far superior, nature cannot be opposed to it.

What would you think if I were to relate something to you concerning nature and which included a statement completely opposed to God's Word. Should you be obliged to believe it? No, you should not. Even if the most educated man in the world told you something concerning nature that was opposed to God's Word, you should not believe it.

Nature cannot ever be contradictory to the Holy Scripture. The Scripture is far superior and there is far more to learn from it in respect to salvation than there is from nature.

Hellenbroek's first question this afternoon is:
"What is God?"

Answer: A perfect and an infinite spirit. John 4:24, "God is a spirit, and they that worship Him must worship Him in spirit and in truth."

That is the way he teaches us from God's Word what God is.

But now, If I were to ask you who God is, what should be your answer?

To answer correctly you should say: "God is one in essence and three in persons, Father, Son and Holy Ghost."

Do you understand now, what a great difference there is between nature, which only teaches that there is a God, and the Bible which teaches both what God is and who God is?

Hellenbroek brings forth still another objection and asks "How can that be, since eyes, ears, hands, and other corporal members are ascribed to Him in the Holy Scriptures?

Answer: All this must be figuratively understood of such properties in God, as bear some resemblance to the use of those human members.

It is especially difficult for you to understand matters spoken of figuratively now. Later, when you become older, you still will not understand the mysteries of the Divine Trinity, but the Lord is able to grant you the faith to believe it.

However, you must try to remember these "Divine Truths" even though some are mere historical facts. It can do you no harm if you do not understand it completely.

I have explained to you in these lessons what God is and who God is, but if I should ask you, "Where does God come from?" what should your answer be?

It happened once upon a time, that an educated man came to Rev. Brakel, who was co-minister in the Rotterdam congregation with Rev. Hellenbroek (you must have heard

23

of Rev. Brakel at one time or another). This man came to Rev. Brakel intent upon entangling him with a matter he thought he could not defend.

He said, "You declare and teach that the world did not always exist, isn't that so?" "Yes", answered Brakel, "The world did not always exist. It was created in the beginning by God."

"So!" said the gentleman, "and where was God before He created the world; where did this God, which you say exists, actually come from?" "Well, sir, Rev. Brakel replied, "God is in eternity, He was there and He remains there. If you would believe God's Word, it is written in Psalm 90 where Moses prays: "Even from everlasting to everlasting, thou art God." Also, a verse from the 90th Psalm speaks of it this way:

"Before the hills in order stood, or earth received her frame, From everlasting Thou art God, to endless years the same."

The aged Rev. Brakel did not defend this or that opinion, no, he only used God's Word as the most effective sword.

Boys and girls, when in the natural course of events, you come in contact with the world, do as he did. If men dispute with you concerning the Divine Truths that you have learned in your youth, never use the defence: this or that minister taught me that. Use only God's Word to subdue them.

The Word of God has been striven against by man and by the devil as long as the world has existed. This is especially true in the New Testament. Have you ever noticed this in the writings of the evangelists?

Matthew begins his book with the account of the generations from Abraham to Christ. Luke begins with the birth of John the Baptist, who was to be the forerunner of the

Messiah. Mark relates plainly how John the Baptist preached in the wilderness. But, who can remember how the evangelist John begins his gospel?

According to certain authorities, John wrote his gospel after the other three evangelists wrote theirs.

In those days the anti-Christ was already strongly manifest in the world. He does not mention the record of the generations, but begins immediately to tell of the source of everything. He comes to grips with the anti-Christ when he says in John 1:1 "In the beginning was the Word, and the Word was with God, and the Word was God. The same was in the beginning with God. All things were made by Him and without Him was not anything made that was made."

The aged John preached fearlessly against all the ever increasing errors of those who did not acknowledge Christ as the Son of God.

Do you see in all this, how the doctrine of the Trinity is so clearly established in God's Word and especially that Christ is always set forth as the only Savior?

You know that the captains of ocean vessels always have a compass on board, don't you?

The needle of the compass always points toward the North even if it is very dark. The seaman oftentimes does not know where he is, but if he has the compass on board, he can always know which way is North and can correct his way accordingly.

God's Word is like a true compass. The Old and New Testaments, throughout, point to Christ alone as the great North Star of safety.

Therefore, don't ever believe now, nor when you become older, that only some things concerning God are in the Bible. The Holy Scripture is so intimately connected with faith in God that it is impossible to separate one from the other.

In our last lesson it was mentioned that God's Word is like a compass. The entire Holy Scripture is intimately connected with faith in God. It is impossible to separate one from the other.

That is why Hellenbroek discusses the lesson entitled "Of God" immediately following the one entitled "The Holy Scripture." You must be willing to acknowledge the Holy Scripture in its entirety as a Divine Book or you cannot believe facts *concerning* God, much less believe *in* Him.

Now, there are many people that say: "If I could understand the Bible I would believe it, but I cannot understand it. How shall I believe what is in it?"

Hellenbroek would say: "That is just exactly the reason why the Holy Scripture is a Divine Book. There are mysteries contained in it that could come of no one but God. Things such as: The entire creation out of nothing in six days, the assuming of the human nature by Christ, etc. are not to be comprehended by man. It is even dangerous to want to understand these mysteries with our natural minds. It would be just as if someone ventured too far by himself in the deep darkness of a forest wherein he did not know the way. He would become hopelessly lost and most likely would never come out alive.

It would be the same in this matter!

If you sat for days and weeks with your hands in front of your face saying, "I want to understand who God is!"

Do you know what would happen?

You would certainly lose your mind. But, what the understanding cannot do, faith can. God's Word does not say that we must understand everything that is written in it, no, it says, "For he that cometh to God must believe that He is, and that He is a rewarder of them that diligently seek Him."

It is impossible to understand God. The Lord speaks of it in His Word through Elihu in Job 36:26: "Behold, God is great, and we know Him not. Neither can the number of His years be searched out."

Not alone would it be impossible to understand God, but it would, in itself, be unfortunate if it were possible.

Why would it be unfortunate?

Well, if we, who are worthless creatures with corrupt minds, could understand God in His Essence and operations, then the Lord would not be what He certainly is.

How can we, finite beings, who have been created by Him, ever come to understand the infinite Creator?

But do you know what would be the greatest blessing in respect to this?

O, boys and girls, it would be wonderful if through that God, about whom you have been taught these simple matters (many of which you did not nor cared to understand), you came to believe in Him. Do you realize what will be very much worse than that you do not understand this lesson?

That you, at some time, will, none the less, have to reckon with this Eternal God.

We shall not discuss these questions any further this noon. This is the last session at which we shall meet as a catechism class this year. Next week, if the Lord spare us, it will be Christmas and the following week New Year's Day. So, we shall not see one another here again this year.

Have you, even just once, in this entire past year, earnestly considered that one day you will stand before a great incomprehensible Divine Being?

Maybe there are boys or girls that are saying to themselves: "Dominie, stop talking about that now. Why are we given a sermon each week in addition to our lesson? We are very well aware of that fact."

I wish that you knew it so well, that you would have no rest day or night until you are reconciled with God. Think about this for a moment. We see one another but an hour each week. So, isn't it worthwhile to remind one another of such an important matter; An eternity without an end lies at stake!

It is true you are still very young and, at the moment, in good health. But, does that mean, therefore, that we need not be mindful of your soul; nor consider that your young lives can be cut off any moment?

Solomon does not say without good reason, "Remember now thy Creator in the days of thy youth, while the evil days come not!"

And, what does he mean with those "evil days?"

He means, when old age and sickness comes; when a person arrives at the end of his life, then that precious time is lost forever.

Last week I visited an old sick man almost 70 years old. He asked me if I would pray for him.

I ask: "For what would you want me to pray?"

"O, Dominie" he said "that I may become well again."

I thought at that time: "Poor man. He has lived 70 years on this earth in an unconverted state; for 70 years he has sinned against the Lord and he still counts it not long enough. Now he is even eager to live a number of years more to — to sin even more!"

This is the way it is with old people. But, so it is with all of us.

This year has almost come to an end. The Lord has spared and kept us in good health, but, is there one among us that has become burdened with sin even a moment during this past year? Has no one experienced how evil and bitter it is to sin against such a kind God?

Has no one come to accept the fact that he is lost and walks in this cursed world without God?

Poor boys and girls. If you do not learn how terrible sin is here, you will soon learn after death; but then it will be a dreadful experience!

God allows a warning to come your way while you are young, but this will also make your responsibility heavier.

The Lord is free of everyone and has been from the beginning of time because He had said, "The day that thou eatest thereof thou shalt surely die." That was sufficient warning. And — what happened? Everyone of us, in our father Adam were disobedient to that command. So, we have deserved corporal, spiritual and eternal death.

We are still living, however, and He has pointed out to us a way of life again, but now through the reconciliation of His Son and our belief in Him.

God, therefore, is not only free from us, but He also makes himself free.

Think about this, even if you cannot understand it completely. It is not necessary either. May you become convinced through the working of the Holy Spirit that you righteously deserve Hell and also that you come to consider it a wonder that you are not there with so many other people including children. Anything we have above that is by grace alone. It may not be saving grace, but yet it is common grace. And how overflowing in abundance it is!

God's Word, God's Day, and His ministers to preach His Word, are all means that He sometimes uses to stop a person who is on the broad way. These means in themselves cannot save us, though, even if we are very punctual in our use of them. I repeat, "the Lord uses them." Only Jesus Christ can be our Savior. We must be made aware of this through light from God.

It would be a blessing if this year did not end as it had begun. Don't you think so, too?

I am sure of this, if the Lord directed His sharp arrow

into your heart, you would seek a place in your home where no one could see you or hear you and you would call out: "O, God, I have sinned against Thee all my life. I am unconverted, and will I now die unconverted?"

I don't mean to imply that if you have had that experience, you are now converted and can be at peace. Oh, no! But it still will be necessary that you first become aware of your deep misery and recognize the fact that we are estranged from God, before there can be a deliverance through justice.

With all my heart I wish that this may become your most necessary concern as this year comes to an end.

The Lord bless the instruction, not alone for instruction sake, but also to the salvation of your never dying souls through the blood of the Mediator.

Lesson 4

The incommunicable attributes of God.

We continue our lessons this afternoon, with Rev. Hellenbroek explaining the attributes of God.

How are God's attributes commonly distinguished?

Answer: Into communicable and incommunicable attributes.

Take notice, it is not meant here that the attributes of God are divided; no, they are God Himself, as he says in the first question. This is easy to prove. For example, Light, Life, Love and the Truth, etc., are all attributes of God. But, in the meantime, God Himself is also called the Light, the Life, the Love and the Truth. Therefore He is that Himself. So, it is clear that God's attributes are not to be separated from God and not to be distinguished from God. They are not something other than God, but truly God Himself, and in Him are all things an eternal perfection.

We call the divine attributes various names because of our limited understanding and because they have a remote resemblance to God's perfections respecting His creatures. For that reason we speak of five incommunicable attributes, namely:

1st. Independency, 2nd. Simplicity, 3rd. Eternity, 4th. Omnipresence, and 5th. Immutability of God. We call this group incommunicable, because there is not the least resemblance of them in any creature.

Hellenbroek also names seven other attributes that are called communicable; they are: God's knowledge, Will, Power, Goodness, Grace, Mercy and Patience.

These attributes are called communicable because there are mere traces or remote likenesses in the creatures. However, they are also infinite and completely incommunicable when related (or ascribed) to God.

In order not to bring about confusion by handling too many things at once, we shall speak this afternoon about the incommunicable attributes.

The first attribute is called Independency.

Hellenbroek says that the Independency of God means He is self existent and self sufficient.

Who is the only independent being?

Only God is independent. He is completely free; not dependent upon a creature, neither in His existence, nor in His work.

And for the very reason that the Triune God is the only independent being and always will be, don't you see, boys and girls, how wicked and God-dishonoring it is for men to declare a country independent?

Maybe some of the older ones among you remember

that in 1913 a great feast was celebrated in the Netherlands, which the people called the Feast of Independence.

There had been no war in 100 years in our country and, in that sense, it was free of all other countries.

It is really wonderful if a country can remain at peace, without interruption for one hundred years, but does that give one reason to say we are independent?

No. In doing so, we dishonor the Lord upon whom we were totally dependent throughout those most privileged years.

Never use that word, therefore, in connection with a person or a country. Remember, independency is an incommunicable attribute of the Divine Being.

Now, I shall ask you a question, about which, you must be very attentive. Who was the very first one in the world to declare man to be independent? Think about this.

Answer: The devil in Paradise.

Right! It was there that man wanted to be free of God and, as a consequence, independent.

Adam and Eve lived there in communion with God. They knew Him by the wind of the day.

The devil, as you all know, is a fallen angel. Since his fall, caused by his revolt against God and his being banned from heaven to the abyss, he held an everlasting hate against God.

He knows very well that there is no possibility of his ever being in God's favor or returning to Heaven.

Do you know what he wants to do now? He has discovered that it is impossible to touch God as God. He lost that struggle. Now he tries to harass God in His works. All the fallen angels (those who became devils) wander about as spirits, and with permission, have the power to show themselves in any form.

The devil went to Eve in this way soon after creation. He

came in the form of a serpent and said: "Yea, hath God said, ye shall not eat of every tree of the garden?"

The woman said unto the serpent, "We may eat of the fruit of the trees of the garden, but of the fruit of the tree which is in the midst of the garden, God hath said, ye shall not eat of it, neither shall ye touch it, lest ye die."

Observe now how slyly the tempter went to work. He didn't begin by saying to Eve "There is no God," or "God knows nothing of it" − no, he acted at least as if he was inclined toward God as Eve was, because he referred directly to God's omniscience in saying, "Ye shall not surely die: For God doth know that in the day ye eat thereof, then your eyes shall be opened, and ye shall be as gods, knowing good and evil."

You all know what the results were. This is not the time to relate this history, but I want to call to your attention, how the devil began ages ago to place the image of "independency" before man − being as God, knowing good and evil.

That charms the poor soul. It entices him to be free from God, loose from all ties and, thus, through desire for independancy became eternally shackled to sin and death.

Do you see now how the devil was a liar "from the beginning", just as Jesus said?

In addition, he confirmed his lies with an oath when he said, "God knows"

When there is a celebration in our cities and villages, the people, oftentimes, make a gateway of ferns and flowers placing beautifully colored lettering, saying this or that, amongst them. Boys and girls, just as these pretty gateways of gold or orange letters entice your heart to go to the feast and you find it so nice that you cannot resist; so it was, figuratively speaking, in Paradise. The devil erected a gateway in Paradise and placed the word "Independency" over the top of it.

This was the allurement or decoy, through which men were made Satan's captive listeners. By our actions, at that time, we renounced the Lord and implied that He was lying in His command that we thought withheld freedom from us.

We want to be in God's place ourselves, knowing all things, good and evil. We want to remove ourselves from the obedience of His command.

So, the devil obtained his purpose, at least in this respect, that man fell from the favor of God.

But, if we were ever dependent upon God, then, surely, it is after our fall. Don't you believe that too?

Because of our desire to elevate ourselves still higher than we were created in God's image, we fell to an inexpressable depth. So now, we are dependent upon God for the smallest of our needs, even if we do not acknowledge Him for them.

We have now mentioned a few things concerning man's dependency.

Would you say the angels are also dependant? I am referring now to the good or predestined angels, not the fallen angels which are now devils.

Yes, the Perfect Spirits attending the throne in heaven as well as the evil angels in Hell are all dependent upon God.

We read throughout God's Word that the good angels are ministering spirits, who by God's command are excluded from sin. They are dependent upon Him in their service to Him before His holy countenance.

Concerning the evil angels: We read in Mark 5 when Jesus met a man "possessed", (a person possessed is one in whom the devil has such great influence, that he is totally under his command) He released him from the devils that were in him. The evil spirits begged Jesus not to torment them before the appointed time.

They knew the Lord Jesus had power over them. They knew also, that it was not yet the day of judgment. That is why they said, "What have we to do with thee, Jesus, thou son of God? Art thou come hither to torment us before the time?"

Yet they were submissive to Him, because they waited for His permission to go into the swine and showed, thereby, their dependence on Him.

The second incommunicable attribute is called the Simplicity of God.

Hellenbroek explains this briefly: That all in God is one, without composition of different parts. Deut. 6:4 "Hear, O Israel: the Lord our God is one Lord."

This simplicity is not meant to be the opposite of pride as when we call a humble person a simple person. No, it means here a one-ness in God without different parts.

The third incommunicable attribute is called Eternity. The word eternity is used in two different senses in God's Word.

Sometimes eternity means the eternity with a beginning but without an end. Sometimes it is spoken of as having no beginning and no end.

Respecting the Divine Being, eternity is expressed in Psalm 90, "From everlasting to everlasting thou art God."

There is, therefore, neither a beginning nor an end. Eternity is as such an incommunicable attribute of God.

As the church speaks of it in Psalm 89, namely, "I will sing of the mercies of the Lord forever;" there is a beginning to that eternity. It will begin directly after natural death. Accordingly, God's children shall enter into eternity with eternal bless that will never end.

On the other hand, there will also be a beginning of eternity for the unconverted. That will be a dreadful eternity; eternally abandoned of God.

After death, whether in eternal bliss or in eternal wretchedness, there will be no succesion of time as there is here, just as there is no succession nor end of time with the Lord.

Do you know where you can prove that to me from God's Word?

Answer: 2 Peter 3:8 "That one day with the Lord is as a thousand years, and a thousand years as one day."

The catechism proceeds, now, with the question, "Where is God?"

Answer: God is present everywhere. This is an attribute called omnipresence and is the 4th incommunicable attribute.

Evidence of this attribute is clear in Jeremiah 23:24 "Can any hide himself in secret places that I shall not see him? saith the Lord. Do not I fill heaven and earth? saith the Lord."

This attribute, Omnipresence, (being present everywhere), is not only to be understood of His operations but also of His essence (His actual being) because He works by virture of His essence.

O, boys and girls, do you ever think about this fact that the Lord is always present at every place in this world?

He can see you anywhere and anytime, even though you are in remote places. He is an all knowing and all seeing God. Do you think about this, boys, when you are busy doing something evil and you say to yourself, "If father or mother just does not see this", that the Lord knows and sees, even though you do it so very quietly?

I am confident, if the all knowing God was always in your thoughts, you would not sin so calmly and easily as you are doing now. Isn't that true?

Now you try to hide all the bad things, as far as possible, from your parents or others, but, remember this, if you hid yourself one hundred yards deep in the earth, the Lord knows exactly the unspoken thoughts that are in your heart. Nothing is hidden from His sight.

I once read about two boys, who were planning to commit a serious crime. One of them said, "Where shall we do it, so that no one will see it?"

"That is something we must think about," said the other. "Wait, I know a fine place were no one can see us."

"But won't God in heaven see us there, too?" said the first boy.

Then his companion became angry and said, "If you must talk that way, we had better not do it, because God is everywhere and in that place, too."

The all knowing God arrested their consciences so much, that they did not dare to execute their plan. Although God knew exactly the evil intention that was in their heart, they were spared from doing the evil deed.

So, boys and girls, never try to seek a place to do evil, where you think no one can see you, because as you remember, Psalm 139 says:

"O, Lord thou hast searched me and known me.
Thou knowest my downsitting and my uprising,
Thou understandest my thoughts afar off.
Thou compassest my path and my lying down,
and art acquainted with all my ways."

As soon as you are tempted to do something that no one should know about, remember that passage. Perhaps, like the two boys, you may be spared of doing evil.

Do you know a better purpose for which to seek a hiding place?

It would be a place to confess all your sins to the Lord and pray that you may come to know how great your sins and miseries are and lament them.

If it would happen that He would make you to feel your sins as they truly are before Him, there would be no small sins, they would all be great sins. Do you know why? Because the sins are done against a kind God.

Listen to me now. I shall try to make you understand how evil it is to sin against God.

You know that we desire and do commit sins as soon as we are born.

Isn't that true? It is because these actual sins are a result of our inherited original sin. But, how do we acquire original sin? Are we created with it? Of course not!

No, we through our own coveteousness and the tempting of the devil have deliberately committed the first sin. We are now so unfortunate, that we find sin to be ever present with us. Before that time we carried the image of God. The image of God, which we possessed, consisted of knowledge, righteousness and holiness, which means: we knew God, had no guilt and were holy.

Through our first sin we lost that image and now carry the image of the devil.

Can a person with the image of the devil be in heaven?

No, the devil himself, because of his revolt, was thrown out of heaven.

What is necessary then?

That we receive the image of God again, that is: that we are at peace with Him. That we become holy again through Christ, that our guilt be taken away, so that we can, in Christ, be pure before God. Then we would have knowledge, righteousness and holiness again.

We see according to the Word of God that man carried the image of God in three different states.

Can you tell me what they are?

38

Answer:

1. The state of integrity before the fall.
2. The state of grace, when God converts a person and once again presents him His image and,
3. In the state of eternal bliss as redeemed souls in heaven.

I hope that you eventually understand the divine attributes of God which were the subject of the few questions you have memorized. Then you will also discover what strength is comprehended in the immutability of God, an incommunicable attribute of God. "For I am the Lord, I change not, therefore ye sons of Jacob are not consumed."

It is obvious God often changes in His explanations.

Our lesson states: "This repentance in God is only a change in His work, not in His will and essence, Numbers 23:19," God is not a man that He should lie; neither the son of man that He should repent."

When it is written, that He changes places; that He comes somewhere and goes away again, it is but a change in the degree to which He shows His presence; not in the real presence itself.

So we see plainly that God's incommunicable attributes are one and the same with His Essence. They are recognized by special features only to accommodate our manner of understanding.

O, how precious all the attributes of God will become to you if God converts you in your lifetime, because these attributes are God Himself.

Also, you will become very conscious of how you miss God and His image even if you are ever so young.

There was once a little girl who was asked why she held God's people in such esteem and went to see them so often. "Oh," she said, "These people have had restored to them something which I still lack." "What is that then?" they asked her.

"They have been restored into communion with the Lord again," she said, "and they know Him, and Christ has taken their guilt away; but, I still carry the image of the devil and am not reconciled with God."

May you also discover this and never have rest, until, through grace, you are restored into God's favor through faith in Christ.

Lesson 5

A Continuation of the Subject — The Attributes of God.

In the lesson previous to the last one, you were asked the question: Wherein must God be known?

Answer: 1st in His Essence, 2nd in His Names, 3rd In His Attributes and 4th in His Persons.

Today we shall continue to concern ourselves with the attributes.

We spoke briefly last week about the five incommunicable attributes and shall now try to speak something of the communicable attributes.

You recited the names of the seven communicable attributes last week, namely: Knowledge, Will, Power, Goodness, Grace, Mercy and Patience. They are *not* called communicable attributes because men posses them in the same manner as they are in God. Oh no, but only because there is a remote resemblance to them in the creature. The first one explained was the Knowledge of God which is that perfection in God whereby He, from eternity, knows everything by Himself in the most perfect manner. This knowledge is all-comprehensive and so, He is omniscient "all-knowing."

Now Hellenbroek asks in question 22:

How is the Will of God distinguished?

Answer: Into the will of His decree, and the will of His Command; or His secret and revealed will.

Before we speak of this further, I shall ask a question.

How many wills does God have?

Answer: One will.

But Hellenbroek talks about a will of His Command and a Will of His Decree; That is actually two. How must I understand that?

I sometimes ask this question just to see if you understand the meaning of Hellenbroek when he asks: "How is the will of God distinguished?" The answer as it is in your lesson is right, but the way I do it is wrong. In fact, God does not have two wills, but His will is distinguished in a secret and revealed will. Now, the will of His decree is unknown to us. Moses said, "The secret things belong unto the Lord our God." It is His eternal purpose, from which He works according to the council of His will.

But the revealed will is the will of His command, which He orders as a rule of our conduct in His Word; according to which we are to behave ourselves. The Bible tells us, "The revealed things belong unto us and our children forever, that we may do all the works of this law." Deut. 29:29."

Do you think we shall be judged by the will of God's decree or by the will of His commmand?

41

Naturally, by the will of His command or the revealed will. The will of His decree is unknown to us. This is a very difficult matter to understand and thousands of people will be shipwrecked on this rock, namely, that God requires something of us that He has, in His council, determined never to give us.

You are still young and caution is needed in this matter to prevent a misunderstanding.

Everyone, whose eyes have been opened, will see that a person will be judged righteously according to the righteousness of God, and that we have freely and continously transgressed the revealed command. In connection with this, there follows this question: What is God's justice?

Answer: That perfection of God, whereby He hates and punishes all sin.

Why does the Lord hate and punish all sin? Is He compelled to do it? or would it be because He so once resolved and now, of course, can do nothing else but follow His fixed decree to punish sin?

No, God is not compelled to do anything. Our answer says: His necessity flows from the most perfect freedom of His will. Hab. 1:13. But, also, it does not follow wholly out of His decree. His decree flows from His being, but His being does not flow from His decree. Nevertheless, God is a decreeing God and His decree cannot be separated from His being. His justice is also His Divine nature and so He hates and punishes sin because, in His essence, He is a just God. Do not ever believe that God hates sin only because He decreed to hate it, and, that He could just as well have not hated it. No, He said himself in Isaiah 61:8 "For I the Lord love judgment and I hate robbery for burnt offering."

By virtue of His just nature, God must hate and punish sin and it is impossible to surrender any of that justice. If He did, He would renounce Himself, because justice is also God.

And how must He punish sin; that is, unrighteousness?
In three ways; namely, corporal, spiritual and eternal.

The eternal punishment is the heaviest to bear, because
then there will be no common grace for support, — which
there is under spiritual and corporal punishment.

Could it be proven from God's Word that being punished
for sin is entirely just?

You are very well aware that we must confirm all our
statements out of God's Word. Without doing that, we
could talk all day and it would be of no value.

Answer: In God's command it was said," In the day that
thou eatest thereof thou shalt surely die."

It is perfectly just, then, that God performs that which
He threatens, is it not?

If there are some of you here that have listened attentively, you could possibly think, "God gave that command
unto all men through Adam and yet there are some that
will not be punished eternally; God has forgiven their sins.
How, then, can He be considered just?"

Hellenbroek anticipated this question too. His answer to
question 30 is: "There God's justice is satisfied in Christ
who endured the punishment of sin for them." His proof
is in Ephesians 1:7 "In whom we have redemption through
His blood, the forgiveness of sins, according to the riches of
His grace."

After the fall He could have righteously condemned the
whole human race, but He had chosen a people that He
desired to save, even though, because of their sins, they are
the objects of His wrath just as all others.

Do you know what else proves that God's justice must
be completely satisfied and that He cannot deviate from His
command?

It is most effectually proven in the suffering and death
of the Lord Jesus. If you may arrive home tonight in good

43

health, you should read quietly and thoughtfully the event of the death of Jesus. You would then observe how God, by virtue of His holy nature, had to punish His own Son with death, because He willingly desired to bear the punishment instead of His elect.

For that reason, it is necessary for everyone, personally, sometime during his lifetime, to experience divine justice. We all know very well this is true because God's Word says so, but we must also experience this in our hearts. That is something quite different from reading it in the Bible or learning it from a question book. If Christ has not borne that righteous wrath for you, do you know what will happen? You will have to bear it yourself, eternally, and that will be terrible. God's justice stands eternal and man will remain eternally guilty. He will then know how important the justice of God is, but it will be too late.

I hope you will consider most earnestly what it shall be to stand before a just and mighty God. Some people have much power in the world; for example, kings, emperors and those in command. But the Lord is above them all, and has an unlimited power in heaven and upon earth.

Question 33, explaining God's goodness as being His kindness in the manifestation of His benefits generally toward all creatures, is followed by the question: "What is God's grace?"

Answer: That goodness of God whereby He shows mercy unto man irrespective of his worthiness.

This is a precious answer. These few words comprehend the salvation of innumerable creatures that have justly deserved death. Grace is the goodness, whereby God benefits man, without consideration of his worthiness or unworthiness.

Now you must give me your close attention:

When the word grace is mentioned in this sense, what is

presupposed? Is it not, that guilt is present? If there is no guilt, there is no place for grace. Grace can never be given as payment for work, for example. Grace has the character of a free gift. It is unearned in comtra -distinction to earning a reward.

It is written in Romans 6:23 "For the wages (reward) of sin is death; but the gift of God is eternal life through Jesus Christ our Lord."

Hold your attention to this text for a little while. You know, of course, what is meant by wages.

Paul talks here to the Romans. At that time, the Roman emperor had an enormous number of soldiers in the service. Each one of these soldiers received their reward at the appointed time. This reward was called "wages."

We could read this text this way: "The reward of sin is death."

We had, previously, talked about God's justice; that all of us have deserved the three-fold death because of our sins; that is the reward we deserve.

That is what Paul wanted to make clear to the Romans. The wages (the reward) of sin is death. But what did he say after that? Listen, now he mentions the word that we have been speaking about; "But the gift of God is eternal life through Jesus Christ our Lord"

Here, you see, he calls grace a gift!

He intends to say we have not earned grace; and, our reward is death. He places grace opposite guilt — and because "sin" means guilt. Where there is sin, there is also guilt; it can be no other way.

This, then, is grace; that God, who, according to our deserts, could have given our reward for our sins in the form of a three fold death, but now, without any consideration of man's merits, He becomes his Benefactor.

That is what grace means here.

45

But now, we come to another question:

How *many* kinds of grace are there?

Answer: There is common grace in regard to all men; and particular and saving grace in regard to the elect.

Common grace is proven out of Matt. 5:45 "He maketh His sun to rise on the evil and on the good." Particular grace is proven from Matt. 11:25 "I thank thee Father, Lord of heaven and earth, because thou hast hid these things from the wise and prudent and hast revealed them unto babes, etc." This answer seems plain enough, but, perhaps some of you do not understand thoroughly, what the difference is between common and particular grace.

We shall use an example. A boy sits here and I ask him: "Are you converted, my boy?"

"No, Dominie, I am not converted" he says.

"So, then you are unconverted; because, it can be only one of the two, isn't that true; there is nothing between. You are, then, unconverted?"

"Yes, Dominie"

"Do you possess, though, the gift of grace that Paul speaks of in Romans 6:23, that is, eternal life?"

"No, Dominie, I do not possess it," he says.

"But, my boy, how can that be? You said that you do not possess the gift of grace that Paul had. You have never been delivered from your sins through Christ?"

"No, Dominie, as far as I know, that has never happened."

"Did you not, then, sin and, even in Paradise deserve death?"

"I am sure I have, Dominie," said the boy.

"Now I am perplexed, because God has said, that the day you are disobedient, you shall surely die. Further, He has bestowed grace on some, because Christ died for them in their stead, but you said you have not received that grace, and you have sinned and deserve to die. How is it, then, that you are still living?"

What kind of an answer would *you* give me regarding that, boys and girls? How can people live, who have never been converted?

Answer: Common grace sustains life until death!

Right! Do you understand, now, that there are two kinds of grace? If a person is converted, he receives particular or saving grace, which is an even much more precious gift and is sufficient for his eternal welfare.

Common grace is merely for this life as a fruit that Christ has earned.

Oh, may you find no peace on this earth until you possess that saving grace, that precious gift, instead of the reward of sin.

Is it a greater wonder to be alive or to be dead? To be healthy and alive, isn't it true? For that reason, we can never appreciate common grace enough either, even though it is insufficient for salvation.

Common grace will be present, generally, over all the world as long as there are elect upon the earth.
(God's people are often characterized as being "wheat" and the world as "chaff".)

As long as there is "wheat" hidden under the "chaff", common grace will be present on the earth. But common grace ceases to exist for the unconverted man when he dies, and will never be restored to him again.

Is there a difference between common grace which men receive here and "the time of grace"? You are well aware that the warning is often given from the pulpit, "Now is the day of grace, now one may still be converted."

You have heard that said at various times, too, haven't you?

Will the time of grace continue, indefinitely, until death comes?

It is not for us to know what God has determined for any one person, so we cannot apply one example to all, but we do read in God's Word that the time of grace has passed, irretrievably, for some persons even though they may still be living. They are special cases but they are certainly there. Do you know of the instances to which I refer? You remember the history of Saul. It is not necessary to relate this. When Saul had been disobedient in allowing King Agag to live, Samuel had to pronounce judgment upon him. It grieved Samuel, as expressed in I Samuel 15:35 "And Samuel came no more to see Saul until the day of his death, nevertheless Samuel mourned for Saul." What follows? Now we come to what I want to tell you, "And the Lord said unto Samuel, how long wilt thou mourn for Saul, seeing I have rejected him?" And in I Samuel 16:14 "But the spirit of the Lord departed from Saul, and an evil spirit from the Lord troubled him."

It is evident, is it not, that from that time forth, the time of grace was passed for Saul?

Yet Saul lived under common grace until the day of his death, having health, food and various privileges. He could never more be converted, however.

It is the same with all those who have sinned against the Holy Ghost. They live under common grace until they die. The time of grace is past for them, too. There is no more hope for their conversion.

This is not the time this afternoon, to speak about the sin against the Holy Ghost. You must not assume, however, because someone lives an ungodly life, he has sinned against the Holy Ghost and will never be converted. Oh no. Those that really have done the unpardonable sin, are never savingly convinced in their conscience and if they but once believe, before their death, that they have committed it, their end is despair. They have intentionally slandered the

48

Holy Ghost, knowing that He is the Holy Ghost. For example, Ananias and Sapphira were aware that they lied intentionally. They wanted to try the Holy Ghost to see whether He would know the amount of money for which they had sold their land.

That was a dreadful sin. That is why Peter, having known this through the Holy Ghost within him, said, "How is it that ye have agreed together to tempt the Spirit of the Lord?"

You must understand now, that this is entirely different than living with the world in all kinds of sin, which are pardonable, even though grievous.

It is still the time of grace for the greatest of sinners. Since we do not know what God's decree for us is until it is revealed, those of us under common grace, who have not sinned against the Holy Ghost, can be converted.

There will be no common grace in hell. You need not think that the devil will permit it there for even one person. Oh no. He does not have it for himself, so he will not allow it for us either. He does not share in the fruits of Christ's merits as do the creatures on earth. Immediately after his first sin it became and remains eternally impossible for him to be restored.

Always remember this, boys and girls: we have not deserved common grace either. It is a gift of Christ's merit and it is a gift effectual only for time, terminating at death. Furthermore, you cannot be saved by it. What then would seem fitting for us to do? We should acknowledge this gift.

I have known two persons who were husband and wife. God converted the woman, but the man remained unconverted. The man was spared, though, through common grace, of becoming hostile toward his wife. He had seen all that had taken place with her and was submissive to it. He went to church, lived among God's people with her and

49

read the Bible and other good books, just as she did.

But later he became sick and was about to die. One day before he passed away, knowing it was to take place, he said to his wife, "God has converted you but I remain unconverted. I have eaten and drank with you; have attended church and had close relationship with God's people but now I must die and be eternally lost. In Adam, I am justly damnable before God."

This man was soundly convinced, through historical faith, of his state and condition before God but it had never been impressed upon his heart.

A little later he said to her, "Please give me some cool water. I may still partake of that through the common grace of Christ's merits. In hell there will be no more benefits of His merits." That pitiable man was soundly convinced of the reality. But, alas, it was only being convinced of the truth. He had never been convinced of his own sin.

We have, in that way, spoken something about common grace.

Hellenbroek asks now: What is God's mercy?

Answer: God's goodness toward a miserable, elect sinner, by which He daily restores him in the state of grace through the Mediator Jesus.

How can it be possible that God can be merciful and still remain just? Does He ignore that justice and, by way of speaking, overlook their sin, because He sees some good in the elect?

We have said often in our previous lessons that it is possible for God to be gracious and merciful to them, only, because His justice is satisfied through Christ. Through Christ He can be merciful unto them, through Christ He can deliver them from the three-fold death, but through Him God can also restore them day by day in the state of grace, just as our answer explains.

Does God's mercy mean the same as His long-suffering or patience?

No, because His mercy is extended to the elect alone in Christ but His patience extends to all people.

God's long-suffering is that goodness of God whereby He delays the well-deserved punishment in order to bring the elect to repentance and to convince the reprobate.

He proves this answer from Romans 2:4, "Or despisest thou the riches of his goodness and forbearance and long-suffering; not knowing that the goodness of God leadeth thee to repentance?"

God is free from all persons, not alone because of our willfull unrestrained disobedience, but also because He makes Himself free.

Therefore, it is not unrighteous if God allows whole generations of savages and heathen to be lost, never having heard of God. God is free of man.

But for whom do you think the punishment will be the heavier, for the blind heathen, that never heard of God's Word, or for the Jews and ourselves, that is, so-called Christians, who die unconverted.

The heathen will be lost as a punishment for sin, but we shall be lost because of the sin of unbelief.

The gospel of redemption has been proclaimed unto us. If we have not been willing to believe it, the punishment will be the heavier.

Does it not become clear, that God postpones the deserved punishment and during that time brings His elect to conversion and convinces the reprobate of his guilt?

You are still young, but even so, confess the truth, have you not noticed how the conscience warns when you have done a wrong?

I am very sure that everyone here, at one time or another, has had a warning given to them. Am I not correct in this?

Sometimes by father or mother, or by means of a sermon, or perhaps when you were sick your conscience spoke to you.

God directs all these callings to us so that we will be without excuse.

It is as someone knocking on a locked door a long time and calling out, "Open the door, let me in!"

Oh, boys and girls, do you intend to let the Lord stand there always; won't you ever listen to Him? Are you going to tramp upon His convictions and warnings, trying to quiet your speaking conscience, but continuing to sin nevertheless?

I know very well that we cannot open our own heart. I do not mean it that way. Conversion comes from God and not from man. But the Lord can justly say: "I have called you and you have neglected to answer." You really do not want to; isn't that so?

May the Lord teach you to cry out, "Lord, turn me and I shall be turned, draw me and we will run after thee!"

Are there some among us, that have been convicted; sometimes crying about their sins and praying in solitude?

I would warn you from jumping, as it were, from the water into the fire. Today crying on account of your sins and tomorrow morning seeking out the fire of sin. Praying on account of sin and then sinning on account of praying. The heavier the conviction in the conscience, the heavier the judgment shall be if you try to quiet it.

Oh, listen no longer to the voice of the deceiver in your heart. The devil tries to draw you and places the world and your young life enticingly before you. But do not believe that he means to be good to you. Do you know what he shall say as soon as you die unconverted? He will say, "Well, boys and girls, why have you listened to me so faithfully? You know very well that I am a liar." He shall laugh and mock with you saying, "You were warned often enough, why have you been so faithful to my desires?"

Oh, if it must come to pass that you are lost, you will surely remember this hour that we have spent together and it will be a cause of shame to you.

I hope and do wish that you do not come to that, oh no, and I pray in submission to God's will for your preservation. I shall surely do it too. However, I must warn you that the long-suffering of God is not meant solely to bring the elect to conversion but also to convince the unconverted, so that they can never say, "We have never been informed of it."

All of you that would rather not hear it here will hear it there eternally and what you never cared to know about here, you will know eternally. You need not think there will be no knowledge in hell!

There will be a clear knowledge of the justice of God and of the guilt of man. That knowledge will be the worm that does not die. That knowledge shall always cause a gnawing in our conscience, and in addition, the fire of God's wrath will never be quenched.

Because of that, may you come to know these things now; with the result that you may be brought to conversion in the time of God's long suffering. May your guilty soul (even if the body is still young) find reconciliation with God through Jesus Christ, "for there is none other name under heaven given among men, whereby we must be saved."

We shall conclude by singing from the first Psalm and close in prayer.

That man is blest who fearing God
From sin restrains his feet
Who will not stand with wicked men
Who shuns the scorners' seat

Lesson 6   A lesson on the three Divine Persons.

Our catechism lesson today deals with the three Divine Persons.

Does this mean that there are three Divine Beings, or three Gods?

No, there is but one God but in that Divine being we distinguish three Divine Persons, which are called Father, Son and Holy Ghost.

We learned in our first lesson, that we can know there is a God by observing nature and from the Holy Scriptures. Can we prove from nature that there are three Divine Persons?

No, and further, we ought not try to do it. Some people and especially writers have attempted to do it. They say: "As in nature root, trunk and branches are one; and, water, snow and ice are one, so also, the three Divine Persons are one."

But I caution you to never say it in that way. It is impossible to equate, created, perishable things with the Divine Being. We have learned that the Divine Trinity is a mystery; not contrary to nature but above it.

Where can we prove this?

Out of the Holy Scripture, which is always the best source of proof.

Before we search out what God's Word teaches us regarding it, I want to know what your thoughts are. You are still very young, but we are gathered together an hour to be instructed, so you have freedom to express your thoughts.

Would the three Divine Persons rate one above another in value or *power?*

Do you think they are as three stripes set one

54

above another in that the Father is higher than the Son and the Son higher than the Holy Ghost?

No, that is absolutely not so and you ought not represent it that way. Do you know what you should read concerning the three Divine Persons? The Athanasian creed. Athanasius lived in the year 333 A.D. and was bishop in Alexandria. Alexandria was the capital of Egypt for a long time. We cannot spare the time now to recite the whole creed. Read it when you are at home tonight. It can be found in the "Doctrinal Standards of the Netherlands Reformed Congregations." It says in part: "And the catholic faith is this: That we worship one God in Trinity and Trinity in unity, neither confounding the persons, nor dividing the substance. For there is one person of the Father, another of the Son and another of the Holy Spirit. But the Godhead of the Father, of the Son, and of the Holy Spirit is all one, the glory equal, the majesty co-eternal. The Father uncreate, the Son uncreate and the Holy Spirit uncreate. The Father eternal, the Son eternal and the Holy Spirit eternal. And yet they are not three eternals but one eternal.

The Father is God, the Son is God and the Holy Spirit is God. And yet they are not three Gods, but one God. And in this Trinity none is before or after another, none is greater or less than another. But the whole three persons are co-eternal and co-equal. So likewise the Father is Lord, the Son Lord and the Holy Spirit is Lord."

The old bishop in the days of the early Christians made it plain for us in this way, that the three Divine Persons are not to be separated from one another. But, can they not be distinguished from one another? You understand, certainly, the difference between things that are completely separated from one another, and things that belong together but are distinguished by themselves.

We can observe plainly in a prayer of the Lord Jesus Christ the distinction in the Divine Persons. In John 14:16 he says: "I will pray the Father and He will give you another comforter. Jesus spoke here to the Father about the Holy Ghost.

Jesus Prayed. To whom did He pray? To the Father. And why did He pray to Him? For the Comforter, that is, the Holy Ghost. The Divine persons are plainly distinguished here. Hellenbroek asks: How is the Trinity proven from the Holy Scripture?

Answer: The three persons are explicitly named in texts both of the old and new testaments. Psalm 33:6 "By the Word (2nd person) of the Lord (1st person) were the heavens made: and all the host of them by the breath of His mouth (3rd person)." And in the New Testament it speaks literally in Matt. 28:19 "Go ye therefore, and teach all nations, baptizing them in the name of the Father and the Son and of the Holy Ghost: teaching them to observe all things whatsoever I have commanded you."

They are truly three Persons, though they are one in being.

The difference is much clearer in the New Testament than in the Old. They are found in texts gathered from the Old Testament but the Persons are not named literally.

That is why the Old Testament is said to be as a shadow. Justus VerMeer mentions in one of his books: "It was for the people living under the Old Testament dispensation as though they carried a heavy lantern with the many offerings and all sorts of ceremonies that they had to perform conscientiously. They went along stooped under the weight of the heavy lantern. Certainly a great many Jews under the Old Testament, because of the detailed ceremonial laws, found them to be heavy tasks and hardly knew their significance. But by way of speaking, there are a few that even-

56

tually put the lantern down and looked in. When they looked carefully they saw that there was a little bright light in there; and the quickened ones, who had faith that all those "shadow services" pointed to Christ, were as they who observed the light in the lantern. Then they courageously took up the heavy burden again and went on further.

So we can know that the Trinity and especially Christ is spoken of in the Old Testament. However, it is like light from the stars in contrast to the bright sunlight in the New Testament. The Lord said to Moses in Exodus 6:2 "I appeared unto Abraham, unto Isaac and unto Jacob by the name of God Almighty, but by my name Jehovah was I not known to them."

The Trinity can be proven from both the Old and the New Testaments.

Now it is asked: "Are they then personally distinct?"

Answer: "Yes, by their personal properties, or manner of subsisting."

Then it is further explained: The personal attribute of God the Father is that He as Father is self-existent.

The personal attribute of the Son is that He is begotten of the Father. Psalm 2:7 "I will declare the decree: The Lord hath said unto me, Thou art my Son: this day have I begotten thee."

The personal attribute of the Holy Ghost is that He proceeds from the Father and the Son. John 15:26 "But when the comforter is come, whom I shall send unto you from the Father, even the Spirit of truth, which proceedeth from the Father, He shall testify of me."

These are called the personal attributes, because they do not belong to the whole essence, but each of them only to one person in particular.

Of the Father, who is called the first person in the Di-

57

vine Essence, it is said "That He as Father is of Himself." That is, not by creation, not through another, but He is Himself without beginning and without end. The Son, nevertheless, is said to be begotten of the Father, which is clear from Psalm 2:7.

But now you must express yourself whether there is a contradiction in God's Word on this point or not.

It is asked: "When is the Son begotten of the Father?"

Answer: From Eternity, Proverbs 8:24 "When there were no depths or fountains, I was brought forth."

Don't you find too that this answer is in conflict with the former where it is said: "This day have I begotten thee?" "From eternity before the depths or fountains existed" is very much different than "This day"; is not this so?

Hellenbroek gives us the solution. He says: "In God is only one eternal and unchangeable day."

How must we understand this now; that the second Person, the Son, is of God the Father?

This is a mystery. It is not contradictory, but far above our nature and impossible for our finite human understanding to comprehend.

Yet, even though we cannot understand them, we believe on the basis of God's Word that it is so.

John the Baptist said, "No man hath seen God at anytime: the only begotten Son, which is in the bosom of the Father, he hath declared Him." John 1:18. The Father shares the same Divine essence with the Son from eternity to eternity. "He is the image of the invisible God," says Paul in Hebrews 1:3, "the first born of all creatures." And in Colossians 2:9 he says: "For in Him dwelleth (in Christ, that is) all the fulness of the Godhead bodily."

Hellenbroek asks now: "Did He not become the Son of God by being born of Mary or by His mediatorship?"

58

"No," says he, "for He was the Son of God before."

He was begotten according to His Divine nature; God out of God, which we cannot comprehend. In respect to His human nature He was ordained. Begotten means: "Same brings forth same." That is to say, the Father imparted His essence to His Son from eternity to eternity.

In respect to His personal attributes as God's Son, (His divine being) they are not His by will alone but out of the essence of the Father.

In respect to His human nature, He was ordained from eternity and took it upon Himself at the appointed time.

These are difficult studies for you, but I must speak to you about these matters even if you cannot understand all of it. Try to remember it. Perhaps, when you get older, you might still receive profit from it. Above all, I wish God would teach these mysteries to your heart. You will then receive them by faith and this subject will contribute to your adoration and admiration of God.

The personal attribute of the Holy Ghost is: that He proceeds (goes out) from the Father and the Son. We have just stated that we must not understand in these personal attributes that the Son or the Holy Ghost are inferior to the Father, so we shall not repeat our discussion of it. It is clearly proven in God's Word, that the Holy Ghost proceeds from the Father. Jesus says in John 15:26 "But when the comforter is come, whom I will send unto you from the Father, even the Spirit of Truth, which proceedeth from the Father, etc."

It is clear in this connection, that He proceeds not only from the Father but also from the Son in that He is also called the Spirit of Christ as in Galatians 4:6, "And because ye are sons, God hath sent forth the Spirit of His Son into your hearts, crying, 'Abba, Father!'"

Soon after the time of the Apostles there was a great

difference of opinion concerning this point between the Eastern and Western churches.

You know that Paul and the other apostles came to Europe to preach the gospel of Christ. As a result, there were congregations established there too, which constituted the first Christian congregations affiliated with the congregations in Palestine.

The congregations in Europe were considered the Western church, and the congregations in and around Jerusalem were called the Eastern Church.

The difference that developed between them concerned this point:

The one part said: "The Holy Ghost proceeds from the Father and the Son"

But the other part said: "The Holy Ghost proceeds from the Father and testifies of the Son."

It became so serious, they were not able to meet in session with one another and because of this one point a schism developed between the two churches.

The differences, however, was not serious; it was only a misunderstanding.

It is clear from God's Word, that the Holy Ghost proceeds from the Father and the Son in respect to His personal attributes or evidences of existence, as we have proved from the quoted texts.

But as for His Divine influence, it is evident that He proceeds from the Father but witnesses of the Son. This is evident in John 15:16; "But when the comforter is come, whom I will send unto you from the father, even the Spirit of Truth, which proceedeth from the Father, He shall testify of me."

Both are correct, therefore; only a distinction must be made.

It is clearly evident all around us, that the Holy Ghost

testifies of the second Person in His divine work in the hearts of the elect.

You know, in an intellectual way, that each Divine Person is recognized for His one distinct work, is not this true?

It is recognized that:

1st. The election is the work of the Father from eternity (however, not without the Son and the Holy Ghost)

2nd. Redemption is the work of the Son.

3rd. The application is the work of the Holy Ghost.

The Holy Ghost, upon the direction from the Father, witnesses in the world.

We cannot see this Divine Spirit with our natural eyes, nor become aware of Him with any of our other physical senses. Yet, He surely and irresistably performs His Divine work in the heart of elect sinners.

He convinces them earnestly of the heinousness of sin, the righteous judgment of God and of the only way of life; that is, in Christ Jesus. This afternoon is not the time to talk specially about the work of the Holy Ghost. Our lesson today concerns the three Divine Persons.

We spoke briefly about it because, while the inward, saving knowledge of God must be experienced in your heart, we must also attain to an intellectual knowledge of it. Who knows what God has in store for you? He can bless it now and in years to come.

We are gathered at this time to inquire into these Divine truths, isn't that so?

Does your father or mother ask, occasionally, what you have learned upon arriving home from catechism? Or don't they ever inquire of you what you do or do not know of the fundamentals of faith?

I hope they do.

If your father would say to you, "well, John, did you go to Catechism?"

61

"Yes father," you would say.

"And of what subject were you taught today?"

"Of the Three Divine Persons, father," you would answer him.

"So, that is an important lesson, John; what did the dominie tell you about it?"

If your father, then, for example, would ask: Can you prove to me from God's Word that the Son and the Holy Ghost are God as well as the Father, what would you give as an answer?

If you had learned your lesson carefully, you would say:

"Well, father, I can point these things out to you very quickly.

1st. I can prove it by their Divine names.

2nd. By their Divine attributes.

3rd. By their Divine works, and

4th. By their Divine honor."

"Now, John," your father would then say, "I would like to have you tell me which Divine names are given to the Son and which to the Holy Ghost."

How many of you know the answer to this?

The name of God was given to Jesus in 1 John 5:20 "And we are in Him that is true, even in His Son Jesus Christ. This is the true God and eternal life."

Secondly: The name of God was given to the Holy Ghost in Acts 5:3&4 where Peter said, "Why hath Satan filled thine heart to lie to the Holy Ghost? — thou hast not lied to men, but unto God."

This is a proof concerning their Divine names.

We also find Divine attributes of the Son and the Holy Ghost in the Holy Scriptures.

Hellenbroek mentions "Eternity" for the second person, Micah 5:1 "Whose goings forth have been from of old, from everlasting."

It is said of the Holy Ghost, that He is omnipresent, Psalm 139:7 "Whither shall I go from thy Spirit?"

It is proved from this Divine Attribute that He, with the Father and the Son is truly God.

It is Said, furthermore, that to them, with the Father, are ascribed Divine Works and, so also, Divine Honor. It is made clear in creation and its preservation that it is of the entire Divine Being and not only of one or two Persons. "Psalm 33:6 "By the word of the Lord were the heavens made; and all the host of them by the breath of his mouth."

We are taught thereby, to worship the entire Divine Being, to believe in them and to be baptized in the name of the three Divine Persons.

Why would Hellenbroek enlarge so extensively upon the proof that the Holy Ghost and the Son are God as well as the Father?

There were people throughout all ages that denied this.

Also, there are writings which teach that the Holy Ghost is no actual Person but only a power of God. This can be answered contrarily from John 14:16 where the Holy Ghost is expressly called "another." This could not be done if He were only a power or "attribute" and, therefore, no real Person.

You can well understand how terrible it is to deny that the Holy Ghost is a Divine Person and to reject the whole doctrine of the Trinity. Do not listen to such wandering spirits, children, because everything concerning life and salvation is based on the pure doctrine of the three Divine Persons.

Now I shall mention something concerning the second Person, which you must remember.

1st. He is one in essence with the Father and the Holy Ghost.

2nd. He is the only eternal, true and natural Son born of the Father.

3rd. He is ordained of the Father from eternity to the office of Mediator.

4th. He took upon Himself, in the fulness of time, the human nature, made of à woman, made under the law.

5th. He is the Immanuel. "God with us," two natures united into a unity of Persons.

There are important matters contained in these five points. Sometimes there are those who teach one of these points of doctrine but deny others.

That is why you must always observe, in your later life, whether men deviate from some of the points in the doctrine of the Divine Persons. Calvin, in his time, had to defend this doctrine against a preacher who acknowledged that the Christ was the only Son of God, but denied that He was eternal.

If men deviate from one of these points of God's Word, the rest of the doctrine is not worthy of credence because it is as a house without foundation.

The time is much too short to talk about all errors that are taught by people concerning the Divine Persons.

We shall conclude this hour that has quickly passed with the consideration of the last question of our lesson.

Is this doctrine necessary unto salvation?

Answer: Yes, because we thereby receive true knowledge of God and learn to seek atonement with the Father as judge in the satisfation of the Son, through the working of the Holy Spirit. This answer is not contrary to God's Word because John said in 1 John 1:3 "That which we have seen and heard declare we unto you, that ye also may have fellowship with us: and truly our fellowship is with the Father and with His Son Jesus Christ." Have you noticed that, in the religious world generally, there is little mention made of the Divine Persons?

You are still young; you may not have experienced it. From now on take notice how little emphasis is placed on the necessity of having a knowledge of the three Divine Persons.

Most of the time the children in Sunday School and in Christian schools are told about the Lord Jesus, but what must a person do with the Lord Jesus if he has no need of a mediator?

And what must I do with a Mediator if I do not know that I have guilt and do not know against whom I have sinned?

How must I come to this knowledge? That is the work of the Holy Spirit. He makes a person aware, for the first time, of the one before whom he is guilty.

God's children shall learn to know the distinct work of each of the three Divine Persons two times in their life. In the very beginning of the saving work of the Holy Spirit, He will show them the first Person as a just judge, whose wrath shall be executed against sin and who will justly demand that His law be fulfilled. The Holy Spirit will so persuadingly convince an elect sinner that God is righteous and he guilty, that he must admit that it would be perfectly just if he would be lost, yes, that he actually is lost because in Adam we already have transgressed God's law. But, as the Holy Spirit so works in him, and the sinner takes over his wretched state, He also uncovers the only way to reconciliation, Jesus Christ. This, then, is the first acquaintance with the three Divine Persons. While this is taking place, however, there is not one person that recognizes it, because if he could see that it was the work of the Holy Spirit, he would run the peril of resting before he became lost. No, that remains unknown to him but it is taking place.

If the Lord, in His sovereignty, works through with such a soul, he is taught that the judged is reconciled through the satisfaction made by Christ, and that now God is His Father in Christ.

Then the Holy Spirit applies the work of the second person to the soul and that soul accepts it by faith.

We point these things out, briefly, even though we know you do not comprehend the full depth of them. Boys and girls, hold to this truth: without satisfaction made by the Surety, it is not possible to become reconciled with the Judge.

The Holy Spirit does not begin in such a way that men can immediately speak of "blessed Lord Jesus," as some men do, nowadays, in speaking to the children. No, He will convince of sin, righteousness and judgment.

After this revelation to the soul, He will be a guide to Christ. For what reason would men need Christ if they do not believe themselves to be guilty?

With all my heart I hope that the Holy Spirit will bring you to a knowledge of the three Divine Persons, while you are in your youth. This is sure: without having gotten knowledge of the First Person through the Third Person, there also shall be no genuine knowledge of the Second Person.

Think about this: even though you are still young, you are not too young to die; so also not too young to be lost and, therefore, also not too young to be converted!

What a privilege it would be if the Holy Spirit began to work savingly in your heart today. It would be to your eternal well being. Then you would surely become aware that you are not only a stranger of God but, also, God's adversary. You would also become aware that it is not possible to have reconciliation with Him without His justice being satisified.

By nature a person would earn what he wants and understand what he must believe. That is so because he has not a true knowledge of the Divine Persons.

There is no place in our hearts for God without God's work there. God must make that place Himself. He makes that place in the heart of every elect person, through the work of the Holy Spirit.

But, what would you think if it happened that the Lord came to work His Spirit in your heart? Would you think He would find you willing or unwilling?

I am of the opinion that some of you think that you are eager to be converted and, that being the case,
would cooperate when He came; isn't that so?

How disappointed you would be if that happened. You would have to learn that you are not merely a dead sinner but also a hostile and perverse sinner.

"Enemies reconciled with God through the death of His Son" is a mystery that will be revealed only to God's people.

You, too, can experience the benefits of the Triune Divine Being through free grace.

So be it.

Lesson 7

Of Gods Decrees and Predestination.

We must talk about a very important subject this afternoon. It is about God's decrees and predestination or foreordaining.

We had mentioned previously in our lessons about the attributes of God and the Three Persons, that God and His attributes are one and the same and that we cannot separate them, but, His attributes can be distinguished.

We tried, also, to make plain to you that the three Divine Persons are not to be separated from one another, but is one Divine Essence distinguished in Father, Son and Holy Spirit.

In like manner, it is also impossible to separate God's Decrees from God. They are the decreeing God Himself. His understanding and will manifest themselves in determining matters outside of Him.

As God is not only a single and a triune God but also an eternal God, without beginning and without end, and, He and His decrees being inseparable, He being the decreeing God,   it naturally follows, God's decrees are also eternal.

That is clear enough; isn't it?

Who can prove from God's Word, that all God's decrees, without exception, were made in eternity?

Answer: Acts 15:18 "Known unto God are all His works from the beginning of the world."

This is clear proof! You are convinced that our faith (belief) must have its foundation in the Holy Scriptures. Hellenbroek handles these matters always using the Bible as his guide.

Now he asks: "To what do the decrees of God extend?" Do they involve many things? Do they involve only some things, or, do they, without exception comprehend all things?

Paul gives us, by the Holy Spirit, an answer to this in Ephesians 1:11 "In whom also we have obtained an inheritance, being predestinated according to the purpose of Him who worketh *all* things after the council of His own will."

God's decree in this instance is called the "council of His will."

The Holy Spirit teaches us that He works *all* things through the means of His Will. There is not one thing that is not comprehended in it.

God's children will learn to love and admire these eternal decrees as being perfectly free as well as supremely wise decrees. The apostle had experienced that and called out in Romans 11:33 "O the depth of the riches both of the wisdom and knowledge of God! how unsearchable are His judgments, and His ways past finding out!"

Can these wise, eternal and free decrees ever be changed?

You have learned in the lesson entitled "The Attributes of God" that immutability is an incommunicable attribute of God. And since God's decrees are the decreeing God Himself, could there be any change brought about in these decrees?

Of course that is impossible because then God Himself would have to change.

That is why the Lord said in Isaiah 46:10 "My council shall stand, and I will do all My pleasure."

We mentioned previously in the lesson on the immutability of God (the unchangeableness of God) that repentance is at times ascribed to God about something He had done; for example, Gen. 6:6 "And it repented the Lord that He had made man on the earth, and it grieved Him at His heart."

69

Does it appear, then, that the Lord is changeable and, therefore, His decrees also?

No, that is not repentance of the decree He had made.

Hellenbroek said: "In God's will we must distinguish a will of His decree and a will of His command."

The will of His eternal decree shall remain steadfast in all things forever. If matters in the world transpire in such a way that they seem contrary to all laws and commandments, His decrees in all these things, none the less, will be fulfilled at the exact time and place.

There are very few persons in this world who adore this doctrine.

God's people, who have been taught to love the Lord above all else, also love His decrees above their own will and become submissive to it, even when it seems that everything is against them.

If all things are decreed by God from eternity, has God also decreed who shall be saved and who shall not be saved?

Answer: Yes, this is called predestination or, fore-.ordination.

The proof for the existence of election is found in Romans 8:30, "Whom He did predestinate, them He also called, etc."

The word "predestination," means, literally speaking, pre-selection, arranging previously or appointing ahead of time.

The decree of predestination is then a decree or a selection of a certain (definite) number of persons that shall be saved, over against others that shall not be saved.

Would this selection (election) be ascribed to the Divine Being in its entirety or to one of the Divine Persons?

In the broad sense, the predestination is an act of the Divine Being as a whole, but in respect to their order of work it is assigned to the Father or the First Person. This is made clear in Ephesians 1:4 "According as He hath chosen us in Him," The word "He" means God the Father and "Him" means His son Jesus Christ.

This election of the Father, in the Son, is applied by the Holy Spirit to the elect. It follows now, since God and His decrees are eternal, that the election is also eternal, because it all is comprehended in God and in His decree. Paul continues in that same text: "According as He hath chosen us in Him before the foundation of the world." That is, then, from eternity.

Now Hellenbroek asks a very profound question. I do not think you will understand all of it, but you should try to remember the words of it.

He asks: "How many parts or acts of God must we distinguish therein?"

Answer: Two; election and reprobation.

Is this to be found in God's Word also?

Yes, in 1 Thess. 5:9 "For God hath not appointed *us* to wrath, (that is the reprobation) but to obtain salvation, (that is election).

The election and the reprobation are, thus, two deeds that are revealed in God's sovereign decree.

But what is the affecting cause of these deeds?

Hellenbroek asks that same question in these words: "For what reason hath God elected the one and not the other?"

Answer: Only for His free and sovereign pleasure. Rom. 9:18 "He hath mercy on whom He will have mercy, and whom He will He hardeneth."

Men cannot give any other explanation that agrees with God's Word than: It is God's Sovereign will. In His Holy decree lies election and reprobation.

Men would think: does it agree with God's virtue of mercy, that there is a reprobation? And contrary-wise, does

71

it agree with the justice of God, that He chose some to salvation?

You should read the answer to this question in the 37 articles of our Confession of Faith.

Guido de Bres, in dealing with the 16th article says: "We believe that all the posterity of Adam being thus fallen into perdition and ruin, by the sin of our first parents, God then did manifest Himself such as He is; that is to say, merciful and just; merciful, since He delivers and preserves from this perdition all, whom He, in His eternal and unchangeable counsel of mere goodness, hath elected in Christ Jesus our Lord, without any respect to their works: just, in leaving others in the fall and perdition wherein they have involved themselves."

What is plainly observed here?

That those, who once shall be saved, are saved out of free grace, flowing out of God's sovereign will for Christ's sake. And that those, that remain lost, shall experience God's justice because of their own sins.

There lies no hardness or injustice in reprobation, because, since we all have sinned, God, with the greatest of justice, without hardness, could have let all men be lost.

There are several kinds of election spoken of in God's Word.

I shall speak a moment of the principal ones. You should try to remember them and recite them to me when I ask about them, if the Lord spare us, next week.

The principal instances of election, spoken of in God's Word, are: 1st: Jesus Christ was elected by God the Father from eternity. He was not elected God or the Second Person in the Divine Being; no, He was God and the Second Person with the Father from eternity.

But, He was elected to be the mediator between God and the elect, and to reconcile the two with each other.

The proof for this election is Isaiah 42:1 "Behold, my servant, whom I uphold; mine elect, etc."

2nd. The angels are elect. They are not God and are not man, but are ministering spirits.

Unto what end are a part of the angels elected? To be saved?

No, because they are saved. However, one part of the angels is predestined or chosen to *remain* saved, that is, to remain standing in contradistinction to another part, that were created equally good and perfect, but were not predestined to be saved.

These, who were properly created angels in heaven, have of their own free will become evil devils in Hell.

But that part of the angels that remained standing and that had not sinned against God, are called elect angels. The support for this is 1 Timothy 5:21 "I charge thee before God, and the Lord Jesus Christ and the elect angels etc."

3rd. It is plainly evident that a nation has been elected.

Israel was elected out of all the peoples of the world to live alone and to be a separate people from whose generations the Messiah would be born.

Does it follow from this, that all the Israelites were elected to be saved?

Certainly not. The Apostle teaches us otherwise. "For they are not all Israel, which are of Israel," he says in Romans 9:6, "The elect have obtained it and the others became hardened."

Yet Israel as a people were elected from eternity above all people. The proof of this is in Deut. 7:6, "For thou art an holy people unto the Lord thy God; the Lord thy God hath chosen thee to be a special people unto himself, above all people that are upon the face of the earth."

4th. There is an election of officials to an office. A person can be chosen to serve in an office in this world and yet not be chosen to salvation.

Saul is an example of this. God had elected him as the one Samuel would anoint to be king.

When you arrive home this evening, read quietly the history in 1 Sam. 9 and 10. You will find there that Samuel said to the people (speaking of Saul): "See ye him whom the Lord hath chosen, that there is none like him among all the people," 1 Sam. 10:24.

But as for his state for eternity, Saul was not a chosen vessel. That was clearly revealed later.

That was so with Judas also. The Lord Jesus said: "Have I not chosen you twelve?" in John 6:70.

He meant the election to office in this case, "choosing" them to perform a task in the world. This had nothing to do with the election to salvation, because the Lord continued by saying: "and one of you is a devil." He said this of Judas Iscariot, for he it is that should betray Him, being one of the twelve," verse 71.

5th. There is an election in general of the whole church of God. In the liberal sense, we could describe this as being the complete inheritance promised to Christ as a reward for His labors. All the elect, as a great assembly together, was the reward for Christ; His inheritance. He said in Psalm 2, "I will declare the decree: the Lord hath said unto me, 'Thou art my Son; this day have I begotten thee. Ask of me and I shall give thee the heathen for thine inheritance, and the uttermost parts of the earth for thy possession.' " This is a universal election of the church comprehended in its entirety.

And, although it is surely true that it is this way, there is much misuse made of it. Even various writers and many preachers of our day stop with this universal election. They say, "There is a determined number elected by God," and that is true. But now, they conclude that one is elect because they see various qualities in themselves or others.

74

For example, if a person is baptized, has a Christian upbringing, makes confession, goes to the Lord's Supper and lives a blameless life, pays each his due, etc, then, from these qualities men conclude they belong to the multitude of the elect.

Do you see, boys and girls, the great peril that is lurking here?

It is certainly true that God's universal church is formed from the great multitude of the elect. But do you know what there is beside that? There is:

6th. A personal (or individual) election. The Lord says: "I know thee by name," Exodus 33:17.

This personal election is a great comfort to all of God's people. Do you know why?

A spiritually awakened, concerned and seeking soul would say: Oh, Lord, I surely believe you have elected a people and also that people are favored; but Lord, would you have elected me: would I belong to that blessed people? Those would be the questions of a person who had been made spiritually alive.

Can a person ever come to know if he is elected personally? What do you think?

Who can give me an answer of proof of personal election from God's Word?

Answer: Romans 9:13, "Jacob have I loved, and Esau have I hated."

Do you hear that now? Their names are all written in God's Book.

That is a source of comfort for God's children; a fountain of joy when by faith they may embrace the assurance that their name is also included with the elect.

May it also become a heavy burden in your life sometime, that you must come to that knowledge.

Maybe there are boys and girls, even now, silently

thinking: "You said in the beginning of this lesson, that God's decree in election and reprobation is unchangeable just as God is unchangeable, so, there is nothing more to do. Actually, I can live just as I want to, because my lot is already cast."

I can realize that such thoughts arise in your minds. Nor do I mean to say, that you must pray to God to elect you. That would be foolishness.

Imagine for a moment, that you entered someone's home and you found the person living there praying aloud. You heard that man asking very fervently and reverently: "Lord, if it please you, will you create the world today —". You would think that man is not in his right mind, wouldn't you?; because, the world is in being already.

But, if request was made for sustenance and strength, health and wisdom, it would be a permissible prayer.

So it would be foolishness to ask the Lord to elect you, because, the election lies unchangeable in God from eternity. But it would be a privilege to have the desire within the heart to ask, "Lord, may I know if I am included with those that Thou hast known!"

He can make this known to you, through grace. O, boys and girls, if this were to take place, you would sink away in astonishment as never before. An elect vessel! That has such a deep meaning.

The Lord had elected Paul both to be an apostle and to salvation long before he was born on earth as Saul.

He did not know this even though he was converted. Ananias did not know it either.

Ananias considered it to be a perilous work to inquire about such a hostile person as Saul was reputed to be. He apparently was afraid that the Lord had made a mistake, because he said: "Lord, you know what evil this man has done. I dare not go to him!"

But the Lord set him at rest and said, "I know it very well, Ananias, just be calm, and go without fear to him because he is a chosen vessel unto Me."

Then Ananias yielded to free grace and went.

And has it not been clearly shown in this Saul of Tarsus, that he was a chosen vessel? Not only to accomplish the work of his office during his lifetime, but also for eternity.

You should read Romans 8 to see what a deep knowledge he had of election. That chapter is called the Golden Chain. Do you know why? Because it forms one golden link onto the other. He begins in eternity with the first; listen: Romans 8:29 "For whom he did foreknow, he also did predestinate." (You must understand, that in the word foreknow he means eternity and with predestinate, he means elect.) That is the first link in eternity. "Moreover, whom He did predestinate, them He also called":

That is the second link, but now he is in time (after creation). He means the internal calling. (the calling to salvation) "And whom He called, them He also justified; and whom He justified, them He also glorified."

"Glorified," He says. So he is now again in eternity where time shall never enter. Do you observe now that Paul formed a golden chain? He formed link to link, beginning in eternity, he goes through time, and then towards eternity which has no end.

Paul had been taught that the whole work of salvation *lay* in the Divine Being, *came out* of that Being, worked through that Being, and *returned again* to that Being.

And do you know what became the greatest wonder for Paul?

That he, too, was taken up in that chain, that his name, too, was marked in that Divine Decree. That was a miracle.

But, our hour is spent. We shall not continue speaking about predestination, even though there is so much more to say about it. For instance, would not the elect become saved just by virtue of being an elect? No, that would be impossible.

The Council of Peace must be reckoned with. The election must be worked out and that could never be done without Christ who took that work upon Himself.

We said last week: without satisfaction we cannot obtain reconciliation. In the designs of God, in the decree of the Triune Divine Being, all the elect are justified and sanctified in Christ. But, that was in the decree.

Now it is also necessary that they become justified through Christ, in this time state, in order to know that they are justified.

We shall speak of this in the following lessons if the Lord spare us.

May the Lord cause your young hearts to become restless through the working of His Spirit, so that you have no rest until you also know you belong to the redeemed of the Lord.

Perhaps the devil tries to make you believe that you are not elect and, so it is not necessary to trouble yourselves about it. But, think about it, boys and girls, he tries this only to draw you further and further away into sin. If you have such thoughts, don't think they are of God because the Lord does not give such thoughts.

If God's Spirit works in your heart, you will surely fall here or there upon your knees saying: "O, Lord, I have lived 14 or 15 years upon this earth. Must I continue living without Thee until I die? Shall I not ever belong to that blessed people that are reconciled to thee? O, Lord, may I find favor with Thee again? I am lost because of sin."

Do you see that could be the voice of God's Spirit! It is not the Spirit of God, however, when the thought is: 'You are not of the elect and so you can live in sin."

78

Think about how fearful it shall be, if you always seek sin with lust and enjoyment!

We justly deserve death when we sin and, yet, don't you feel in your heart that you would much rather serve sin than shun it?

The devil and your evil heart are saying: "You can't do anything about it. If you are a castaway, you will never be converted anyway —," but will a person be lost because he is not elected, or because he has love for sin above love for God?

I think the latter, don't you believe so, too?

Cannot the Lord say righteously: "You do not want to come to me?"

If your conscience is still open, you will all agree with me in this.

From my heart I wish that God in His boundless good pleasure, would cause each one of you, personally, to stop in your way, and would call you by name, just as He did to Saul on the way to Damascus.

I know that you, even as he, would fall prostrate before Him, without further resistance, asking: "Who art thou, Lord?"

O, may that become a reality, to God's honor, and to profit for your precious soul.

Lesson 8

Concerning Creation

As we proceed with our catechism lessons we come this afternoon to the one entitled "Creation."

Last week we dealt with a few questions regarding God's decrees. In connection with that, it is now asked: "Doth God also put His decrees into effect?"

Answer: Yes, in time by His works.

I hope all of you remember what we said in our first lesson, namely: God's works in time are twofold. First, His works in nature and, second, His works in grace.

Further, His works in nature are divided into two parts, namely: first, His works of creation and, second, His works of providence.

We see here, then, a sequence.

God established His decrees in eternity, but He works out all these decrees in time in various ways.

The execution of those eternal decrees concerning the work of creation and providence was also brought about.

Which of those two, do you think had to be revealed first?

I shall give an example first, then you may give me the answer.

A house that is built and carefully maintained by its owner manifests two things: First, the house was erected. Secondly, the house was kept in good condition. But, what was necessarily the first work?

Building the house; isn't that true? He could not maintain it before it existed.

The work of creation must take place first, otherwise, the work of providence could not follow. Providence is the sustenance, cooperation and ruling of all creation.

Now it is asked: What is it to create?

Answer: To produce or give existence to something, by an omnipotent act of a simple will.

The truth of this answer is proven out of Rev. 4:11 "For thou hast created all things, and for thy pleasure they are and were created."

This almighty deed was not the work of only one of the divine persons; no, the creation is the work of a Triune God as it is plainly read in Psalm 33:6, "By the Word of the Lord were the heavens made; and all the host of them by the breath of his mouth."

Concerning the order of work in creation, it is said the Father stands in the forground, just as it is said of the Son in the work of redemption and of the Holy Ghost in the work of sanctification.

Considering it in the broadest sense we speak of it in this way: The Triune God created the World.

And *when* did He do this?

Hellenbroek says it very briefly, "In the beginning."

This answer embraces the first words of the Holy Scriptures: "In the beginning God created the heaven and the earth. And the earth was without form and void; and darkness was upon the face of the deep. And the Spirit of God moved upon the face of the waters.

And God said, "Let there be light; and there was light."

The first three verses of Genesis 1 speak of it just this way.

We find the answers to these four questions in Gods Word: First — Who has created all things? Answer: God. Second — Of what are all things made? Answer: Out of nothing. Third — By what means has He done this? Answer: Through His power. Fourth — For what reason did God create the world? Answer: For His own glory.

There are very many people in the world who do not

believe God's Word is truth. Or, if they voice agreement in speaking about it, they want to give an explanation that is in accordance with their own notions.

When you become older you, too, will hear or read about certain educated people who suggest: "There is an eternal fluttering matter and all the separate parts or cells just grew and continued developing until they took the form of a plant or animal. This growing process took a long time involving many thousands of years. The matter continually improved until it became what it is now."

If these people give pretense in believing God's Word, they explain that the six days of creation are six periods of time, each one consisting of many hundreds of years. "And so," they say, "God has created all things, in that He created the first matter and, further, let all things develop."

Boys and girls, perhaps sometime in the future, you will hear or read many things that are contrary to the simple explanations given in the lessons by Rev. Hellenbroek.

But consider this, these lessons are the true doctrine, founded upon God's Word. Hold firmly to them, even though it may be only with an historical faith. Don't follow along with the varied proposals of people who do not believe in God and who bring into question the authority of His Word.

The Lord tells us plainly in His infallible Word: "In the beginning God created the heaven and the earth," and then follow the achievements He accomplished in the first six days.

Isn't it plain from the great creation alone, that there is a creator?

If we were to visit a place where there is an especially fine building, we would, at first, thoughtfully admire that showpiece, but eventually we would ask: "Who is the architect of this magnificent building?" We would have high regard for the man who brought about this work. Don't you agree?

So also, the whole creation should fill us with reverence and awe. He is worthy of all honor as the planner and executor of all creation.

Now in nature, it is impossible for the most expert of builders to make something if he does not have materials.

The great Creator, however, created everything from nothing. That was omnipotence.

Paul was not among those that say that there was an eternal living cell that formed into a completed object after thousands of years. No, He said in Romans 4:17 "And calleth those things which be not as though they were."

Hellenbroek says, "Respecting the matter, in a moment, and respecting the farther disposition of them, in six days."

Now, I would like to ask something:

When God created the light and the other things in the succeeding days that followed, did the earth, with all that was on it and in it, contribute to or hinder the creation? Or, did it simply remain the way it was? The latter we call "being passive."

What are your thoughts on this matter?

The world did not contribute and neither did it hinder. It was a creation but had no acting strength either for or against.

It was as clay in the hands of God, the great Potter. He spake, and it was done; He commanded, and it stood fast.

It states, "In the beginning." God was from eternity.

There never was a beginning with Him.

But according to His eternal decree, He wanted to create "time." We could say it this way: In the beginning when God opened time and made a continuation of it, days, nights, light and darkness came into being.

The first thing He created in heaven and on earth was

light. That was necessary, because without light, what would the rest of creation be? Our human minds cannot comprehend what light actually is. How valuable it is in the natural creation.

Now, each day follows another; there is sun and moon, trees, beasts, etc.

But, what would you think to be the greatest thing created?

You should read Genesis 1&2 very carefully, this evening.

You will notice there that just before God created the greatest work, He said something that He never had said before.

Again and again it states, after it was evening and morning: "God said" etc., and then follows what he brought forth.

But on the sixth day it states something else. Just read in verse 26 "And God said: Let us make man in our image, after our likeness, etc."

Is not that a wonderful decree?

The holy Divine Being refers to Himself, for the first time after all that creating, in the plural: "Us," Father, Son and Holy Ghost. As if the emphasis is laid upon this: That of all that He had created in the six days, He now would create the ornament of it all.

Not incomprehensible light, not seas, great powerful beasts or magnificent plants, no, now it would be something totally different; now something in God's own likeness! You must think about that for a moment.

And that was — man.

I hope all of you know how He did this and what substance He used.

God tells us briefly: "And the Lord God formed man of the dust of the ground, and breathed into his nostrils the breath of life; and man became a living soul" Genesis 2:7.

He called this first person "Adam," that is "Earth man."

He created Adam to be the head of the whole human race.

One for all, or: All in one. That is also the meaning of the words that Paul said to the Athenians (Acts 17:26) "And hath made of one blood all nations of men etc."

But what about Eve? Was she created to be a "head" of the human race?

No, she was named Eve, which means: Mother of all living. Only Adam was established as the responsible head of his whole posterity.

Now just observe closely that the Lord has something to say to us in all His dealings.

Eve, as you know, was not formed separately as Adam was, but God used a part out of Adam's body.

What *did* He use? A piece of his hand or foot? No, He used a rib. The Bible says: "And the rib, which the Lord God had taken from man, made He a woman and brought her unto the man." (Gen. 2:22)

Just what does this mean?

That man, even though he was created first and given a place as the principal one, may never despise the woman as a lesser creature. She was made out of his rib, a part of the body close to his heart. In that way God has brought the wife in close union with the man; as two creatures from one making.

And Adam said, upon awakening, "This is now bone of my bones, and flesh of my flesh: she shall be called Woman, because she was taken out of Man."

He saw that this creature was not an animal or a plant, but, even as he, a person. Bone of his bones.

We see two things in the creation of Adam. God said: "Let us make man." He would, then, give execution to His decree through the act of creation. What do we see in that execution?

First, God took something, and, second, He did something. He took, (figuratively speaking, because God does not have natural hands but, for our way of understanding, it is stated "He took") dust and formed a body. But a person cannot consist of a dead stiff body, no, therefore; second, He did something: He breathed the breath of life into his nostrils; and man became a living soul.

But was this all? Didn't God do more in the creation of man than these two things?

It was wonderful that He formed a body using a means and gave it a soul without means, but what was even greater? Read Genesis 1:27 "So God created man in His own image, in the image of God created He him; male and female created He them."

"And God saw everything that He made, and, behold, it was very good." Gen. 1:31.

Now, do you think that man cooperated with or was in opposition to this creation?

The sun didn't say "I want to be the sun"; the rivers didn't say, "We want to be rivers"; and Adam didn't say "I want to be a man." Nothing of the sort.

The Triune God created everything, not only according to His infinite power, but, also according to His sovereign power. Everything was passive under His hand; out of nothing, through His boundless power, to His own glory.

Would there be an indication that God was weary, since the Lord rested on the seventh day?

No, but it is meant to say: He ceased creating. "The Creator of the ends of the earth fainteth not, neither is weary" Isaiah 40:28. He rested on that day and hallowed it only because He Himself ceased on that day from all the works that He had made. Reverently speaking, God observed the first Sabbath or "Rest Day," after six days of creating, with Adam and Eve. There was none other than these two created persons with whom He could observe the Sabbath. It was not because He was tired of His work but because God had accomplished all the work He had set out to do. And, because He wanted to rest on the seventh day, He hallowed it for all the creatures that would follow and commanded that they, too, should hallow that day.

Boys and girls, have you ever earnestly thought about how serious it is to be a person?

Trees, plants, beasts, etc. all belong to God's creation, but to be a person is quite another matter.

Do you know what is most precious in a person? His body is very beautiful, but, the living soul which God has placed in it, is most valuable. The soul is immortal and, even though the body dies, the spirit of life never dies.

Actually, a person has a beginning but not an ending; the soul being immortal. The body, which will be given back again in the judgment day, will also be immortal.

Our lesson time is coming to a close! We shall talk no further about the creation. If the Lord spare, we hope to continue next week with this lesson and to say something about the creation of angels.

Take these thoughts of the lesson home with you this afternoon and consider how great a matter it is to be born as a person here in this world.

When we, in our thoughts, walk through Paradise, we see the finest plants and fruits, magnificent animals — each one a model of perfect beauty. But, what was the very finest of them all? Amidst the entire great divine creation, man was the jewel, a rational creature, placed above all animals, formed with an immortal soul. But what made him so exceptional?

He carried the image of God.

You would ask, perhaps, "Does God have a body such as ours?"

No, God does not consist of matter or substance. The image of God consists in this, that man knew God; he had communication with the Divine Being and knew His voice in the wind of the day.

Man was pure. There was no sin, therefore, also no guilt and, of course, no shame; for shame implies guilt and guilt implies sin.

These had no place there; it was a perfect situation.

But — look at this same world today, the world that was created so perfect.

Take notice of man, who still carries the same body that God formed out of the dust!

"What has changed?" you, perhaps, would want to say. Fundamentally, sin has come between the creature and his Creator and has made an eternal separation between them.

We do not have God's image anymore, because we do not know Him. That knowledge is lost because of sin.

Instead of the very finest of creation, a person now walks on this earth as the most unfortunate of all creation.

It is not that we have another body but we no longer have God's image but, instead, we have the image of devils.

What is it that we, none the less, have not lost? We have become wretched, that is true, but, we have remained man. We remain rational creatures with an immortal soul; our soul has not been blotted out of existence by sin.

I would now propose three things to which you must give consideration.

What would a person prefer; to go to heaven, to go to hell or to stay on earth?

Naturally, not to go to Hell, no, that would be a ghastly dark place.

And heaven? Yes – that seems to be very nice; streets of gold and gates of pearls – that must be grand to live there. But, as it is said, there is only perfection there. All is pure and holy and nothing shall enter there that is impure or that speaks lies.

A holy God shall be King there. No, we could not endure such holiness. What is remaining, then?

Boys and girls, tell it honestly the way you feel in your heart. Wouldn't you rather always stay on this earth? I know surely, that you will answer, "Yes." O, if that could only be. Most people, by far, would rather stay on this earth forever.

If you want to remain friends with everyone, you must not talk too much about Heaven, and less about Hell. Talking about the earth is most acceptable. If they can but keep what they have now; eating, drinking, a way of making a living and, then, a life without obligations, for their part, the devils may keep Hell and God, Heaven.

Don't you believe that too?

But that is not the way it will be, even though men wish it.

Now your conscience makes you afraid, doesn't it, when you have been naughty or disobedient and a severe storm comes up at night, or you suddenly become ill? You have a feeling, then, that something bad will happen; your conscience accuses you.

But, that usually does not last long. When the shower is over, or the sickness gone, then the fear is also gone, isn't it true? Except when God takes hold. Then you cannot get away anymore.

Then everything you hear now and with which you agree in mind and conscience will become actuality and that is considerably different than mere agreement. You will never be able to go in the old ways again even if you try it with all your youthful love of life.

Are there among you those to whom it has truly happened; those who have feared they live without God in this world?

O I hope that the "draw bridge" is raised forever; that you will never be able to find your desire in sin again even if your natural desires are so inclined.

May the Lord give grace in making those, who are secure in themselves, insecure and those who are insecure, keep them insecure. May He then apply the merits of Christ, through the Holy Spirit, unto you so that you may find reconciliation through faith and Christ's meritorious work alone.

Never rest in your unrest or conviction; no, that will not satisfy for your guilt. Remember, only the blood of the Mediator can restore the breach between God and your guilty soul.

We can, through Christ, receive again the image of God which we have willfully lost.

May the Triune Creator of heaven and earth recreate your heart and spirit to the praise of His Name which is magnificent.

So be it.

Lesson 9

Creation

Since we had not discussed all the questions on creation last week, we shall, with God's help, attempt to go further.

For a moment, I shall review briefly:

Who is the creator of all things? The Triune God.

Out of what has He created it? Out of nothing.

Through what means? Through His omnipotence.

For what reason? For His own sake and to His own glory.

We mentioned: "Some people explain the six days of creation as six periods of time."

We do not accept this. God's Word teaches us: "And the evening and the morning were the first day, second day, third day etc." We must hold stedfast to the declarations of God's Word. God completed the whole creation in six ordinary days of 24 hours; opened and closed by morning and evening.

The Lord did not create all these things because He had need of them. No, it would then have been a creation out of compulsion.

He created only because He so desired; merely through His sovereign unlimited power (omnipotence) He completed it.

What were the principal creatures that God brought into being?

Men and angels.

We have said earlier: (but are reviewing it a moment to sharpen your memory), God created man on the sixth day as the crown of creation. He referred to himself for the first time in the plural as He set about doing this work: "Come, let Us make man."

God created the whole of mankind in the first man, which is evident in Acts 17:25 & 26 "He giveth to all life and breath and all things; and hath made of one blood all nations of men for to dwell on all the face of the earth."

It is also clear in the account of creation that God created man in two parts, namely, body and soul (spirit). The body by way of means (from dust of the earth) and the soul without means (the soul came immediately from God, for He breathed a living soul into them).

The Bible talks about "spirit" and then again about "soul." We must consider these as having the same meaning, because the soul is a spirit that never dies (immortal) whereby we live and exercise reason, according to Hellenbroek.

Last week we talked about the creation of man; so, we shall now try to talk about the creation of angels.

Our lesson asks: Are the angels also created?

Answer: Yes. Psalm 104:4 says: "He makes His angels spirits."

What are angels, actually?

Paul gives us a clear answer to that in Hebrews 1:14. "Are they not all ministering spirits, sent forth to minister for them who shall be heirs of salvation?"

Hellenbroek asks further: "When were the angels created?"

He answers: "Probably on the first day" God's Word is not explicit in this. There is only a reflection of it referred to in Job 38:4, 6 & 7 where God said to Job, "Where wast thou when I laid the foundations of the earth? declare, if thou hast understanding. Who hath laid the measures thereof?

Whereupon are the foundations thereof fastened? or who laid the corner stone thereof?"

The Lord asked Job all this. He spoke with Him about the great work of creation and especially in these verses about the creation of the earth. He then follows immediately with: "When the morning stars sang together, and all the sons of God shouted for joy."

The words, "sons of God" and probably the word "morning star" mean the angels whom God had created for His praise.

In as much as the Lord speaks of it in connection with the creation of the earth it leads us to believe that the angels could have been created at the same time: on the first day.

We shall not involve ourselves any deeper; the hidden things are for the Lord. We might better be silent concerning matters on which God's Word is silent.

To what can we give a more certain answer, however?

To the question whether the angels were created good.

Without hesitation we can say "yes" about that, because, "God saw everything that He had made, and behold it was very good." The angels were included there.

If it is sure, then, that all the angels were created perfect, you would say: "Where do the devils come from?"

Would God have created the devils?

No, that is impossible; He would then be the creator of evil.

What happened then?

The angels were all created good, but they did not all remain good. One group of them fell away from God and became devils in Hell.

Can that be proven from God's Word?

Surely, just read it in the epistle of Jude:6 "And the angels which kept not their first estate, but left their own

93

habitation, He hath reserved in everlasting chains under darkness unto the judgment of the great day."

Some people teach that the evil angels were not created perfect but carried a germ of sin.

You must never believe this. It follows (according to that theory) that God created them with a sinful germ and so He is the creator of devils.

That is in direct conflict with the Truth. He is the Creator of the angels.

A part of the angels did not remain standing in their perfect state in which they were created. They had, with their unrestrained volition, stood up against their Creator.

But the Triune God stood above them and punished their uprising by casting them out of heaven.

Peter said very plainly in 2 Peter 2:4 "God spared not the angels that sinned, but cast them down into Hell and delivered them into chains of darkness, to be reserved unto judgment."

So, the first sin was begun by an angel.

Now, you must pay careful attention.

It is a very difficult matter to present and a yet more difficult matter to understand. None the less, I want to say something of it in connection with our lesson.

You must not believe that sin was created even if the first sin was perpetrated by a created angel.

No, everything that God created has self-dependency; is something that has the ability to stand.

Sin, however, is not a self dependent thing. Sin is something that has no tangible existence. It was not created by God nor did it have a place in creation. So, then it had no right to be there.

What was sin, then, in its original state?

Sin, in its original state, is a deviation from good.

Even if it is impossible for you to understand all this, do

not dismiss it from your thoughts.

The true source of sin is something beyond our comprehension. But there is one thing very definite, and do not forget it, that the creature is the cause of evil and not God.

It is generally said, that the sin causing the angels to fall involved pride.

Who knows why?

This is derived from a remark made by one of the fallen angels (an angel that had become a devil) to Eve when he said, "Ye shall be as gods."

He proposed that man be equal to God. He desired to have man sin the sin that had brought him from being a good angel to being a devil; that sin, rising out of terrible pride, was wishing to be equal to God. This statement is not contrary to God's Word. It is plain that Satan was not satisfied with the position in which God had created him as "angel." That was what Jude surely meant, too, in his letter when he said, "And the angels which kept not their first estate, but left their own habitation etc." Jude :6.

Isn't it clear in this text that they were not satisfied with their beginning; that is, with the position of good angels as God had created them?

In that proposal to Eve, Satan betrayed the fact that he wanted to be equal to God.

But, just because of that, he forfeited his own dwelling place in heaven and became a devil in hell.

Devil actually means "Satan." And Satan means: someone that stands in opposition; the adversary of God.

So it was an angel who became an opponent of God and as such brought sin into the world.

The word devil is usually used in the singular, but it is plain in God's Word that more than one angel was involved in the rebellion, because the evil one himself said to Jesus, "My name is legion; for we are many." Mark 5:9

In respect to the character and consequences, the fall of Satan is more terrible than the fall of man. Understand this thoroughly now, I do not mean that our fall is not the most terrible. We know that, but in respect to the consequences, the fall of Satan is irreparable.

They continued to be "spirits" as they were, but became "devils" which they were not originally.

Also, Satan sinned without being tempted, while man did so being tempted.

The sin committed by the devil is unforgivable. They are kept with bands until the great day of judgment.

So, we have explained something about the fall of the angels and the first sin perpetrated by them.

But now, what does the Holy Scripture teach us about the other angels that were predestined to remain in their original state?

They are neither God or man but are the ministering (serving) spirits sent forth to serve the heirs of salvation.

You must not think that there were two kinds of angels: good and evil. No; God created only good angels. Yet one part of them stood completely free, that is, to stand or fall, while the other part was predestined to remain standing, as we have already stated in the lesson on predestination.

Which one of you can tell me what the word "angel" means? It means messenger or ambassador. God endowed them with understanding, will and strength. Even though they are spirits, without a body, they can, upon God's command take on a body to bring about His purpose.

They are innumerable. We can observe this in Daniel 7 where we read: "Thousand Thousands ministered unto Him and ten thousand times ten thousand stood before Him."

Just think of this. What an innumerable multitude of

angels standing in the service of the Divine Being. They are created spirits without bodies. Eternally they surround His throne, carrying out His instructions.

Also, He created this whole legion of angels to minister to His elect creatures and to serve them at His command.

Boys and girls, do you observe how the formation of such spirits was an important work in creation?

What difference is there in the creation of angels and the creation of people?

Come, think about this; who has noticed the difference between the two?

We stated last week that man was created one for all. The whole human race, then, came forth from this one person. It comes about in a natural way.

We said that Adam was created as "head"; he was the forerunner, the first of all men.

But was that so with the angels too?

No, the spirits were created individually, each one separately by itself. Not even one angel has ever been born; they have all been created.

This is also plain from the words of Jesus to the Saducees, when He said that God's people shall be as the angels of God in heaven, that do not possess a material body neither do they marry or multiply.

God's Word makes a distinction between angels, though. We are told about two archangels. Archangel means: chief of angels or: grand angels. They are Michael and Gabriel. Sometimes they are referred to as cherubim or seraphim. O, it is impossible to explain all the mysteries of the angels!

This is certain: God created them for two important purposes. First, to glorify Himself, the God in heaven. Second, to be of service to the elect on earth.

Someday the angels will come with Christ on the clouds. That will be the great judgment day.

97

We find throughout all God's Word, various services of the angels. There is, especially, much mentioned in the book of Revelation. When He does come, He will be surrounded with many thousands of angels who will, with great swiftness, obey His commands.

But now, if the angels have such an important destiny shouldn't we honor them?

No, absolutely not. We ought only to esteem them. The Roman Catholic church honors them even though it is explicitly forbidden to do so in God's Word. When the apostle John, in Rev. 22:8, had heard and seen all the angel had shown him, he fell down before his feet to worship him but the angel said, "See thou do it not; for I am thy fellowservant, etc., worship God!"

Think about what was said here; what does this actually mean? The spiritual creature from the throne said he was no more than John, a person living on the earth; he said, "I am thy fellowservant."

It is plain that John was recognized as an elect vessel and an apostle called of God in Christ. The angel would never had been able to say "fellowservant," looking upon him as a fallen man.

Whose voice do you think will ring the loudest (by way of speaking) in that blissful eternity: the voices of the elect millions of angels, who kept their first estate and remained standing in obedience, or the great multitude of elect creatures, who, notwithstanding their disobedience and fall from God, were, while on earth, redeemed to eternal salvation?

I believe the latter, don't you, too?

Just read in Revelations 5 this evening. In verse 11 we read, "And I beheld and I heard the voice of many angels round about the throne, etc., and the number of them was ten thousand times ten thousand, and thousands of thousands saying with a loud voice, 'Worthy is the Lamb that was slain to receive power and riches and wisdom and strength and honor and glory and blessing," etc.

That is what the millions of created elect spirits round about the throne said. But, what is written there about the elect creatures that are in heaven? " – and they sung a new song, saying, 'Thou art worthy to take the book, etc. for thou wast slain, and hast redeemed us to God by thy blood out of every kindred and tongue, and people and nation, etc.' " in verse 9.

Don't you believe, too, that the voices of God's delivered people shall ring above the angels' song?

They are redeemed from the earth through His blood and released out of such a great need and from death itself.

That is not so of the Holy angels!

But there is, nevertheless, a perfect harmony between them. A pure, beautiful, perfectly beautiful song to the praise of a Triune God!

For what reason do the angels glorify God eternally? Because of sovereign grace? No. They never fell, so it was not necessary to redeem them. But they will glorify God eternally for His predestination, whereby they were ordained to remain standing.

The angels will give Him honor for electing love, but God's people will honor Him for His redeeming love; and will also glorify Him for free grace, and for the merits of His blood applied to them.

There will be no discord between them, however. Even though the reasons for their songs are different, and one is deeper than the other (to use words you can understand) they have but one purpose: that is, the praise of the Triune God.

Isaiah, by faith, spoke of it in Isaiah 51:11 "Therefore

the redeemed of the Lord shall return, and come with singing unto Zion; and everlasting joy shall be upon their head."

That will be an occupation! Eternally, without end, glorifying God in fellowship with legions of angels who are doing the same.

Do you appreciate now, boys and girls, how significant creation was? Especially the creation of men and angels?

All the other creatures were not appointed to live eternally. Only spirits and people shall never have an end.

Do you know what was God's intention concerning this?

In Genesis 2:3 it is written: "God rested from all His work which He created and made" to hallow it (to make it holy).

Do you see, that was His purpose! To fulfill that eternal decree which He had made to glorify Himself in the most perfect way!

To that end He predestinated legions of angels. To that end He saved a great multitude of people, that no one could count, only to fulfill His purpose and work.

But now, what do you think would be the most important matter for us?

You have heard of the various things pertaining to creation: the decree of creation, the work, the execution of it and its purpose.

There are but two places for the angels. This is true for people also.

The angels which sinned became devils; eternally cast away from God. Their place is now in an abyss.

What about people who sin?

Rev. Ledeboer in catechising asked his little children, "Where do the children go that remain unconverted?"

Answer: "To Hell with the devils there."

Because of our fall that is righteously the place for all of us.

We hope to speak of "The Fall Of Man" more fully in a following lesson.

But heaven is the abiding place for the good angels; The same heaven where the faithful in Christ will be assembled.

Sinful creatures, neither angels nor men, shall ever be able to enter heaven.

In God's immediate presence there will be eternal perfection.

Our class time is spent again and you must go to your homes.

I hope that God will give you meditation upon the creation to the extent you have never had before!

Depend upon it; it will be one way or the other: after death it will be eternally with the angels in heaven or with the devils in hell. There will be no other places after death.

The church of Rome teaches that there is a purgatory, a "vestibule" to heaven, but we cannot find that in God's Word. It is, therefore, not true.

Have you ever had an impression, boys and girls, what it is to be rational creatures, having a soul and body created by God, good and pure, adorned with the image of God, and as such, being the greatest work of creation? And, now further, through sin we become one with Satan, the fallen angel; just as he, wanting to be as God and because of that proud desire, is righteously separated from God eternally, so are we, except we be reconciled with God.

A person has not become a brute beast (one without intelligence) through sin, no, he remains a rational creature; retains his immortal soul.

He has, through sin, fallen in the direction of devilishness.

The Lord Jesus said to the Pharisees: "Ye are of your father the devil and the lusts of your father ye will do. He was a murderer from the beginning and abode not in the truth."

101

He dared to say it plainly. Did the Pharisees believe this? I fear they did not. They were so hostile that they said Jesus had a devil.

But would we by nature believe that truth?

No more than they. I said last week; "When God created the earth, it neither assisted nor hindered. It was passive. "But, when God converts a person, is that person passive too? No, it is not and it will never be that way! A person is in roaring enmity against God and will never yield to Him without a struggle. It takes the irresistible force of the Holy Spirit.

When we read of Felix it appears he was inclined toward Paul at the beginning. At least, he let him proceed without interruption. As long as Paul told only the experiences of his life, he listened to him calmly, but as soon as Paul began to talk about: a just God who tries us for our sins and shall punish us in the coming judgment — Felix didn't want any more of it, and so he said, "Go thy way for this time; When I have a more convenient season, I will call for thee."

He did not want to hear that. Would that only be so with Felix?

The answer would be no, wouldn't it? Everyone experiences that he would rather not hear of God's judgments. Yet, they shall come one day!

I hope that the Lord will hold judgment in the court of your soul before you die, otherwise you will have to stand with body and soul in judgment in that great Day.

And, I hope you may learn to condemn yourselves here and assent to the just judgment of the Lord.

The devils will never do that. They will always remain in the state of dreadful hatred and enmity against God's judgments.

But the grace of God can make you bow before Him. O, that would be the greatest gain of your whole life. May He give this to you for Jesus' sake.

So be it.

Lesson 10

Concerning Providence

Building a house and maintaining a house are two different matters. Building must take place before maintaining the structure can follow.

Creation, too, came first. After God had created all things, did He cease to care for His creatures?

"No, there is still a continual operation of Divine Providence," answers Hellenbroek.

It is often said: "Everyone should be able to confirm the answers they give by using God's Word. Who knows where the word "providence" can be found in the Bible?

You would not feel very good about it if I were to send you home with the assignment to look for that word in the Bible, because the word "providence" is not to be found literally in God's Word.* The meaning however is there.

Providence is the name of that work of God whereby He upholds all that He had created and brings it to the destiny He had resolved for it from eternity. We find in Genesis 22 that Abraham called the place, where he was able to offer up the ram instead of his son Isaac, "Jehovah-jireh": as it is said to this day, in the mount of the Lord is shall be seen (In the mount of the Lord it will be provided).

This is what is meant by it: The Lord controls all things.

Even if the word is not used literally, as we are accustomed to see it, the Holy Scripture often speaks about the acts of Divine Providence.

In how many ways can the Providence of God be distinguished?

* In Acts 24:2 the word providence means prudence.

In the broadest sense, in three ways:

1. In preservation
2. In cooperation
3. In the government of all the creation.

Now Hellenbroek asks: What is preservation?

Answer: The almighty power of God, whereby He continueth all things in being.

He proves this from Hebrews 1:3 "Who upholdeth all things by the word of His power."

And what is His cooperation?

Answer: God's almighty power, whereby He influences all the motions and operations of His creatures.

Can it be proved?

Surely, in 1 Cor. 12:6 "And there are diversities of operations, but it is the same God which worketh all in all."

What is the 3rd one, the government of God?

Answer: That mighty power whereby He directs everything to a certain determinate end. Psalm 93:1 "The Lord reigneth: — also the world is stablished, that it cannot be moved."

These three things, Preservation, Cooperation and Government must never be separated from one another in God's Providence; do not ever forget that.

It is not intended to mean that there are three providences.

No, there is but one God and only one Divine Providence, and, within that framework, these three things cannot be separated from each other because each one does its work by means of the other two.

The Providence of God does not mean that God only foresees all things but that He also provides for all things; evidently, everything is comprehended in His decree.

To what, do you think, does the power of God extend? Over very many things or just a few things?

It extends, without distinction, over everything. Not only to things that pertain to a person's salvation, but also to the smallest things in nature.

Who can give me an example?

Answer: Jesus said in Matt. 10:30 "Yea, the hairs of your head are all numbered." Can you think of anything smaller?

This example is sufficient to show that not one thing is outside of the Providence of God.

The work of Providence is plainly observed from John 5 in the history of that man who lay sick 38 years.

Jesus said in verse 8, "Rise, take up thy bed and walk." Then it states in verse 9, "And immediately the man was made whole, and took up his bed and walked; and on the same day was the sabbath."

When the Jews heard that Jesus had healed on the sabbath day ', they considered it very wicked of Him. It was so bad, that it says in Verse 16: "therefore the Jews sought to slay Him because He had done these things on the sabbath day."

But what did Jesus answer them; He did not make lengthy excuses to try to free Himself. No, He gave a very short answer saying: "My father worketh hitherto and I work." And as the Jews became even more angry because of this answer, the Lord made it plain to them what He meant: "Verily, I say unto you, The Son can do nothing of Himself, but what He seeth the Father do; for what things soever He doeth, these also doeth the Son likewise."

What did Jesus mean by this?

He would say: "You Scribes and Pharisees believe that God created the world, isn't it true? If the Triune God has created the world, it naturally follows that the Triune God maintains (upholds) the World too. This maintenance is the work of the Divine Providence. I am sure none of you believe that God, after He had completed all creation in six

105

days, had nothing more to do with it after that time." (I said it now just as you would expect the Lord Jesus to say it to the Jews.)

Just imagine that God, in order to keep the sabbath the way you understand it, did nothing from Friday night until the sabbath was past and then, repeatedly, withheld His providential care each following sabbath. What would happen then?

Naturally, everything would die. If God would withdraw His preserving hand from man and beast on the sabbath day, everything would die. We receive life and all that is necessary for life from moment to moment.

That is why the Lord Jesus said;" "My Father works (in providential preservation and cooperation) and I also work!" The Jews understood from this that Jesus was saying He too was God, therefore, they more and more tried to find ways to kill Him. Not only because they thought He violated the sabbath day but also because He said that God was His own Father, thereby making Himself equal with God.

The scribes believed they loved God and therefore kept the sabbath out of love for Him. They thought, because they loved God, they must hate Jesus. They viewed Him as a sabbath breaker.

But the Lord Jesus made it clear to them, that if He was a sabbath breaker, God the Father was, too. For that reason He said, "He that does not honor the Son does not honor the Father who has sent Him."

When that woman, whose body was stooped for eighteen years, was healed, the ruler of the synogogue said the same as the scribes. He said to the crowd: "There are six days in which men ought to work; in them, therefore, come and be healed and not on the sabbath day." But the Lord answered him; "Thou hypocrite, doth not each one of you on the sabbath loose his ox or his ass from the stall and lead him away to watering?"

Then all those that stood in opposition to Him were ashamed.

Do not these texts prove clearly that Divine Providence is the work of a Triune God? And it is plain from the words, "My Father worketh hitherto and I work," that it has never been interrupted one single day since the beginning of creation.

Can the work of providence be proven in any other way than by the Word of God?

Yes it can. Providence can be clearly proven from nature too.

We could start with day and night in which there is no variation. The seasons of the year, Summer, Winter, Autumn and Spring which have always followed one another at exact times for ages. The ebb and flow in the seas and rivers which continue on and on. All plants, trees and beasts which, under His direction, are kept in their various kinds and continued in their existence. Everything remains as He has created it. People remain people, even though they are so wicked. They do not become beasts, at least, not in regard to their bodies. The beasts do not become people, be they ever so noble.

He also maintains the beasts according to their kinds. The horses do not become cows, nor do the cows become sheep; no, age after age, the creator continues the whole creation in their kinds and races, just as He had created them on the earth.

People try very often to change all this, and with God's permission, it happens once in a while that they cultivate a new kind of plant or flower. That has taken place with animals too. A person is responsible for his deeds. The providence of God, however, keeps everything in their own kinds just as they were originally created.

What reverence we would have for God's providence if we had eyes to behold all this. What do you think this world would look like without this sustenance?

Think of this for a moment; — two men built themselves homes. They both used the same materials and had the same carpenters do the work. The homes were identical in style. In this way everything was the same. They began to live in them at the same time too. One of the men maintained his home in the proper way but the other did nothing to it. The second one's home took on an untidy appearance. Wouldn't everyone be able to see, after ten years of aging, which of the two houses had the best care? I think so. The one was completely dilapitated, even though it started out in excellent condition at the beginning just as the other one had.

There are many who do not maintain their homes, but the Lord is not neglectful of His creation in that way. He sustains and directs everything, to the smallest detail in the most complete manner.

The next question asks: Does the Providence of God extend to our life and death?

Answer: Yes; the time thereof is also determined by Him. Job 14:5 "Seeing his days are determined, the number of his months is with Thee, Thou hast appointed his bounds that he cannot pass."

With respect to God's providence, a person cannot lengthen or shorten his life. The time of death is firmly established, right to the minute. But with respect to ourselves we can shorten our lives. If anyone deprives himself of life or dies because of recklessness, he shortens his life. This is a great evil.

From God's side it would be the right time, but, we may never say: "God has decreed it so and therefore it is not a sin for me!" When someone shortens his life, the time is definitely known by God and the deed happened under providence; but yet, such a person comes to judgment before he was called of God. Reverently speaking, the Lord could say, in such a case, "I command, at the firmly established time, birth and death, because it is appointed for man once to die and then the judgment, but who has made you to die? Man, you have come to judgment without being called." A murderer can receive forgiveness of sin, but how can a self murderer expect to receive forgiveness? He has taken upon himself to cut off the time of grace.

There is a text in the Bible which I would like you to explain to me. In Psalm 55:23 it says, "Bloody and deceitful men shall not live out half their days." How should I understand this text?

We have just said: The hour of the birth and death of all people is known and determined. There is nothing we can do to shorten or lengthen it.

It is not only those who make an end of their lives who are considered "deceitful"; there are many more deceitful and wicked people who would never do that. How must this be understood, then?

Even if men do not take their lives directly by hanging themselves or by drowning, they can, nevertheless, shorten their lives.

If someone, for example, through an unrestrained life of drinking or other activity neglects his body and ruins his health, don't you think that would be considered shortening his life?

If men, in recklessness, swim too deep in the water and drown, or climb too high when it is not necessary and fall to their death, wouldn't that be the same as a suicide? I say it would be, if done in recklessness.

Taking it in this sense, the wicked shall not live out half their days.

There are many examples of this and I shall relate for

your instruction, an example which I have experienced.

When I was a boy living in Zeeland with my parents, there was a terribly wicked young man, 16 years old, living in a small village. Every Saturday and Sunday evening he was intoxicated and often during the week too. His parents had a dreadful amount of grief because of him. He went to all the festivals and fairs being held in the neighborhood and sometimes lay all night in a drunken condition on the sea dike or some other place.

Naturally, his body became completely neglected by such an intemperate and destructive life.

This continued until his nineteenth year when he was drafted. He was rejected, however, because his body was too wasted to serve as soldier in the service. I knew him very well and worked with him very often. He had medicine in his pockets most all the time which he had gotten from the doctor. At that time he was only 20 years old. Yet he dragged himself along through life until he became almost 35 years old. In the meantime the Lord had called me to preach and one day this man asked for me to come to see him. I found him lying on a sickbed at his sister's home. His parents had passed away.

But, oh, how miserable I found him! I had always known him well and had deep compassion with him. There he lay with swollen arms and legs, his eyes bulged out of his head and his whole body was swollen from drinking. He suffered dreadfully.

I said, "Boy, boy, it has come very far, hasn't it; and now shall it be death after all this?"

Yes, death came very fast. That was the end of a life that was ruined in youth.

Wouldn't you think that this boy had shortened his life? His time was firmly established, but from his side he did not live out half his days.

Boys, and girls, you are still young but I relate this example as one to abhor.

Though it is terrible, remember this your whole life long. Sin is ruinous, not only for the body but also for the soul. Also, while God's Providence influences and directs our lives and brings about the day of our death, yet, considering it from our side, we can shorten our lives.

Do not misuse the bodies that God has given us to use.

The next question Hellenbroek asks is, "Since God has determined everything in His Providence, is it not then in vain to use the means for preserving life?"

He answers, "No; God has decreed these means to that end, and He giveth man a willing mind to use them."

It is, for that reason, a difficult matter for us to believe that God's providence also extends over sin, and yet it does.

Hellenbroek taught it. He said, "God permits it, limits it and directs it to a certain end." Genesis 50:20 "Ye thought evil, but God meant it unto good."

This does not mean that God causes sin. A holy God cannot be the cause of anything sinful. He hates and punishes sin.

Now you need not think that all sins are openly punished here on earth. O, no; sometimes not even of the most wicked persons.

Yet the Lord upon occasion punishes sin openly so that others will fear to commit that sin.

I still remember what happened some time ago. A certain converted man, who was a leader in his church, preached to the congregation on Sundays. He had children all of whom were comparatively obedient and gave no offence in the congregation, all of them except one. One of the boys was terribly wicked. He cared for nothing and went his own way. His father tried everything to persuade him to obedience but nothing helped. It happened that his father had an appointment to speak in their village church on a Sunday afternoon. The entire family went to church and of course this boy had to go with them, too. He did not care about going because it was mid-summer and such beautiful weather that afternoon. He went with them though, and as usual he sneaked into the back of the church because he did not want to sit with the other members of the family. When his father had preached a few minutes, he slunk out of the church and went swimming with his chums. They mocked amongst themselves that it was such an unusually nice day and much too warm to be listening to a sermon.

After the church service was over, and the elder and his family were back home, one of his children standing at a window said, "Look father; there is such a lot of commotion in the village!" One of the family asked a passerby what was happening. "I heard that someone drowned, but I do not know who," the man said. "Are all of our boys home?" asked the father. "Yes, fortunately — or — no, one is not yet, but he was with us in church, so it cannot be he."

That is what they thought.

But soon after a group of men came directly to the house carrying a body — it was he — drowned while swimming; they had just recovered his body.

That was the boy who ran away from the sermon his father was preaching on Sunday afternoon in order to fulfill his own desires. The poor father pulled the hairs from his head in mourning over his son who had gone into eternity.

Wouldn't you think that boy had shortened his life?

He certainly did! God had not called him to go swimming on Sunday afternoon. He should have remained in church. In this way he deliberately ran to his death. There was an example of how the wicked shall not live out half their days.

Boys, remember the case of this boy. Do not mock with warnings and do not play recklessly with your lives.

There is nothing wrong with swimming when it is done in a way permitted; if it is necessary for our vocation or to help others. But in the time in which we live there is a tendency to misuse so many things.

Men use their minds which God has given them for their own profit, for all sorts of inventions, as it were, to provoke the Lord and to exalt man as a god.

Wouldn't you think that those people are self-murderers of whom we often hear that they fell to their death in an airplane?

I believe firmly, that they themselves will be tried before God's judgment seat as self-murderers because we have no indication from God's Word or from God's children in this world that God has called them to fly through the air.

God has given the earth to the children of men on which to do their work. And the Lord Jesus gave an example that we may sail upon the water. He actually did this himself, but we do not find anything to serve as an approval of airplanes or other means of air travel.

It is true God has decreed these machines as instruments for the death of some people but from their side they have shortened their lives.

The next question is, Does the providence of God direct the most voluntary things?

Answer: Yes, even our very thoughts.

Doesn't that destroy the free will of man?

No, this direction is not compulsion but inclining to a ready willingness.

Maybe you too have heard the saying, "Thoughts are free." It is intended to mean: No one can be punished for having certain thoughts; you may not say or do certain things but can think what you want without punishment.

Is that true?

It is true that police, father or mother cannot punish you for evil thoughts, even if you murdered someone in your thoughts because they do not know it. But are the sinful thoughts unknown and unpunished by God?

Think about this. Thoughts are no more exempt than words or deeds in God's view. He is an all-knowing and all-seeing God. His providence extends over the tiniest things but also over the most deeply concealed things.

Since our time is about gone, we cannot treat each question separately.

Boys and girls, remember what has been said of this subject even though it is brought to you only briefly.

I am saying it in concern for your never dying souls.

Perhaps most of you have never had, even for a moment, an idea of the value it has for your soul.

And are there some present who have often felt in their conscience that there is something wrong? Have you felt admonished inwardly when you are about to do something which you know is not right?

Do not suppress that feeling in order to do it anyway! Do not smother the voice of your conscience by going on and committing sins against God and your own conscience.

Perhaps you are thinking now, "I can do nothing but what is tainted with sin and you have said yourself we could not be saved even if we lived perfectly, so, what good does it do?"

It is true you would not go to heaven even if, by way of speaking, you did not even one sin from this moment until your death.

Must I say then, "Boys, go ahead and live carelessly, it does not help anyway to listen to God's Word and to your conscience"?

The situation would be very disagreeable when soon I

must stand with you and you with me before God's Judgment seat, wouldn't it?

I have said many times before, "It is an evil time in which we are living; you have a wicked heart and live in an evil world."

When the measure of ungodliness in a nation is full, God will come with His judgments to that nation. We saw this in Russia, Germany, Belgium and France. Thousands fell in battle when God came with the World war. The measure was full.

The Netherlands was spared then, but if the Netherlands continues in sin and in despising God, the Lord will go through with the Netherlands, too. The measure will become full in respect to our nation, too.

It is just the same with a person as it is with a nation. A person doesn't have to become old for his measure of sin to be full. No, that can happen while he is still young. Just think of the son of that elder.

I hope and wish that the Lord may spare you from resting in an open conscience. This is what I mean: if you are easily affected under warnings and do not dare to be disobedient, that you do not have the misunderstanding that everything will be all right and that you can die securely. No, in order to live and die comfortably, what we need is not primarily an open conscience, but the Lord Jesus as our Mediator. He alone is the way through which God reconciles man unto Himself.

And yet I hope the Lord will continue speaking to your conscience and that you will not disregard the things you have been taught.

Lesson 11

Of the Covenant of Works

We learned from the previous lessons that the Triune God created the earth. He created it in the beginning from nothing by His power for His own sake and to His own glory. We also learned that the work of Creation came first and the work of providence afterward. When Hellenbroek finished the explanation of Divine Providence in regard to all the creation, he asks this question: Has God any other particular direction respecting man?

Answer: Yes, He governs them in a covenant way.

How many of you know what a covenant is?

A covenant is an agreement between two or more persons. It is evident, then, that two parties or persons are needed to make a covenant.

How many covenants are mentioned in the Holy Scriptures?

Two. There is a covenant of works and a covenant of grace.

And which covenant was first revealed to man?

God made the covenant of works with Adam before the fall; this is, then, the first one to be revealed. The covenant of grace was made in eternity, but was not revealed to Adam until after the fall.

Both covenants have a "head" with whom they are made. Who knows who was the head of the covenant of works and who is the head of the covenant of grace?

Adam was created by God in the state of rectitude. He was made in the image of God and was perfect. He was the "head" of all persons that would be born after him. But besides the fact that he was the father of the whole human

116

race, God made a covenant with him and appointed him head of that covenant; that is to say, he represents all mankind. In this way God, through Adam, establishes the covenant with all people yet to come.

Perhaps this is still difficult for you to understand but that would not be reason for us to omit the entire lesson, would it?

In the simplest terms we could say: God created man, one for all or all in one. God created the angels one for one. Each for himself. After their creation not one was added to them. Their number never increased or decreased by way of birth or death, because spirits neither are given birth nor do they die.

Just as God created Adam one for all, so he also establishes the covenant of works with him as the principal one, but at the same time, it is established with all men in him as the head.

Now, covenants always contain conditions to which there is an obligation.

What was the condition set forth in the covenant of works? We could also consider this a requirement, and this is: perfect obedience to the law.

To the law? Had there been a law given at that time; I thought that the law was given to Moses on Mount Sinai sometime later?

The law was presented again at that time in 10 commandments, but God had created in Adam's heart a knowledge that he should love God with all his heart, with all his soul and with all his mind and his neighbor as himself. Adam carried this consciousness about with him. He could do this because God gave him the ability to love Him above all else.

Men call this innate (inborn) knowledge; the law of love.

How shall we present it to you in the simplest way; Give me close attention:

1. God established a covenant with Adam and with all of us in him, that is, He made an agreement.

2. God placed a condition in that covenant which we call a requirement, and what is this?

3. That Adam must be obedient to the law of love. But how could Adam know which law is meant for him to obey?

4. God created the knowledge of that law in his heart; that he must love God above all else and his neighbor as himself.

5. God promised eternal life to Adam (and to all men in him) upon the fulfillment of this requirement.

6. This promise was confirmed by means of a visable token (or sacrament) which was the tree of life. The Lord was saying: Just as surely as you see the tree of life in the garden of Paradise, just so surely I promise you eternal life if you remain obedient to me.

7. On the other hand He threatened death upon transgression. And lastly, He added:

8. A probationary command, that is: He not only commands love for God in their heart but they must show it through an actual deed too. The Lord informed them of the tree in the garden, the fruit of which they may not eat. In this way they would show that they wanted to remain obedient to God. If they ate of it, their actions would show that they did not respect the ban and the requirements of the covenant that God had set up with them.

The tree was called: The tree of knowledge of good and evil. This means: Through this tree it would be revealed whether they would sin or not. It was tangible proof whether Adam wanted to remain obedient to God or not. If he really wanted to remain obedient to God he would never eat of that tree.

Who can name the twelve points regarding this matter in exact order? Try to list them, because it will be necessary soon to grasp the meaning of this lesson in order to understand the lesson that follows.

1. Who made the covenant, God or Adam?

Answer: God with Adam.

2. What do we call this covenant?

Answer: The covenant of works

3. Was it instituted only with Adam?

Answer: It was instituted with Adam personally but with all men in him as head of the covenant.

4. What is Adam properly called?

Answer: Adam is called the representative head of the covenant.

5. Did God place conditions in that covenant?

Answer: Yes, He required obedience from Adam.

6. In what way must he be obedient?

Answer: To love God above all else, etc.

7. What kind of obedience is this?

Answer: An obedience to the law of love.

8. Did God promise something upon his obedience to this law?

Answer: Yes, God promised him eternal life.

9. How did God confirm this promise?

Answer: Through a visible symbol, which we call a sacrament. This was the tree of life that was placed in the center of the garden.

10. What did God threaten if he did not remain obedient?

Answer: Death in its fullest sense, that is: Physical, spiritual and eternal.

11. Did God give Adam opportunity to manifest his obedience in a real way?

Answer: Yes, God gave him a probationary command, the symbol of which was the tree of knowledge of good and evil through which he could show whether he wanted to obey God or not.

12. What difference was there between God and Adam in respect to their being parties of this covenant?

Answer: God was and is a holy righteous, sovereign, almighty, boundless, omniscient, omnipresent, eternal and triune Being, without beginning and without ending.

But Adam was created a tangible creature; and, even though he was perfect, he was able to fall. In respect to his person, he had a beginning. He was the pinnacle of creation. God, on the other hand, was not created and is incapable of doing evil.

You must remember these points. You will be able to put them to good use in the following lesson.

I shall ask something now, about which each of you may feel free to speak your mind.

God convenanted with Adam and with us in him. We all understand that now. But why did God use the tree of knowledge of good and evil as the means for a probationary command?

Did not God do that for the love that He had for man?

Can anyone make clear to me that God did actually give that probationary command out of love?

I shall try for a moment to do that for you.

Here is an example: A father and mother have a small child. As long as that child is very small it doesn't understand anything of what it may do or may not do.

As it grows older, the father and mother often say to their child, "Be careful, you must not do that!" The child gradually comes to understand what is wrong and what is not.

(The conscience speaks too, but we are not talking of that aspect right now.) I am only using this common situation as an example. But now if the parents never directed the child in what was good or bad and allowed the child to grow up that way, what would happen?

A situation might develop that such a child would take something that did not belong to him. That child could say

120

to the police when they come to punish him for stealing, "I did not know this was forbidden. My father never told me it was wrong."

It would bring shame upon such parents, but an excuse for the child.

In another instance; if the parents had cautioned against stealing and other sins and then the child was caught in the act, they could justly say, "Child, child how often we warned you and yet you did it anyway. It is just and proper that you be punished."

It could never be said by the child, "I did not know it."

This is plain enough is it not?

The first parents were unkind to their child in not warning him against this evil but the latter had done their duty in love.

These are just simple examples, because we can not compare human happenings with Divine. They are merely given so that you children can grasp the meaning a little better.

If the Lord had not said to Adam, "The day that thou eatest thereof you shall surely die," Adam would then have sinned ignorantly in the eating of it and would have been able to defend himself saying, "I did not know that the tree was meant for my probation."

The fact that He did was an expression of God's love. He pointed out the danger of sin and threatened the consequences of that sin prior to the act.

In this way no one can excuse himself.

Adam, as an individual and also as head of the human race, representing us all as head of the covenant of works, would have received eternal life (according to the promise) if he had not sinned. But since he has fallen, we too are righteously lost in him. And because we are justly lost through that first sin (that we have done in him) we shall also be lost after our natural death unless redeemed by Christ while in this life.

What is the only way of escape for every person from that three-fold death?

That we be brought out of Adam our original head, in whom we are condemned before God, and that we be transplanted into Christ. Christ is the head of a much better covenant, the Covenant of Grace. Christ can not break that covenant as Adam did the Covenant of Works. Therefore, those that are in Christ, included in the Covanant of Grace, shall never be lost.

When the tragic event took place in Adams' race there followed nothing but continuous disaster.

But it is now in gracious Divine hands and it shall always be well for those who are chosen to have a part in it.

I read in a book this statement, 'The devil, in his hatred to God, tried to dig a hole under the Covenant of Works so that the foundation would cave in. He did succeed with God's permission, to get man to listen to him.

But he will never be able to undermine the Covenant of Grace because Christ, the eternal Son of God, is the foundation and the head of it."

That is the way it is and it is the comfort of all God's people.

Although it has been proven that the devil is a liar, he persistantly tries to lull a person to sleep with more lies. He said to Eve, "You will not die if you eat of it, but you will become like God."

We see every day before our very eyes that that was a lie, because men do die. And yet — now be honest, are you genuinely sincere in believing that you must die?

I am certain that you would much rather think about all sorts of mirthful things than you would about death. At least this is true of most of you.

That happens because a person in his fallen state would rather continue listening to the voice of the devil than to the truth. He does not want to die, but to live. Isn't that so?

We could have lived; lived eternally if we merely had kept God's command. We could have kept God's command faithfully (considering our side of the matter) because we had received the moral excellence to keep it.

We shall leave it at this point this afternoon and hope to continue the next time we meet. Our absence from one another will be one week longer than usual, if the Lord spares us, because next Friday is "Good Friday" and next Sunday is Easter.

I hope, boys and girls, that these esteemed days for the church do not become sin-days for you in which you, even more than usual, seek out all sorts of idle amusements.

O, if you received, for one moment, an impression in your souls what happened on that Friday, now nineteen hundred twenty two years ago, you would not have a desire to look at the worldly amusements with even one glance.

It was then that the holy, perfect Son of God hung on a cross between heaven and earth in order to obtain favor of a holy God for creatures that had lost that favor through breaking of the covenant of works.

If Good Friday had not taken place, the other solemn days such as Easter, Ascension Day and Pentecost could not have followed.

And even though you are very young it is possible that He has accomplished that for you. Isn't that so?

I hope you may never consider yourself to be happy or joyful until you have had the assurance that His blood has been shed for your guilty soul.

Do not think I begrudge you happiness in this life. O, no, if you bowed your head like a bulrush and went about all day wearing black but had no true sorrow to God, it would have no profit.

I only wish for you "that godly sorrow, that worketh repentance to salvation not to be repented of", in your never dying soul.

May the Lord take that which I have expressed and impress it upon your minds and hearts.

He alone can place within your heart that which I have laid on it. May He do it for His Name's Sake. So be it.

Lesson 12

Of The Image Of God

God governed man by means of a covenant when he was in the state of rectitude (uprightness). God gave a command and a promise. By this, man knew he could obtain or lose eternal life.

The question is now: Was man capable of keeping that covenant.

Answer: Yes, God had created him capable to keep it.

Just as the Triune God had created everything else good and upright, He had also done so with man. And who was it that saw that everything was good?

We read in Genesis 1, "And God saw everything He had made and, behold, it was very good."

This is in itself proof that man was created good and upright.

Nevertheless, Hellenbroek asks a question that is a bit strange; don't you find it so? He asks: "Was not man created in a simple state of nature, between good and evil?"

You must explain to me what Hellenbroek means by this. What does it mean to be between good and evil?

There have always been erroneous beliefs concerning this

124

point. During Hellenbroek's life, and even before and after his time, the Jesuits (and remonstrants) taught that man was created neither good nor evil.

They try to explain that man was like a piece of white paper on which nothing was written, good nor evil. If we believe this, then we evidently do not believe God's Word. It tells us that we were created after God's Image; That is, very good.

What conclusion do we come to if we believe that man was created in a neutral state (neither good nor evil)?

1st. If a person was never completely good, then he also never became completely evil, but had sinned only because he was not perfect.

2nd. If he had not become completely evil, then he did not become dead in sin and has no need of a mediator to reconcile him to God.

They do speak of the Lord Jesus, but they use Him as an assisting mediator; not as a complete savior.

It is self evident; if men deny the total state of death in Adam, they also deny the complete satisfaction in Christ. These two matters are inseparably bound together.

Do you see now what the result is if we do not believe that Adam lost everything when he disobeyed?

There are many people who confess with their mouth that they are spiritually dead and have completely lost God's image, but their every day living reveals that they have never accepted it in their hearts.

Instead of going to God *through* Christ, they go to God *with* Christ. (In their imagination of course, because in actuality it is impossible.)

I shall. try to make it clear just what I mean with an example. There was a man who had very much debt. Since he had nothing with which to pay, he was about to let his creditors sell all his belongings. Before it came that far, however, a friend came along who was willing to pay all his debts and he actually did that.

The whole world knew that this man was bankrupt and had nothing but debt. They also knew someone paid all the debts for this man.

That is one case. But now there is a second man who had just as much debt as the first man. This man, too, had a friend who would help him. But, the debtor said to his friend, "Give me your money. I have yet a small amount myself and, if I put yours with mine, I can satisfy my creditors."

This second man paid off the debt himself with the money of his surety. In this way he remained a respectable person in the eyes of all who knew him.

Do you see the difference?

The first was totally dependent on his surety to pay the debt for him without any help from himself. But the second man still had something left which, when added to the money of his surety and by paying the debt personally, (by means of his surety) remained a respectable man. This doctrine was initially brought in by Pelagius. When you become somewhat older, you should study the books of Alexander Comrie regarding this matter. He fought violently against these errors of Pelagius and showed how dangerous they were.

I can give another example. Just suppose that a ship was wrecked in a severe storm. Two men were the last to survive on the wreck but finally it sank completely and both were left in the water. One of the men noticed a lifebouy he could take hold of. At last he was able to swim safely to shore.

The other man soon became unconscious because of exhaustion and it seemed he must drown. But the captain of a lifeboat noticed him and pulled him aboard.

126

When he came to consciousness on shore he saw his companion safely situated. They both had experienced exactly the same danger, both placed in the same water and now both had been saved. What was the difference?

The one had the ability to save himself, but the other lost all his strength and was certain to drown unless rescued by another. Therein lies the difference.

In every day life this is not critical because, as in the example, both were rescued. But in spiritual life no one can be saved who saves himself *with* Christ. God the Father shall say, "I never knew you." He only recognizes His Son and the sinner *in* His Son.

Isn't it a great sin and terribly deceptive to conclude that we have not lost God's image completely?

It is for this reason that Hellenbroek asks the question, namely, "Was not man created in a simple (neutral) state of nature between good and evil?" Then he goes further and says, "Wherein did the image of God consist?

Answer: In knowledge, righteousness and holiness.

Doesn't the image refer to the outward shape of the body?

No, because God has no body.

Adam received a perfect physical body from God, but that was not the image of God. The image of God does not consist of a visible body, but does consist of the communicable attributes of God. These were imparted to Adam.

They were: 1st, knowledge. Adam knew God in His essence. He possessed a divine knowledge of the Triune God. The New Testament clearly proves this to be true.

Every elect person has God's image, which he had lost through sin, restored to him again in Christ. That is why Hellenbroek says, "Prove that the image of God consisted in knowledge." The answer lies in Colossians 3:10, "And have put on the new man, which is renewed in knowledge, after the image of Him that created him."

The 2nd and 3rd attributes are: Righteousness and true holiness. Ephesians 4:24, "And that ye put on the new man, which after God is created in righteousness and true holiness."

Where did the image of God have its source?

Since there were three divine and perfect attributes, their source was from God Himself. It can be no other way than that Adam possessed perfect knowledge, perfect righteousness and perfect holiness. A perfect God gave to the perfect man these three perfect attributes. Even though, however, Adam was given God's image, he did not become a God. He remained a person. Boys and girls, pay attention now to what I want to say, because this is a difficult point in our lesson.

Adam was perfect. He received the image of God from a perfect God. He possessed it. That image had its source in God. And yet Adam did not become God by possessing that image. Why not, do you suppose?

Adam became a person in creation. He himself had made neither his body nor his soul. They both had been created by God. In addition to soul and body he received the image of God. Gen. 1:27, "God created man in his own image, in the image of God created He him; male and female created He them."

He possessed this image, then, not of himself; it was the gift of God. It had been given to him. And because it was a thing given to him, he did not become a god. This image was simply a gift which he, a perfect creature, received from his Creator. Also, by sinning, he could lose this image.

Adam was immortal. He possessed the image of God as long as he remained obedient to God. Death was threatened only if sin entered in. "In the day thou eatest thereof thou shalt surely die." Because it was a gift it could be lost.

If you have the book of Arnoldus Rotterdam at home, you should read the chapter on "The Image of God". The article this man wrote is very comprehensive. He says we must view the image of God, which Adam carried, in both the broad and narrow sense and has given a very clear description of it. He says in reference to the words "image" and "likeness" in the scripture verse, "Let us make man in our image after our likeness", that they are intended to be understood as a resembling image; an image that closely conforms to God.

Why would both words have been used? Would it not have been sufficient to say either "image" or "likeness"?

Answer: No, even though they are essentially the same, every image is not a likeness and every likeness is not an image.

God wanted to use both words in order to impress upon our minds that man was created in God's image in such a way that he was like God in His Communicable attributes, knowledge, righteousness and holiness.

And, on the other hand, this image is so in conformity to God that that likeness was as it were an impression or a representation of God. It is clear that there are four things required in an image:

1. An *original* according to which something is portrayed.

2. A *subject* through which the likeness appears.

3. An *impression* which the original presents.

4. The *resemblance* between the original and the likeness.

1. The original is God's attribute of knowledge, righteousness and holiness. God created man according to that image.

2. The subject was the soul of man. God impressed these perfections upon the soul.

3. The impression is the image which Adam carried, in other words, the pure image of God, knowledge, righteousness and holiness.

4. The resemblance is the genuine conformity between the attributes impressed upon the soul of Adam as the image of God.

That is why it is said God created man in His image and likeness, purely conformable to His image.

Now you must not think that I mean that image and likeness are two things. No, they mean the same thing. The word "likeness" serves to explain the word "image". Both words used together mean, "A close resembling image."

Do you understand now, what a magnificent state the state of rectitude was in which man carried God's image and likeness?

That is what he lost in his disobedience.

But the elect begin to receive that Divine image again through Christ and in Christ. By grace they receive a beginning of Divine knowledge, righteousness and holiness in the Mediator. One day after their death, they will again bear the perfect image of God.

But those who are not converted to God during their lifetime will be eternally without that image.

Boys and girls, have you ever carefully considered the fact that you are living in this world without the image of God? You still have the same natural body. I mean our body has not changed its form. Also, you have the same never dying soul which God has given. But we have lost God's likeness and not a single attribute remains. Yet a Holy God will justly demand His image of us when we come to die and stand in the last judgment, because He has placed us upon this earth adorned with His image and has never taken it away from us. We have faithlessly sinned it away.

Man, being the image bearer of God, was the jewel of all creation. The likeness which he carried by virtue of God's attributes and shared with a perfect God made him the noblest of all creatures.

By virtue of that image he was also established as king of creation and received power over all creatures.

It is not that the image of God consists in the exercising of power over the beasts, no, because that power over the beasts will not be needed in heaven and yet God's image will be there in the most perfect way. The dominion over the beasts in the state of rectitude was an effect or a result of the image of God. Also, as long as Adam carried the image he was immortal. Indeed, while he carried these divine attributes perfectly, how could he die?

But now man walks in the great creation as the most shameful, instead of the most magnificent, creature. Unless he obtains salvation in Christ he is without that grand gift eternally.

I walked a few hours one splendid evening along a quiet gravel road near the Belgian border.

It was an exceptionally nice quiet evening. There was a great deal of pasture on both sides of the road in which the cattle were calmly grazing or sleeping. Everything was so peaceful and pretty. It was as if there never had been any sin in the world.

But all of a sudden I heard cannon roar in the distance (it was during World War I). The cannon roared unceasingly. It was much better heard in the quiet of the night than during the day.

Then I thought, "Now, that is sin". The creation remains as it was, but man has ruined everything by sin. Right here is peace and quiet. The animals are lying or grazing in the pasture. The clear sky was full of twinkling stars and it was so nice a person would think he was in Paradise.

But out there in the distance, hell vomited death and destruction. Thousands of persons fell dead or were maimed and blood flowed as water. God's creatures, that once were the ornaments of creation, were out there murdering one another.

That shows how horrible a creature man has become, much worse than the beasts.

Girls and boys, do you ever think of what sin has caused?

Sin is a pleasure for a person in his natural state. That is why it will be so terrible for an unconverted person to die. Death removes all this pleasure from him. In hell a person continues to sin but the pleasure of it ceases.

O, then, God at their awakening will despise their image (Psalm 73:20) for they bear the image of the devil. Men, too, forsook God and were disobedient to Him just as the devil had been.

But when God's people die, death will free them from their greatest burden.

When grace was given to them, sin became a burden instead of pleasure. Death will be a welcome messenger to them then for it will lift from them their heaviest burden.

Boys and girls, we must go home. Our hour is spent. Has sin become a burden to you too, or, is it still your pleasure?

When I visit here or there, it is not necessary for me to ask the people if they are sinners. I know they are because we all are. But I may enquire if sin is a burden or a pleasure to them.

By nature we all are dead sinners and living enemies of God. But here and there amongst these dead sinners are sinners who are spiritually alive.

Often times sinners such as these will seek out a place alone in their homes or out of doors crying out, "O, God, I have offended Thee. I no longer have Thy holy image. I

132

have sinned in every way, and, what is worse, sin is my greatest pleasure!"

Boys and girls, even though you are still young you are not too young to die. This is because you were born in sin.

Search within yourselves to determine whether you are dead or living sinners.

Be assured that it is necessary to determine that you are a living sinner before God. In no other way will sin be a burden to you.

What a fearful death you will have if sin always remains a pleasure to you!

After death, God's children will be satisfied to the full with the divine likeness in eternal bliss. Without the possibility of losing His likeness again, they will glorify God in a perfect manner, above all sin and above all desires and burdens.

May the Lord awaken within you a holy jealousy of these blessed people. May you learn to love them, not because they are going to heaven, but because they are reconciled with God and are once again adorned with His image.

May He speak to you for the first time or by renewal to give up the satisfaction you have in sin and in yourself. Also, to preserve you from being satisfied in a self-made religion or a self-acquired piety.

If with Luther you chastised your body and shortened your life and walked to Rome in your bare feet, even that shall never move God to help you. No, children, God is eternally affected in Himself to glorify His grace in the elect and also to elevate His honor to the highest splendor.

May He create within you that desire to love Him above even your own life, then you will cherish your soul as if it were your most precious possession.

So be it.

133

Lesson 13

The Fall Of Man

We were taught in our lesson on the Covenant of Works that the Triune God entered into an agreement (covenant) with Adam.

The great Creator made man one of His principal creatures. He created all the angels as separate individuals at the time of creation. Man was created one for all and all for one. Dust was used in creating his body while his spirit was created without the use of materials or means.

God established man in a very privileged position in Paradise. He was well acquainted with God and had the ability to obey Him.

Man was perfect in every way and very rich. He had the freedom to eat of every tree in the garden of Eden except one. This tree stood in the center of the garden; of this tree he was forbidden to eat.

Would that tree have had a bad or poisonous fruit on it? What would be your thoughts on that?

No, that was not the reason man was forbidden by God to eat of it. What then?

God had given Adam a probationary command to see if he would be obedient to Him or not. The sin would not lie in the fruit but in the transgression of the commandment, not to eat of it.

How many things do we see in this command that God gave to Adam?

Answer: Three things. 1st. God made a demand. 2nd He made a promise. 3rd. He also made a threat.

Concerning the first point, God demanded perfect obedience from Adam in keeping the law of love, the precept which God had created within his heart.

Secondly, He promised eternal life upon the fulfillment of His law, that is, when obedience became clearly evident.

Thirdly, He threatened death in its fullest sense upon disobedience: "For in the day that thou eatest thereof thou shalt surely die."

In the original text it is written: "For in the day that thou eatest thereof dying thou shalt die."

That means: To die a threefold death; physical, spiritual and eternal.

These three are bound together in an inseparable way.

After Adam sinned, it would be impossible for his body to die and his soul to live on eternally.

It was also impossible that he remain physically alive throughout time while spiritually dead; that is, without communion with God and without His favor.

That is certainly not hard to understand, is it?

Adam, who was a perfect and rational creature knew full well that as soon as he became disobedient he would die the threefold death.

Who actually originated this covenant?

All of you know that a covenant is a mutual agreement between two or more persons. But one certain person must initiate a proposal in order to make a covenant.

We discussed these matters in former lessons but it is probably necessary and surely profitable to repeat these important details.

The covenant transaction proceeded from God alone, but as would naturally follow, Adam accepted the covenant freely; this being the result of his integrity.

The first covenant was called the Covenant of Works because through obedience Adam could obtain eternal life for himself and all his posterity.

The covenant provided the opportunity and means to show that he would continue with this covenant faithfully by not eating of this tree.

The requirement God placed upon him was not heavy to bear. He had received in his perfect state the ability to be obedient. He was created according to God's image.

Our lesson this afternoon asks "Does man still possess that image?"

Answer: No, he lost it by sin.

This answer tells us also that Adam (and we with him) violated the covenant. What reasons could Adam have had to break the covenant?

Was there insufficient food in the garden that made it necessary for him to eat of the forbidden fruit?

No, that was not the reason. Solomon says in Proverbs 6:30, "Men do not despise a thief if he steal to satisfy his soul when he is hungry; but if he be found, he shall restore sevenfold; he shall give all the substance of his house."

Stealing is always sin, but a person who is hungry, or in dire need, is inclined to obtain what is needed, and does steal bread to feed himself, yet such a person is not considered as contemptable as one who has stolen willfully. You all agree with Soloman in that, do you not?

While in Paradise, Adam had not the least need. There was a delightful abundance to sustain his body.

Was it necessary then, for Adam to steal in order to satisfy hunger? No, it was a wanton disobedience when he took the fruit and ate it. There is, therefore, no excuse for his sin. He knew full well that he could lose his magnificent situation, because the Lord had spoken plainly to him about it.

Do you remember who was the first one ever to speak of death?

Death had been spoken of before death or misery even existed. Who had done that, the devil, man or God?

136

Not man. Adam knew nothing of death or misery while in Paradise. There was no place for death in the state of rectitude.

Neither had the devil spoken of it, because he had come after Adam had entered into the command of obedience.

In the use of the words, "You shall surely die," the Lord was the first to speak of death.

The serpent referred to this word when he said to Eve, "You will not surely die."

Who was the first liar in the world?

The devil. His first lie was that man would not die if he ate of the tree of the Knowledge of Good and Evil.

Who can tell me what purpose the devil had in causing our first parents to eat of that fruit?

Answer: He wanted to tempt Eve.

That is true, but the devil had an ulterior motive with his tempting. He wanted to attack God in this manner. He wanted not only to bring about the mortality of man but also tried to bring God's purpose of creation to destruction.

That is why he said to Eve, "Yea, hath not God said, Ye shall not eat of every tree of the garden?"

Do you see through the base accusation contained in this question? It is as if he wanted to say, "You mustn't believe that this is really true: God knows if you eat of it you will not die, but you will be like God, knowing good and evil. That covenant is cruel."

I shall try to make it clear to you by way of an example how the devil did his work.

There was a man who had a son, but also an enemy. The father gave his son a warning by saying to him, "Remember, my son, These are the things you may do, but this and that you may not do." After explanation of those matters he gave a warning and some directions to his son so that there would be no misunderstanding about this.

137

Now the enemy of the man cunningly inquired of the warning the father had given to the son and thought within himself, "I cannot rule over the father, he is my greatest enemy and my superior but I shall try to harm him through his son."

He went to the son and questioning him, said, "Didn't your father say it was all right for you to do that?"

The son replied, "No, my father forbids me to do that; he does allow me to do many things, but that particular thing I am forbidden to do."

"Come, come," said the enemy, "your father knows better; it is not so that it is forbidden. You just go ahead and do it without fear, because he knows, too, that you shall have some profit in doing it."

Each one of you will understand that the boy stands between two forces; either he must remain faithful to his father and consider this man to be a liar, or, proceed to do what he says and consider his father to be a liar. He cannot believe both at the same time.

The boy, of course, did not know that the man who was trying to deceive him was an enemy of his father, nevertheless, he had a duty to obey his father and not this man.

But the boy paid heed to the enemy and, in so doing, just as much as said to the father, "I do not believe you. You are the liar. This man tells me the opposite of what you said, and I believe him."

That is about what took place in Paradise, too, isn't it? And so the devil attained his goal; at least he thought he had. He used man to attack God. He was not successful because the Lord suffered no loss because of our fall. He accomplished His intention for which He had created man.

Who had suffered harm then?

Well, man suffered the harm. The first question in our

lesson testifies to that: "Doth man still possess that image?"

Answer: No, he lost it by sin.

And the last question is: "What consequences had this sin on Adam and Eve?"

Answer:

1st. The loss of God's image.

2nd. Awareness of nakedness.

3rd. Horror of conscience.

4th. Expulsion from Paradise.

5th. Death itself.

In this way we have wilfully torn ourselves away from God and by our deeds we have said to our Creator: "I dissolve the covenant you have made with me. I believe the devil. I will serve him."

Adam knew very well what was going to be the result because God had spoken of death and had said it would be the result of disobedience.

I once read a story about a sailor, who had been converted to God. Actually, it is dangerous to explain spiritual things with natural examples, but because you are still young, you probably will find it easier to understand the meaning of our lesson. It was an English sailor, John Newton, who gave the following account:

"I imagined I was on board a ship at sea. It was a very large ship. I was not acquainted with very many people on it. It was at that time a distinguished looking man approached me and said, 'John, here is an expensive ring, would you want it? There is a perpetual good fortune bound to it. I shall put it on your finger, but you may not take it off because your happiness depends upon it being on your finger. Take good care of it.' "

"I put the ring on," the sailor continued his story, "and I believed what the man had said. Somewhat later, however, a stranger came to me and said, 'Well, John, what a handsome ring you have on your finger. Who gave it to you?'

I told him the circumstances, and when I had finished telling what the gentleman had said, the stranger threw back his shoulders in contempt and said disdainfully, 'Hm, you say this is a good fortune ring? Don't believe it friend, it is only a story the man is telling you, nothing else; believe me, John, you would have better fortune if you take the ring off than if you keep it on.' The stranger spoke so friendly and persistantly that I believed him, with the result, I removed the ring and threw it into the sea. Now that the stranger had achieved his purpose, he went his way and again I stood alone.

Immediately the feeling came to me that I had been unfaithful because of the promise I had made to take care of the ring. I had listened to a tempter who had come to me in the disguise of a friend. I had much regret but I could not recover the ring.

While I anxiously reflected upon the fact that I had foolhardily perverted my good fortune, the gentleman who gave me the ring came by and said, 'You look so dejected; what has happened? What do I see; where is the ring?'

Shaking with anguish I related what had happened, justifying myself, saying that, while I did not know the stranger, he had introduced himself in such a nice manner.

The gentleman rebuked me seriously and reminded me of the gross unthankfulness that I had shown. He also found the stranger and told him he would experience terrible results for his base dealings.

Finally, he turned to me again and said, 'You have lost your good fortune because of your rashness. If you had kept the ring you would have earned good fortune. But now I am determined to do something else. My son will recover the ring from the bottom of the sea and bring it back to me. He will recover this good fortune which you would have received had you kept the ring. You will never be given the ring again. I shall keep it for you, because I have now come to see that you cannot be trusted with it. You will receive good fortune, not because you deserve it but because I love you.

My son wants to do the necessary work for you in bringing the ring back to me because He loves you, too."

The sailor told, in the foregoing account, an illustration of the fall of Adam, the violation of the covenant, the results of which nullify any possibility of anyone earning eternal life again. On the other hand, the covenant of grace in Christ is much more sure than the covenant of works ever was in Adam. God's children, the elect, receive eternal life which they could not earn, preserve, nor lose. Christ has obtained and will guard it securely for them.

We have already mentioned in our lesson on the Covenant of Works that, although the devil tempted Adam, Adam fell of his own free choice. This is so because the devil, having no power over Adam's will, could only suggest it. There was no coercion here on the devil's part but only an unconscionable disobedience on Adam's part.

Have you ever read how John Bunyan describes the temptation of the devil? When you come home, ask if you may read the book entitled "The Holy War." Bunyan describes there how the devil held council with the fallen angels on the best method to bring man to sin. They used temptation. Man of his own free choice yielded and sinned.

When was the first time that they were aware of their sin?

Read Genesis 3, too, this evening; you will find the answer there; "– and gave also unto her husband with her; and he did eat. And the eyes of them both were opened and

141

they knew that they were naked; and they sewed fig leaves together, and made themselves aprons."

And what then? Did God leave them to their lot, with no more concern for them?

No, they heard the voice of the Lord God while walking in the garden in the cool of the day. Then Adam and his wife hid themselves from the presence of the Lord among the trees of the garden. But there was no place so secluded among the trees that God could not find them. The Lord God called Adam and said to him, "Where are you?"

What did Adam answer? Did he say, "I am full of fear because I have broken the covenant?" No. He was not that honest. Immediately he tried to find ways of escape and said, "I heard thy voice in the garden and I was afraid because I was naked."

Read the conversation that followed, and you would see that Adam was not willing to accept the blame.

What is the meaning of the words, "Adam was naked"; does that mean that he had no clothing on his body?

It means that, but something else too.

Before man sinned he was clothed with the holy image of God. The Divine attributes of God, knowledge, righteousness and holiness had been imparted to him. Adam had to acknowledge that he now had actually lost that image and stood naked before the eyes of God.

He endeavored to cover himself with a garment of leaves he had made for himself. But, did the Lord consider their garment appropriate?

No, because, after the Lord had pronounced the curse and punishment, as we read in verse 21, "Unto Adam also and to his wife did the Lord God make coats of skins and clothed them."

The covering that Adam had made for himself could not at all fulfill the requirements, so the Lord made a robe for him; not of leaves that perish, but of skins, which signifies that it would require shed (sacrificial) blood. An animal must be killed in order to obtain a skin.

It also signified that Adam could not clothe himself with the righteousness of Christ. God's Word is very emphatic in this: "Unto Adam and to his wife did the Lord God make coats of skins and clothed them."

He would not have put the coat of skins over Adam's leaves, no; God unclothed Adam of his own covering and then clothed him again.

Boys and girls, that will also be necessary for each of us. Have you ever thought about what it means to stand naked before God?

Imagine that tomorrow at 12 o'clock noon, when the streets are crowded with people, you, being naked, were placed in the public square across from the cathedral so that children and adults would see you. Wouldn't you feel terribly ashamed? I think you would want to hide yourself beneath the pavement. This is merely in consideration of *people* seeing you.

By nature we all now stand naked, in Adam, before a holy God.

Each one of us have taken off the coat of virtue that God had given us.

Do you understand now why we must be clothed?

Because of sin. It was not necessary in Paradise. Only after sin came was it necessary to clothe our bodies. It is not an honor that we wear clothes. Contrariwise, it is a great shame. We would not have been ashamed of the nakedness of our bodies, if we had not lost the image of God. Everything would have remained holy and without sin.

O, if only more thought were given to the dreadful reason why we wear clothes! Would we still desire to display ourselves with these clothes?

143

I think that then the simplest kind of material would satisfy because even the fact that we wear clothes testifies that we are separated from God and have sinned against Him.

On the other hand, it is a favor of common grace that we may have covering for our bodies. We have lost all right to any sustenance because we have sinned.

Have you ever given thought to this in respect to our clothes too? In one respect it is a shame to wear clothes and in another a privilege.

Owing to our fall we all wear the cloak of sin, but through the merits of Christ everyone is also covered with common (or universal) grace.

Always remember, boys & girls, that you are clothed this way.

A young lady once asked me, "Pastor, what kind of clothes should I wear?" I replied, "Clothe yourself in such a way that you are not a laughing stock to the world nor an offence to God's people. Thus, plain, modest, and yet not ridiculous."

But, though we wear clothing for our bodies in addition to the cloak of common grace, would they be sufficient covering before the face of God?

No, they cannot possibly be, because they cannot endure beyond death, for then they will be taken away from us. If we do not possess the cloak of Christ's righteousness at that time we shall stand naked before our Maker.

What can we conclude from this? Listen attentively to these four things:

1. In the state of innocence we were clothed with the holy image of God.

2. We lost that image through the fall and became clothed with a covering of sin and shame.

144

3. However, our lives are also covered with the cloak of common grace since the fall.

4. We must be clothed with the righteousness of Christ in order to be able to stand before God. The cloak of common grace does not extend beyond death. It will no longer be effectual and it will cease irrevocably.

It is necessary, therefore, that you truly accept the fact that you stand naked before God because of willful disobedience. Even if you never could admit this during your young lifetime, you will surely find it so when you come to die.

The Lord Jesus said to the Jews, that men in the day of judgment shall say to the mountains, "Fall on us" and to the hills, "Cover us." Luke 23:30.

But, children, mountains or hills will not be able to cover your naked soul!

Then it will be fully revealed how great our sins and disobediences were.

May you learn to fear sin as well as to fear its results. By nature all men fear the results of sin.

Last week I stood by the death bed of an old man. He had such dreadful fear. One had to feel sorry for him. His wife and children stood round about his bed crying. He could hardly speak anymore. He searched around with large hollow eyes and in an almost unintelligible voice asked me to say a prayer. I asked him before proceeding, "For what should I pray?"

What do you think the man's answer was? He could hardly talk because he lay dying, but haltingly he said, " To – become – well, that – I need not die, but – live."

Poor man. He had never once accepted the fact that death comes as the result of sin. Now the result of sin was present, but he did not want to face it. His desire was to live and continue in sin.

But the precious time of conversion was past for that man. He died a short time later.

We all stood round about him. There was nothing more the doctor or the minister could do; his wife and children were unable to do anything for him. He had to bear the penalty of sin all alone. He had to appear before God — and now naked, without a covering for his poor guilty soul.

Do you see now that the devil was certainly a liar when he said, "Ye shall not surely die?"

Tell me truthfully now, you see or hear of people dying all around you everyday and you know that the judgment day is coming when we must stand before Jesus, but, do you really believe that that day is coming?

I can plainly see that you do not actually believe it, for you live as though it will never come to pass.

Perhaps in your thoughts you say, "I wish that you would stop talking about that matter. It is repeated every week and it is so depressing to listen to your talk about death and eternity."

But one day you will have to deal with the matter even though it is depressing.

I hope and wish that you do not die as that man did. If you do, your conscience will be opened as you have never experienced it before. And in spite of your desire that we should not discuss such things now, you will certainly have to acknowledge, "Our pastor talked to us about these matters. Now it has become a dreadful reality!"

A great number of people, nowadays, think that these matters should not be discussed, especially not with children. They say that it detracts from their happiness.

But the Lord said to the prophet, "If you do not speak to them of it, I shall require their blood from thy hand." Death is no myth and death and hell after death even less. Do you think there is only a heaven and no damnation? God's infallible word speaks of both.

O, boys and girls, if you should die without being clothed with the righteousness of Christ, you will certainly enter the place of torment because death is an unceasing punishment for disobedience.

There will not be one drop of water for relief, nor one drop of love, nor one drop of mercy! Nor will there be mercy for one another but, instead, eternal hatred, terrible envy and despair, cursing and slandering. Every sin committed in thought, word and deed from birth until your death shall burn on your open consciences like big fiery words and the wrath of God will kindle a fire that can never be quenched.

The Lord's own words in speaking of the unconverted are, "And these shall go away into everlasting punishment but the righteous into life eternal."

May you personally accept your "fall in Adam" and become the guilty one before God through His work in your heart.

You are still in the day of grace. You can still be reconciled with God through Christ. May He bestow that upon you before it is too late.

So be it.

Lesson 14

Original Sin

Hellenbroek begins the lesson this afternoon with a very important question.

Last week we discussed Adam's fall and now, without any reference to it at all, asks, "Doth Adam's sin also affect us?"

He answers, "Yes; it is imputed to us."

And why?

Answer: Because Adam was the head of the covenant; and therein considered as representing all his posterity. Romans 5:12, "Wherefore, as by one man sin entered into the world, and death by sin; and so death passed upon all men, for that all have sinned."

Perhaps some of you have reflected upon the question we had in a previous lesson; I mean the one which asks, "By whom was Adam deceived?"

Answer: By his wife. She gave him, and he did eat.

Haven't you thought: "In that case, properly speaking, only Eve had sinned and Adam was not guilty of transgression; only the woman"?

It is true as Paul says in 1 Timothy 2:14: "And Adam was not deceived, but the woman being deceived was in the transgression." Wouldn't it be unjust to charge Adam with this sin which Eve had done?

No, because, in the first place, Adam was the one with whom God had made the covenant; not Eve. Adam was a principal, with God, in the covenant.

2nd. Even though Eve was the first to be deceived, Adam, personally, had taken part in the sin. Instead of reprimanding his wife and refusing the fruit, it is said, "She gave also unto her husband with her, and he did eat." He agreed to Eve's conduct and so with her became responsible for the sin.

That is why Hellenbroek asks in the first question on Original Sin, "Doth *Adam's* sin also affect us?" He does not mention Eve's sin. Adam was a head in three respects.

1. He was the head of the Covenant of Works.
2. He was the head of the whole human race.
3. He was the head of the marriage with Eve.

Before we proceed any further in our lesson, I want to ask you an out of the ordinary question.

Are we charged with Adam's sin because he was the head of the Covenant of Works?

This is not an easy question for anyone and I am sure it is a bit complicated for you. But, it is a very serious question in that it has a bearing on the principal parts of our doctrine.

A little later in life it would be profitable for you to search into Dr. Comrie's writings on the various errors that prevail on this point. I shall attempt to explain something about this briefly.

There are people holding to erroneous doctrines who teach that God has not required that all men be condemned for the sin of one person. These people believe it would be hard-hearted and unjust. This is not a new doctrine. On, no; Pelaguis was the first to occupy himself with this point of doctrine.

Who knows when this man lived?

Answer: It was during the time of Dr. Comrie.

You are mistaken about that, but Dr. Comrie did write much in opposition to the Pelagians. The doctrine of

Pelagius had been actively taught and believed during the time of Comrie and is being taught now also but, actually, the man died ages ago.

Pelagius was born in England in the year 354 A.D. He was a monk and lived in a cloister. He abstained from all enjoyments. In the year 400 he journeyed Eastward toward Rome, Milan and Carthage. While in Rome he wrote books in which he said not only that no one has original (or inherited) sin, but also that everyone born since the fall is born without sin; that all men sin now because of the power of temptation. He said a person sins by imitation.

This is what Pelagius wrote and taught. It is only natural that he attracted many followers during his lifetime and since his death. He acknowledged that Christ had come upon this earth, but said that He had come to give a good example which everyone should follow.

In that same time Augustine was also in Italy and directly opposed the teachings of Pelagius. Augustine taught in accordance to the correct viewpoint: That God's Word teaches that man is spiritually dead because of original sin and as a consequence not one child is born without guilt.

A man named Socinus was born many years after the time of Pelagius and revived the Pelagian teaching. He denied the existence of original sin. Of course he could not deny that man must die; everyone sees it take place. According to him, "Death was not the result of Adam's sin which was imputed to us, but, because Adam is the head of the people, we are his natural children. And, because Adam died, we, being his descendants, must also die."

Socinus is very definite in his writings about this matter. He says, "Even though it is true all creatures proceeding from Adam must die, it is not because the guilt of Adam is imposed upon them, but because they are his descendants."

Do you understand now why I put this question to you, "Are we charged with Adam's sin because he is the head of the whole human race, or, because he was the head of the covenant of works?"

Pelagius, Socinus and the Remonstrants taught that we do not die because the sin of Adam is imputed to us but because we are his descendants. In other words, Adam was the father of all people but was not our representative in the Covenant of Works.

It follows then, if he is not our representative head, (wherein God views him as though the whole human race is in him) then his actions cannot be made chargeable to us.

Do you understand this?

You know that in the government of nations, presidents, kings and queens have ambassadors in other countries. These ambassadors represent them there or are there in behalf of the heads of government.

When an ambassador makes a statement, it is accepted as though the king or president had made it.

We could regard an ambassador as a representative. He is a type of the person for whom he substitutes.

That is why Adam is often spoken of as our "representative head" and so, a representative of us all. God regarded Adam as though He saw before Himself all persons who were yet to come. Therein lies the difference between being the head of the covenant and being the head of all people.

If by virtue of creation he was simply the forerunner of all his descendants, and God had not made him head of the covenant, he would have only been answerable for himself as a person. His obedience would have had no value, nor his sin done any injury to the generations following him. But that is the way the Remonstrants believe. They say, "We must die because our father Adam died, not because he was our representative in the Covenant of Works."

But Hellenbroek, being opposed to all these erroneous opinions, composed his lessons in strict accordance to God's Word and the confessions of the true church. He asks in question 3: What kind of sin do we derive from Adam?

Answer: Original sin. Psalm 51:5 "Behold, I was shapen in iniquity, and in sin did my mother conceive me."

And then he comes to the important essence of the matter: "How does original sin become ours?"

Answer: By imputation and heredity. You will observe that he does not say: "God does not require that every person be punished for the sin of Adam."

He does say very plainly, "Original sin is imputed to us; just as if it were our own sin." And it is our own sin because Adam was our representative while in the state of rectitude.

Original sin is said to have two parts; 1st, guilt of sin, 2nd, pollution of sin.

For which of these are we held directly accountable?

The guilt of sin. That is to say: just as soon as Adam received and ate of the fruit and was disobedient, in that very moment, that disobedience (the guilt of that sin) was imputed to the whole human race.

Who knows where that can be proved from God's Word?

Answer: Romans 5:19, "For as by one man's disobedience, many were made sinners, so by the obedience of one shall many be made righteous."

This text clearly demonstrates that the first sin was imputed directly to us because it says, "Many were made sinners".

Were all of Adam's sins imputed to us or just the first one?

Only the first one. Since Adam lived for nine hundred thirty years, he must have committed innumerable sins. God did not impute them to us because they were actual sins committed by Adam himself as fruits of his fall. This is because of the depravity within him; a condition brought about by his fall. Only Adam's first sin was imputed to us, but not his subsequent sins.

Why is it that he only is responsible for his actual sins?

Well, as soon as Adam fell, he forfeited his office as head of the covenant and he no longer represents his descendants.

What is the guilt of sin?

Answer: A subjection to punishment for Adam's sin.

Romans 5:18 clearly testifies of this: "Therefore by the offence of one, judgment came upon all men to condemnation etc."

The fact that babies die is proof that original sin exists.

They have not committed actual sins, for which deeds they would be guilty before God.

Death was threatened only as a punishment for sin.

Why should these little babies die except that the guilt of sin was imputed to them?

Paul explained this to the Romans, also, in Romans 5:14, "Nevertheless death reigned from Adam to Moses, even over them that had not sinned after the similitude of Adam's transgression."

The apostle means to include newly born babies here. Babies who had not committed any actual sins against God, as Adam had done in his day. They had to die, nevertheless, which is positive proof that they have original sin.

They receive the punishment of death for this sin.

We have considered the various aspects of original sin, but, now, what about pollution of sin?

Answer: We inherit the pollution of sin from our parents. Everyone, Christ excepted, has the pollution of sin just as everyone has original sin. Christ had neither original or actual sin.

Job said, "Who can bring a clean thing out of an unclean? Not one." Job 14:4.

The pollution of sin is a corruption which cleaves to us and has extended itself throughout the whole human race.

A person is not only guilty because of the guilt of sin but he is also loathsome in God's sight from birth until death because of the pollution of sin.

That is why this sin is called original sin. We inherit it from our sinful parents and ultimately from Adam. No one, save the Lord Jesus, is excepted. Isn't it plainly evident that we carry the original sin of Adam and do not sin only by imitation as the Remonstrants teach?

Do you think a child who was set aside from birth, allowed to grow up apart from all people so that he would see no evil example, would grow up a perfect person?

Don't you believe it! That child would show evidences of corruption as all others do. Since the fall, sin no longer comes from outside of the man but is situated within and throughout his whole existence. Man and sin have united. Sin has become a part of man.

Sin works from the inside and is manifest on the outside.

Adam and Eve were the only ones into whom sin came from the outside. They were sinless, having been created without the germ of sin. It could be no other way, because "God saw everything that He had made, and, behold, it was very good."

The Holy Spirit inspired the writing of Ezekiel (Ezekiel 16) to show clearly how loathsome a person is to Him because of original sin. In verse 5 we read, "Thou wast cast out in the open field, to the loathing of thy person, in the day that thou wast born."

It doesn't say, "You were laid on the door step of a home." No, because a child would not be there long; it would soon be taken in.

154

But, "Cast out in the open field," where no one passes by.

What is our prospect, then, with original sin?

The Lord had said, "Dying, you shall die", and that is our due reward.

We are loathsome in God's holy sight. By original sin we, in the first place, become spiritually dead at our natural birth. This is a state of separation from God's favor and we lie impotent in sin.

Secondly, by original sin we experience physical death, which separates soul and body.

Thirdly, by original sin we are subject to eternal death, that is, an eternal suffering of punishment in hell, a punishment of pain and also a punishment of want. This will be everlasting.

What are your thoughts about this now? Isn't it a momentous happening when a person is born into this world?

Just as surely as a person is born with a real body, so certainly does he come into the world with guilt and pollution of sin. This makes him condemnable in God's sight.

The Lord had placed us originally upon this earth without sin and according to His holy likeness, but we have taken sin upon ourselves. The devil did not force sin upon us; he merely proposed it to us. Besides, we had the inherent ability to maintain our favorable relationship with God. For this reason God is entirely free. Eternal life would have been the reward for obedience, consequently eternal death was the reward for disobedience.

May you learn to clearly see and accept these serious matters through the convincing and saving work of the Spirit of God. By nature a person will not accept or admit his guilt and pollution. No, never.

155

Be truthful about it now, don't you feel, too, that sin is a delight which you would rather not take leave of?

Have you ever noticed how corrupt and filthy your own nature is?

I hope that which is now your delight may become a heavy burden to you. Only free grace can accomplish this. A work of conscience can cause distress, but it will never cause a true grief for sin. Only the presence of the Holy Spirit in the elect soul will convict it of sin. This includes original sin with its guilt and pollution.

May this same Spirit bless these imperfect instructions to your young lives.

Lesson 15

Actual Sin and The Punishment of Sin.

Last week we were given instructions on Original Sin. The title of this lesson is "Actual Sin and the Punishment of Sin."

What, is the meaning of Actual Sin?

Actual sins are those we unceasingly commit from our birth. James 3:2, in many things "We offend all."

In what way do we commit actual sins?

Answer: In thoughts, words and deeds.

Verify that it is with thoughts.

Answer: Proverbs 6:18 "A heart that deviseth wicked imaginations."

Can you prove that it is with words?

Answer: Matt. 12:36 "But I say unto you, That every idle word that men shall speak, they shall give account thereof in the day of judgment."

Prove that it is with deeds.

Matt 15:19 "For out of the heart proceed evil thoughts, murders, adulteries, fornications, thefts, false witness, blasphemies."

What is the source of these actual sins? Adam was not created with them and yet everyone sins everyday in many ways beginning from the day of their birth.

Actual sins are the fruits or results of original sin.

Symbolically, original sin is the tree and actual sins are the fruit. It is natural, then, for Hellenbroek to ask, "Are all men by nature in a state of misery?" The answer is, "Yes."

Christ was the only person who did not possess original sin and consequently no actual sins. He, being God, willingly assumed human nature and was not born the way other people are conceived and born.

Everyone then is a miserable creature, by virtue of the fact that we have original sin and are polluted with it, being totally unable to do anything but sin, even until death. Don't you agree?

And wherein lies the greatest misery of all for a person?

Rev. Ledeboer points out in his catechism book that the greatest misery lies in the fact that one is not aware of his misery.

He is correct in this observation; don't you think so, too?

Our complete insensitivity to our miserable state proves that we are spiritually dead and impotent under our sins. That is why our lesson says, "Man's misery consists in three things: in sin, in impotence under it and in punishment."

Under the influence of original sin and actual sin, he is incapable of any spiritual good.

In everyday living, if a man falls down from a height and breaks an arm or leg, that man is painfully conscious of his fall.

His broken limb is painful. Why does he feel pain? Because he is physically alive. If he had been killed in the fall, even if he had broken both arms and both legs, he would not have been aware of it.

Feeling can be present only when there is life.

By nature we are all born spiritually dead, so as a result we do not have the least feeling or burden of our miserable state or loathsomeness before God.

That is why the impotence and unawareness of our misery is the misery in our misery.

Actual sins can be classified in two types:

1st — Sins of omission and

2nd — Sins of commission.

If your father or mother would say to you this evening, "John or Marie, please do this" and you do not do it, but walk away instead, it would be a sin of omission. Contrariwise, if it were said, "Remember what I told you. You may not do that" but you proceed to do it anyway, it would be a sin of commission.

This is the way it is between God and man too.

Last week we spoke briefly about original sin, the cause of all sins, but now the results of original sin follow exactly the same pattern. God had commanded Adam to do something and He also forbade him to do something.

He did not obey the commands and he did that which he was forbidden to do. Adam's first sin, then, was a sin of omission and a sin of commission. That is the way it always is in actual sins. What a person should do he does not do, and what he should not do, that he does.

If you think carefully about it, man being spiritually dead, without any consciousness of his situation, is the same as a corpse having no sensation when placed in fire or water. A person might say, "Are then not all God's commandments, threatenings and promises in vain so that it will not help any even if a person is warned?"

158

The answer presented to us this afternoon says, "No; for these are means whereby God will operate upon man as a rational creature to the discharge of his duty."

The Lord is slow to anger, continually "nourishing the tree" and, from His side, pointing out man's obligation so that there can be no excuse.

So then, since man has original and actual sins, the very least of them deserving death, are there none that can be forgiven?

None can be forgiven in itself. In Christ they can be except those against the Holy Ghost as is plain from James 2:10 "For whosoever shall keep the whole law, and yet offend in one point, he is guilty of all."

All sins, no matter how terrible they are, can be forgiven in Christ, with the exception of the sin against the Holy Ghost.

Why cannot this sin be forgiven?

This is a very serious matter, so give your close attention.

The Lord Jesus, when He was still upon earth, told His disciples that sorrow would fill their heart because He would be leaving them. If He did not leave them, the Holy Ghost would not come to them, but if He did leave them He would send Him to them. He said, "And when He is come, He will reprove the world of sin and of righteousness and of judgment."

The work of the Holy Ghost is, then, to convict and convince sinners of their sins. In general or in a universal sense, all men, elect as well as reprobate, have sinned against a Triune God. This is so because, while God is one God, He is also a Triune Being.

A person can sin against each individual Divine Person as well as against the Divine Being.

If a man sin against God the Father, the Holy Spirit

convinces the sinner of it and his sin can be forgiven in Christ.

So also if one sins against the Son, the Holy Spirit convinces of that sin and it will be forgiven in Christ. But, what if one sins against the Holy Spirit?

The Father does not convince of sin nor does the Son. It is not in the order of their operation to do so. Since it is sin against the Holy Ghost, He does not convict either.

The person who sins against the Holy Ghost will not be convicted or convinced of even one sin and, — since conversion or true saving work cannot take place without true conviction, that person will never be saved. That is why the sin against the Holy Ghost is unpardonable.

Would not that person, in whom that sin has taken place, feel badly or have sorrow about it?

No, we have regret about our sins only when we have been convinced or convicted of them. If I have not been convicted of something, I have no burden or distress about it either.

That is why there is no regret or unrest felt by the person who has done the unpardonable sin.

Their heart is hardened and they continue without any true conviction until they die.

They have quenched the Holy Spirit and He will never convict them for their conversion. Further, if their conscience is stricken prior to death it will be most terrible for them and they will die in complete despair. It is most dreadful when it becomes evident.

Some people are often seized upon with the thought that they have committed the unpardonable sin and as a consequence they fear they will not ever be converted.

But, though they are fearful of it, they surely have not committed it because their conscience speaks and they are very much concerned.

To despise warnings, to grieve the Holy Spirit, to go contrary to admonitions, to engage in sin and the activities of the world are all certainly grievous sins. It will not go well for a person to continue in such a way against proper teaching and even his own better judgment. But even so, they are sins which can be forgiven. The sin against the Holy Ghost has not been committed.

On the other hand, you should not think that it is not so bad to sin just because those sins can be forgiven.

A sin in itself is not forgivable. O, no. If you want to see how dreadful sin is, just think of the first sin ever committed. That was the revolt of the angels against God. That sin transformed angels in heaven to devils in hell. Since there was no mediator for them, their sin cannot be forgiven.

The sin of Adam estranged the whole human race from God, making them heirs of wretchedness, unless reconciliation is accomplished for them in Christ.

Do you see now, why not one sin, in itself, is forgivable?

The Psalmist says, "But there is forgiveness with Thee, that Thou mayest be feared."

Can anyone give an example from God's Word that proves that the sin against the Holy Ghost is unforgivable?

Can anyone relate just one instance?

When you come home this evening, read Acts 5.

You will read there that Peter said to Ananias, "Why hath Satan filled thine heart to lie to the Holy Ghost. Why hast thou conceived this thing in thine heart? Thou hast not lied unto men but unto God."

It is obvious in this case that they held back the money not alone because of stinginess, but, with premeditated design to test whether it was really true that the Spirit would know this. They doubted the deity of the Holy Ghost. This is evident in the words of Peter spoken to

Sapphira, "How is it that ye have agreed together to tempt the Spirit of the Lord?"

This was an intentional tempting of God on the part of Ananias and Sapphira to determine whether the Holy Ghost was truly the All-knowing God.

The answer that was given by the wife reveals clearly that they had not the least sorrow or remorse about their sin.

When Peter questioned her she said, without emotion, "Yea, for so much."

The sin against the Holy Ghost takes place with an intentional design without ever having remorse for it.

It should be understood that this sin can only be committed by reprobates. By the grace of God, the elect are preserved from this sin, even though they may live terrible lives committing all other kind of sins.

You need not infer from this that all reprobates commit the unpardonable sin. Absolutely not. There are thousands of people who, though they have never committed the sin against the Holy Spirit, die unconverted, and are lost.

Hellenbroek asks in the 15th question, "Is the Covenant of Works abolished by sin?"

Answer: Yes, respecting its power to justify.

What does he mean by this statement?

As long as man remained bound to the Covenant of Works, that is, remained obedient, this covenant possessed the power to justify him. He would receive eternal life upon doing all its requirements.

Now that man has broken this, however, he will never obtain eternal life by his own keeping of the Covenant of Works. In respect to its ability to save or justify someone, it is powerless.

But in what way was it *not* abolished?

In the claim that it has upon man. The Lord can righteously require perfect obedience of us which we ourselves had covenanted to give Him in the Covenant of Works. Sin did not cancel this claim upon us.

I shall endeavor to make this understood by means of an example. There is a rich man who asks a poor man whether he would like to work in his garden and whether he had the ability to do it. "Yes," answered the poor man, "I am healthy and have strong arms, but I have not any tools."

"That matters not," said the rich man, "I have all the tools you will need."

He gave the tools to him and instructed him what to do. The poor man accepted all the conditions set forth by the rich man and went to work.

The rich man could reasonably require that the work be done well. The poor man had the strength and tools and was delighted in the agreement they had made. It went quite well for a few days, but it happened that the worker became intoxicated. Because of that condition, he was unable to do his work.

Does the rich man, because of this drunkenness, have any right to demand that his garden be worked on? This is the purpose, you will remember, for which he had employed this man, and to which the worker had consented. I think he has this right. The worker made himself unfit to carry out his gardening obligations by his sinful behavior. It would be only right if he would not be paid, but, does his obligation to his employer cease? Absolutely not!

In this way, too, the Covenant of Works is annulled as to its ability to justify anyone, but is not done away with in holding us responsible for its requirements.

The inference reached at the end of this lesson is: Outside of Satan, there is not a more tragic creature than natural man.

Boys and girls, if God would arrest you and you then became aware of the sins within your heart, you would have to agree with this answer wholeheartedly.

O, then you would not be able to go through this life as easy and careless as you do now.

Consider for a moment the blessings you still have. God gives you, from moment to moment, physical well-being, food, shelter and all the necessities of life.

Do you have any right to these things? No, and yet God does not cease in His benefits towards you. What has been your response to Him regarding this matter?

Imagine for a moment a certain gentleman lives in this village who has many laborers. Everyday he sends directives to have all sorts of good things brought to the families of these men and does good deeds for them all the time. For this he receives, as thanks, nothing but mockery, scorn and contempt. Wouldn't the benefits of this man soon stop? I think he would, within a very short time, cease from his well doing, discharge them from their employment and say, "Those ungrateful creatures! I have done only good to them and they do nothing but evil in return."

But what is the situation between God and man?

There is no example to describe that!

Sin has earned a three-fold death. If you would try to find an example of this exactly as it is, you would exclaim, "O, sin, sin, sin; sin is so abominable!"

May the Lord cause you to sense what damage and shame it has caused.

Generally, we fear to do great sins, only because shame will be brought upon us. But God's people experience that sin, when committed, brings the greatest shame upon God and for that reason, a shame upon men for committing them. Solomon says, "Sin is a reproach to any people" Proverbs 14:34. We say in addition; Sin is a murderer of God. Maybe you would ask, "Can God be murdered?"

No, but the first sin was an attack upon God. Man wanted to be as God, so it amounts to this: I want God

164

dethroned and myself raised upon it; not that it is possible, but it is what we would like.

That is why it has been said that sin is "God destroying." Since sin is disgraceful to God and hurtful to ourselves, I do hope you will hate sin in even the slightest thoughts.

Then the truth of the catechism lesson, "There is not a more tragic creature than natural man, Satan excepted" will be more than a memorization experience and you will be able to say it from the bottom of your heart.

May God bless this truth through the application of the Holy Spirit for Jesus' sake.

So be it.

Lesson 16

Of The Covenant Of Grace

Our lesson this afternoon deals with the subject: The Covenant of Grace.

Our previous lesson taught us that the covenant of works had been broken in respect to its power to bring righteousness to anyone. Eternal life can no longer be received through that first covenant.

You are aware that God the Lord had communion with man in the state of righteousness. But when the first covenant was broken, that communion was also broken; no longer can there be communion with a holy God. Man will meet God but it will be in judgement. Man will meet God where man is sinner and God is judge but there will be no communion with Him. An everlasting cleavage has come between. Is man, then, forever separated from God because of the breaking of the covenant of works?

No. The first question in our lesson runs as follows: Has there been another covenant put into effect in place of the covenant of works?

Answer: Yes; the covenant of grace.

With the question: When was that covenant established?, Hellenbroek answers: Immediately after the fall. He means by this that it was *revealed* immediately after the fall. God's Word is unmistakable about this fact; that it was established in eternity but revealed to man immediately after the fall. The text in Genesis 3:15 is clear, "And I will put enmity between thee and the woman and between thy seed and her seed; It shall bruise thy head and thou shalt bruise His heel."

We have explained in previous lessons where and when the covenant of works had its place, but now what about the covenant of grace?

Answer: The covenant of grace is the way by which God through Christ becomes the property of the sinner and by which the sinner in turn becomes the property of God. Jeremiah 31:33.

We discern three parts to this answer:

1st. The sinner. 2nd., God. 3rd., Christ. Since the fall, God and man, as sinner, cannot have communion with one another. But there is a third party revealed in this covenant of grace whereby they can be reconciled.

Who is this third party? He is the second person in the Divine Essence, who, out of unrestrained love desired to be the mediator of the covenant of grace.

This covenant between the Divine Persons was prepared and securely established in eternity to be the way in which God would become, through Christ (the mediator of the covenant) the possession of the sinner and vice versa, the sinner (through Christ) the possession of God.

The Lord speaks plainly in John 14:6 "I am the way, the

truth, and the life: no man cometh unto the Father but by me." What is meant here is, God cannot have communion with sinners in the covenant of grace with no one less than Christ, the mediator, and through Him alone as intercessor.

Jesus is the Way for the elect in the election, the Way in the calling, the Way in regeneration, the Way in justification, the Way in sanctification and also the Way to and in glorification.

He was the Way, is the Way, and remains the Way, the Truth and the Life for His people in time and eternity.

The covenant of grace was put into effect for the elect *only.*

External callings have a part in the temporal covenant privileges bestowed universally, but not in the essential things; not in the reconciliation with God and eternal life.

Our catechism now asks: What does God require in this covenant?

Answer: That which God requires in it is also a promise of the covenant, namely, faith in Jesus Christ. What else does He promise?

Grace here in this life and eternal life hereafter. Acts 16:31., "Believe on the Lord Jesus Christ and thou shalt be saved, and thy house."

The Pharisees and the Scribes were in bitter opposition to this covenant of grace. They sought their salvation in the works of the law, not by faith in Christ.

Paul wrote to the Romans: "Israel, which followed after the law of righteousness, hath not attained to the law of righteousness.

Wherefore? Because they sought it not by faith, but as it were by the works of the law. For they stumbled at that stumblingstone."

Paul meant to say this: You gentiles, thru faith, have been reconciled with God in Christ and have part in the benefits of the covenant of grace. But the Jews, being enemies of Christ, are determined not to believe in Him. For that reason they benefit in the temporal convenant privileges pertaining to this life, but not in the actual covenant itself. That is why he said, "What advantage then hath the Jew? or what profit is there of circumcision? Much everyway: chiefly, because that unto them were committed the oracles of God."

Paul would say, the outward privileges that the Jews had, by virtue of the covenant God had made with Abraham, were very great. But on the other hand, it is plain to see, the Jews were by no means all established in the covenant as respecting salvation, because what does he say in Romans 9?" They are not all Israel which are of Israel: Neither, because they are the seed of Abraham, are they all children."

And in Romans 11:7 he says, "What then? Israel hath not obtained that which he seeketh for; but the election hath obtained it, and the rest were blinded."

Do you understand now, that the covenant of grace was in fact, established with the elect only? This had occured in eternity, but God made it known to them in time. He calls them with an internal saving call and makes room in their hearts for His work. Would the Lord have had provisions or conditions in the covenant of grace? Yes, he had; and who knows what these conditions were?

Sit quietly and listen attentively, then I shall try to make it clear to you.

God the Father, God the Son and God the Holy Ghost acted upon the plan and intentions that God had eternally, which were: First, to transcend His honor to the highest degree and secondly, to bring to salvation a multitude of the elect.

But now how would God receive His honor and man

come to salvation, considering man had become so shamefully disobedient after God had created him in His image? Wouldn't you say that is impossible? His justice must be satisfied and man had put shame upon it. His virtues are to be glorified, but instead, insults were brought upon them.

By virtue of His Divine nature a holy God·has nothing to do with sin. What was needed, then, in this situation?

A mediator was needed who could satisfy the Divine requirements. So, a council was held in eternity by the Divine Persons arranging for the Surety, for the elect.

The Father was the motivating cause in these negotiations. The Son established Himself as mediator and the Holy Ghost took upon Himself to execute the whole matter.

Did the Father require certain conditions to be met in these negotiations?

Yes, He required complete fulfillment of His pure virtues.

And as the second Person took upon Himself to fulfill these requirements, the Father promised Him, as recompence, the elect as His inheritance.

Who can confirm this from God's Word?

Answer: Psalm 2:8 "Ask of me, and I shall give thee the heathen for thine inheritance, and the uttermost parts of the earth for thy possession."

The covenant of grace in itself, then, does not merit anything. It is impossible. God in the covenant promised Christ the elect, and He promised the elect Christ, grace, and eternal life. He will surely give this to all of His own. Would He say this and not fulfill His promise? Would He speak and not confirm it?

The Covenant of Grace has been essentially the same throughout all ages. All believers under the Old Testament dispensation as well as those under the New Testament have part in the benefits of the covenant of grace. "Jesus Christ, the same yesterday, and today, and forever." Hebrews 13:8.

So, it is very definite on God's side that He views the children of the covenant solely in the Mediator of the Covenant. When that appointed time approaches, when God of His own accord, embraces a sinner in that covenant, the Holy Spirit begins the saving work of conviction. Hellenbroek states in the answer to question 9: "God first comes to him (in the internal calling) when He kindly and beseechingly invites him."

Having been wrought upon by the Holy Spirit in this way, the elect sinner cannot but be completely subdued and made willingly submissive. "I drew them with cords of a man, with bands of love."

The sinner then has no choice but by grace to submit to the Lord, taking Him as his possession.

No matter how unwilling and hostile he may be, the Holy Spirit instills a new nature within him so that he now willingly and by faith consents to all God does.

I hope that each one of you may experience, personally, the essence of this lesson on the covenant of Grace.

The explanation of the questions and answers being quite lengthy, the time has, consequently, passed by quickly.

If the Lord will spare us, we shall see one another again in two weeks, because next week is Pentacost.

When it is Christmas time, what is then the common saying? Jesus came upon earth, so it is said, "God with us." When it is Easter we say, "God for us", and at Pentacost, "God in us". Three thousand souls were converted under one sermon at that time. Boys and girls, how many sermons have you heard in your lifetime? How often have the Christmas, Easter and Pentacost seasons come and gone in your life? You have celebrated those days, probably, 14, 15 or 16 times and, —still without conversion.

Imagine for a moment that you were present at Jerusalem with those devout Jews on Pentacost day, when the Holy Ghost descended and you witnessed the salvation of three thousand persons congregated there.

What profit would this conversion of others be for you, if you were not included? Absolutely nothing.

That is why it is so necessary that the Holy Spirit be the victor in your life. If you never experience this during your lifetime, you will come to discover at death that the Lord has wrought out salvation but you have lost it eternally.

Maybe you have been told the account of emperor Julian in the history of the early christians. Julian's father had been shamefully murdered by his uncle. Now that he was an-orphan, the murderer of his father endeavored to rear him sanctimoniously in the christian religion. It was only natural that Julian hated his "christian" uncle, because he knew very well that his uncle had murdered his father and taken over the reign.

When Julian became older, he began to inquire into pagan religions and studied night and day in books written by Greek philosophers.

Since he did not know the true God, not having been born again through the power of the Spirit of God, he never became acquainted with the principle of genuine faith.

He formed opinions on the christian doctrines influenced solely by the false religion of his uncle.

When he became a man he emerged as a valiant general and, after many triumphs in battles, was summoned by the Roman Legions to be Kaizer in the year 361.

He reigned over this great empire for two years, oppressing the christians as much as possible and restored heathendom to its former place of honor. His hatred of

Christ was so intense, that he always used the words of Christ in a sacriligious way.

For instance, when christians came to the court of justice to complain that something had been stolen from them, he answered them mockingly, "Why do you complain about this? Didn't your master teach you that when men take away your coat to let them have your cloak also?"

He called all christians "fisherman disciples" because they were followers of the apostles, most of whom were fishermen by trade.

After he had reigned in that way for two years war erupted again with the Persians. At first, it appeared he was being victorious, but he finally was seriously wounded with a spear.

Some historians relate that he removed the spear from his wound himself, caught some of the flowing blood in his hand, threw it into the air, calling out, "That despised Nazerine is victorious after all!"

In his last moments he talked with some heathen philosophers about the exalted nature of the soul.

He comforted the generals and friends standing weeping about him by saying he would return his life to the creator from Whom he had received it. He then asked for a drink of water and — died.

That was the end of Julian the apostate. In spite of his apostasy to heathendom and his hardness of heart, he was compelled to confess that Jesus Christ had been the victor.

Boys and girls, I hope you may acknowledge, during your lifetime, not only in conscience but with your whole heart thru the new life within you, instilled there by the Holy Spirit, that the Lord has been the victor over you.

May the Lord grant this to you out of free grace for His Name Sake.

Lesson 17

The Mediator of The Covenant

This lesson has much in common with the lesson on the covenant of grace. You can understand that when Hellenbroek speaks about the Mediator of the covenant, he is not referring to the covenant of works. The covenant of works needed no mediator.

What covenant is then referred to here?

Answer: The covenant of grace.

In our lesson on the covenant of grace, a few weeks ago, we directed your attention to the fact that when man sinned, he withdrew himself away from God.

Fellowship could no longer exist between them. The two must be eternally separated. However, it was resolved from eternity in the Divine Triune Essence that the Second Person should be the Mediator between God and man, establishing the covenant of grace. The covenant of grace was now the way by which God through Christ would become the sinner's possession and he God's possession.

The first question this afternoon is: Who is the Mediator of this covenant?

Answer: The Lord Jesus Christ. 1 Timothy 2:5. "For there is one God, and one Mediator between God and men, the man Christ Jesus."

Is He a Mediator of intercession only, or of reconciliation also?

Answer: Also of reconciliation; for thus it follows in the same text, "Who gave himself a ransom for all" 1 - Timothy 2:6.

What does Hellenbroek mean with this question when he

173

says: a mediator of intercession only?

Does anyone know?

We read in God's Word about Moses, the man of God, who stood between God and the children of Israel. Had Moses been a mediator for Israel there or not?

Certainly he was. He was, however, a mediator only of intercession because he prayed continually to God for the people.

He was not a mediator of reconciliation. That would be impossible because Moses was of like passions, with all the sin laden Israelites. He could not make satisfaction for himself or anyone else, therefore he could bring about no reconciliation.

Jesus Christ the Son of God, Who willingly took upon Himself our human nature is the only Mediator of intercession and of reconciliation.

He made perfect satisfaction to his Father for His people in all that was required; satisfaction to holy justice.

Without satisfaction, reconciliation was impossible, but now reconciliation flows out of satisfaction.

It is not a superfluous question then, to differentiate between a mediator of intercession only, or a mediator of intercession *and* reconciliation.

How can we prove that our Lord Jesus Christ is the true Mediator or Messiah?

This question is given special emphasis because Jews deny this.

When Jesus was on earth in His human nature they would not believe that He was the Messiah who was to come and they still do not believe it.

That is why our lesson states: He is the true Mediator because all is fulfilled in Him that was prophesied of the

Messiah. He came at the proper time; that is to say:

1. Before the sceptre was departed from Judah, in accordance to Gen. 49:10 "The sceptre shall not depart from Judah, nor a lawgiver from between his feet, until Shiloh come; and unto him shall the gathering of the people be."

2. While the second temple was yet standing. Haggai 2:7: "And the desire of all nations shall come (for Christ, that is); and I will fill this house with glory."

This is not the temple which Solomon had built, which is referred to as the first temple, but the temple which was built in the time of Nehemiah.

This temple, in which Christ was present and out of which He cast all them that sold and bought merchandise, was burned down shortly after His stay on earth and there never has been a temple like it since in Jerusalem. This is a clear testimony that this prophecy was fulfilled in Christ Jesus.

3. When the seventy weeks were expired in accordance to Daniel 9:24.

Maybe you are saying to yourself: the time between Daniel and Christ was surely more than 70 weeks!

That is so, but, years instead of weeks is to be understood here. Each "week" counts for 7 years instead of 7 days; so 70 x 7 years is 490 years.

The fulfillment of this was seen in Christ's coming at the exact time it was prophesied, and so everything was fulfilled in Him at the exact time and place according to prophecy.

We could present even more Old Testament prophecies which have been fulfilled in the New Testament in Christ, for example: That He was to be born in Bethlehem according to Micah 5:2, "But thou, Bethlehem Ephratah, though thou be little among the thousands of Judah, yet out of thee shall He come forth unto me that is to be ruler in Israel."

And who can tell me where it was prophesied in the Old Testament that the Lord Jesus had to flee from Herod into Egypt? It states in Matt. 2:13 "When he arose, he took the young child and his mother by night and departed into Egypt: and was there until the death of Herod: that it might be fulfilled which was spoken of the Lord by the prophet, saying, 'Out of Egypt have I called my Son.' " Hosea 11:1.

Do you see that even that hasty departure was prophesied in the Old Testament? We could use our complete hour with various prophecies and their respective fulfillments, but we shall let these suffice.

Even though it is so clearly evident from these instances that He is the true Messiah that had been promised, the Jews have not submitted to Him, *nor believe* in Him. They have bumped themselves against the stone of "stumbling".

And — this too was prophesied in Isaiah 8:14. "He shall be for a sanctuary; but for a rock of offense to both the houses of Israel." (Romans 9:33)

They disowned Him as God, in His mediatorialship, and as a result they disowned Him in His names, in His offices, in His natures, in His states and in His benefits.

They will not acknowledge the covenant of Grace, even though they claim to be children of Abraham. Also, they did not believe that Christ had no original sin but

176

considered Him to be born in the same manner as every one else, because they said in hatred, "Art thou greater than our father Abraham, which is dead? and the prophets are dead; whom makest thou thyself?" These poor people had not the least realization that this Jesus was the Divine Lamb that must be slain for the sins of the elect. That in Him alone, since He was the mediator of the covenant, the two diverse parties could be reconciled again. In Him God could have communion with His creatures again; His sinful creatures who had fallen so deeply.

Listen now to what I have to say. Can God have communion with sin?

No, never, that is eternally impossible, but He can have communion with the sinner through the Mediator, because He views them completely covered in their Surety who accomplished that which they were not able to do.

In order to do that He must have no original sin and, of course, no actual sins. In order for this to be possible He had to be God and man simultaneously.

What does Paul say about this in the letter to the Hebrews? "For such an high priest became us, who is holy, harmless, undefiled, separate from sinners, etc. Heb. 7:26.

Who can prove to me from God's Word that Jesus had no original sin? Come now, sharpen your minds, what did we say about this at Christmas time?

Answer: "Therefore also that holy thing which shall be born of thee shall be called the Son of God."

Correct!, you have a good memory. Now, who knows where it is shown that he had no actual sins?

Answer: In John 8:46, "Which of you convinceth me of sin? and if I say the truth, why do ye not believe me?"

177

Do you understand that now? There you have two proofs that the Mediator was born without sin and that He lived without committing sin. Now I shall question you about three things:

1st. Did Jesus, the Mediator, come for the whole world?

2nd. Did He come for the church universal?

3rd. Did He come for each elect individual?

You are still quite young for this, but please give me your attention. Which one of the three is correct? Is only one correct? Two? Or would all three be truths?

All three are truths but they must be correctly understood.

The 1st: In a certain sense, Christ came for the whole world. Not in a saving way but only in respect to His merits in a general sense. If Christ had not come on this world it could not have remained standing. Divine justice would never permit a sinner to exist except the Mediator had shed His blood upon this earth for the elect's sake.

Understand clearly what I am saying now, I do not mean that He shed His blood for all people in the way of salvation. No, that happened soley for His Church. But, the whole world shares in the benefits of it having their food and livelyhood as long as the elect are upon the earth. The only reason the world continues is to bring in all the elect. When that is accomplished the end shall come.

Secondly, Christ came into the world for the whole church universally. John 3:16 states: "For God so loved the world, that he gave His only begotten Son, etc."

Which "world" is intended here? The world of the elect is meant here. God gave His Son out of love for that whole multitude. But,

Thirdly, The Mediator came for each elect individual. It becomes a personal matter for each of them; not one of general concern. What comfort can there be for a person who believes with all his heart that the whole Church will be saved, but he personally lacks the assurance that Christ has shed His blood for him?

None at all. That is very clear. That is why we are able to say that the works of God are twofold: First, works done in eternity; they are:

Decree, predestination and covenant of grace. These works are revealed in God's time outwardly and are seen.

Second: works done in time. These are works of creation in nature, and re-creation (regeneration) in grace when He brings a person to conversion.

When the Lord converts a sinner to Himself it will be a work that is clearly evident. Don't you believe so too?

The Holy Spirit makes such a person susceptable for the grace that Christ has acquired for His people. They are not aware of the covenant of grace nor of the Mediator of the covenant for themselves. God's Spirit teaches them to believe they are separated from God with an eternal separation.

But if it is a saving and continuing conviction, they will become aware that God the Father is the eternal motivating force in the election of the Mediator. The Lord Jesus said again and again, "That the world may believe that thou hast sent me."

They learn to believe on the basis of God's Word that the Mediator:

1st. Is revealed in the eternal council of peace. "See, I come, O God."

2nd. Is revealed in the promise immediately after the fall. "It shall bruise thy head."

3rd. Is fore-told by the Patriarchs and the Prophets throughout the Old Testament.

4th. Is finally revealed in the fulness of time in the crib of Bethlehem. But, what does such a person feel to be so necessary? That this Mediator of the covenant be revealed in his own soul.

So, we have had a brief look at who this Mediator of the covenant is and when He came. Now I would pose one question more for your consideration to be answered at our next session, if we may be spared until next week. The question is:

Why is Jesus the Mediator?

Now you have something to think about this week. If you cannot arrive at the answer by yourself you can feel free to ask your father or mother about it.

There is definitely an answer for this question, because, for every "wherefore" there is a "therefore".

We are speaking only briefly about these important matters, which I am trying to impress upon your minds. I hope, boys and girls, that each of you personally finds a need in your heart for this Mediator.

If in everyday life, a rich man would pay a huge debt for a poor man, that poor man would be made very happy, wouldn't he? I would think so. But if he is an honest and upright person, for what would he have the highest regard; the profit he has gotten from the rich man, the kindness he has been shown, or for the actual person who had paid the debt for him and relieved him of great care?

Properly, he would regard the person most highly, wouldn't you think so too?

The Holy Spirit instills love for the person of the Mediator in God's people and they worship Him for Himself.

In our natural state we have no desire within our hearts for a Mediator. What need have we of one?

If a person is blind, dumb or deaf, he still has need for food, sleep and clothing. And for what reason?

Because he has life even though he is handicapped.

But does a dead person need the necessities of life?

No, because he is not only blind, dumb or deaf but entirely without life. We do not say that a person who has died is deaf or dumb. No, we simply say he is dead.

It is the same with a person spiritually too. Each one of you are sitting here present before me; you have not yet passed on to eternal death, for then hell would be the place of your abode. You are not intellectually dead either, because you have sound minds; you are not beasts but persons. Neither are you physically dead because your body lives. It functions and develops.

But what is actually the case?

You are spiritually dead. It is not just a spiritual deficiency, for then you might be able to remedy the situation. No, completely dead, hostile and powerless. Without realization of your great wretchedness, walking over the earth, as if bound with chains, you are a captive of sin, the devil, and your own evil heart. You are living in spiritual death, and unless the Lord prevent, you will pass away in spiritual death. Spiritual death can not be annulled once physical death has taken place.

Isn't that a wretched state to be in?

Don't flatter yourself with the thought, that it perhaps

will not be quite so bad and that nothing more will transpire after this life.

According to God's Word a person has an eternal existance. As soon as a baby is born into the world, it is born for eternity. When we die, our bodies are placed in a grave where it decomposes, but in the Judgement Day every soul will receive a body again; one that is incorruptable which will never decompose or be consumed.

May you learn to have a need for the Mediator of the covenant for your surety before you must appear before the Judge.

If He once becomes a necessity to you, He will also become indispensable, and, God can bestow, through faith, that He become precious to you. May He grant that to you out of free grace.

So let it be.

Lesson 18·

Of His Names (Jesus and Christ).

The first question in our lesson today is: Wherein must the Mediator be known? The answer is: 1. In His names, 2. In His offices, 3. In His natures, 4. In His states, 5. In His benefits.

This afternoon we shall begin by considering the first one; His names.

The two most common names are Jesus and Christ. The first, Jesus, is a Hebrew name. The second, Christ, is a Greek name.

By whom was the name of "Jesus" first mentioned?

That name was mentioned before He was born as man upon earth. The angel said to Joseph, "Thou shalt call His name Jesus; for He shall save His people from their sins." What is the meaning of this name then? Jesus means "Savior".

You might say, why did the angel mention only the name "Jesus".

The Son of God has so many names, He could equally as well have mentioned another name.

Who can recall some of the names in the Bible which have reference to the Lord Jesus?

Answer: Son of David, Immanuel, Messiah, Redeemer, Savior, Alpha and Omega, Christ, The Lion out of the tribe of Judah.

That is good, all of these names and many more were given to the Mediator. Why would the angel, then, have only mentioned Jesus and Savior? Could not he have mentioned another name?

Yes, but these names were employed because He came into the world to save His people from their sins. For what is it to save?

Answer: To deliver a person from the greatest evil and make him a partaker of the supreme good.

Do you understand that now? That is the reason he named Him "Jesus".

That is the purpose for which He came upon this earth; to deliver His people from the greatest evil, which is sin, and to make them partakers of the supreme good, which is God's favor.

Whereby doth He affect that?

By acquiring and actually applying salvation.

183

How did He merit salvation? He merited this with His perfect obedience to all that the Father required of Him. It is in this way that He became the basis of eternal salvation unto all who are obedient to Him.

But, even though He has merited that for them, is that sufficient? Do they have comfort in that alone?

No, His meritorious work, without anything more, would give them no comfort. He does more. He actually applies His merits to them. Hellenbroek gives as proof for this, John 10:28, "And I give unto them eternal life; and they shall never perish, neither shall any man pluck them out of my hand."

Now we might think, "If Jesus has merited salvation for someone, that is certainly sufficient; can the "meriting" and the "applying" be separated from each other?

The answer is, "No; He surely and only applies salvation to those for whom He has merited it."

Application of salvation has no dependency at all upon ourselves; that is to say: we cannot take the merits of Christ out of ourselves whenever we want to. No, the application depends upon the effectual operation of Divine grace.

We mentioned last week that we are all born spiritually dead and, comprehended in this fact of course, is that we are all born sinners. That is certainly evident enough isn't it? Bear this in mind for a moment while I ask you a question.

The name of Jesus signifies: Savior, and salvation is necessary for sinners only. Anyone who is not a sinner has no need for a Savior. Now all of you agreed a moment ago that all persons are born sinners. Does this mean that all persons are saved by Jesus?

I see several shaking their heads and others calling aloud: "no, dominie". You evidently do not believe this, do you. Now you must, then, explain to me how this is to be understood.

You say all men are sinners and Jesus means "Savior", who has come to save sinners by meriting and applying salvation, and yet all sinners are not saved. How can that be?

Listen; I shall give you an example: If tomorrow morning, I went throughout the village and asked at each home if sinners lived there, I am sure that, by far, most would answer "yes". Don't you think so too? But if I at the same time asked these people, "Has Jesus atoned for your sins and saved you?", perhaps there would be very few, who would venture to say; yes.

Wherein lies the difference? Well, it is very apparent that there are two kinds of sinners in the world. The first kind are those who are born sinners but who have not the least regard or grief concerning it. These are dead sinners. The second kind are living sinners who truly believe in their hearts that they are sinners and find it to be a grievous burden. The Spirit of God exposes the deadness by giving life to such a soul; exposes darkness by giving light; and enmity by giving love. This soul is then discovered to the person and to God.

That is when he, as a dead sinner, discovers his need for a Savior.

I am confident, should God convert you, you too would call out, "I never knew, standing before a Holy God, how dead a sinner I am."

You can be confident, when this happens, there will be a definite breaking away from sin and the world.

Through the same discovering work of the Holy Spirit, wherein they find themselves to be dead sinners, they also find they cannot out of themselves appropriate unto themselves the merits of Christ, and that the application of those merits depends entirely upon the Holy Spirits efficacious influence and Divine grace.

Beside the Mediator being called Jesus, there is often added "Christ", which means messiah in the Hebrew language. John 1:41, "We have found the Messias, which is being interpreted, the Christ." That is to say, "Anointed".

Now we shall test you to see if you have learned your questions well this afternoon.

Of how many parts doth this anointing consist?

Answer: of two parts; His appointment, and His being qualified to His mediatorial office.

The name Christ signifies "Anointed".

Who hath appointed and qualified Him?

Answer: God the Father.

Wherewith is Christ anointed or qualified?

Answer: With the Holy Ghost.

Unto what offices was He anointed?

Answer: Three, prophet, priest and king.

There now, who can recite this in its entirety?

God the father did the anointing, God the Son is the anointed one and God the Holy Spirit is the unction (or anointment)! Christ was not anointed to be God's Son. No, because He was His Son; one in essence with the Father and the Holy Spirit. He was anointed to be the Mediator. In Proverbs 8:23 He says, "I was set up from everlasting, from the beginning, or ever the earth was."

Hellenbroek explains now: His anointing consists of two parts.

1st. His ordination and 2nd. His qualification to His mediatorial office.

These are two different matters. These are dogmas of eternal truths and are as a foundation for our faith. For that reason we shall speak briefly about each of them.

There is quite a difference between ordaining and qualifying.

God the Father *ordained* His Son in eternity, that is: He appointed or consecrated Him to be Mediator according to both His divine and human natures.

But He was *qualified* in the fulness of time when He was born upon earth as a person.

Only in His human nature is He made qualified. In the divine nature no qualification could take place. As God He is perfect and incapable of being made qualified.

Why is His ordination or consecration to the mediatorship, according to both His Divine and human natures, called an anointing?

Answer: Because under the Old Testament men were ordained and installed to certain offices by being "anointed" to them.

And His being made qualified, in respect to His human nature, is also called an "anointing" because God by His anointing infused the qualifications necessary for those offices.

David is a good example of this. David was but an ordinary boy. The men of his day did not accord him special honor as he was but the youngest of eight sons. This was evident enough, for they did not send for him to come home when Samuel came but quietly left him in the pasture with the sheep. He amused himself there with his harp and the songs he composed. For this reason it was very remote that he would be envisioned as a future king!

Never-the-less, he was chosen of God from all eternity to that office. How was this to be brought about? If it depended upon his father and brothers he would never be anything more than a shepherd.

But — nothing will take place without the supreme command of the Lord. Nor is anything more certain to transpire than the word of His command.

Samuel had to go to Jesse the Bethlehemite with his horn filled with oil. The oldest sons, who also seemed best suited to Samuel were passed by. He saw what appeared to the eye; handsomeness, tall stature, courageousness. But, the Lord looks upon the heart!

Young David had to be brought in and the Lord said to Samuel: "Arise, anoint him, for this is he".

Then Samuel took the horn of oil, and anointed him in the midst of his brethren.

Do you know what else is written there? You must pay attention now; just read the history of this in Samuel 16 this evening.

The young shepherd received, simultaneously, upon his anointing, qualification for the office he would administer. In verse 13 there follows: "And the Spirit of the Lord came upon David from that day forward".

The anointing was the means for the divine preparation to the office of king. So then, according to God's Word, both the ordination and qualifying of Christ is called an anointing.

Now we stated at the beginning, "He was anointed through the Father and became anointed with the Holy

Spirit". But can the statement, "He became anointed with the Holy Spirit" be proven from God's Word too?

This is clear in Acts 10:28, "How God anointed Jesus of Nazareth with the Holy Ghost and with power".

Wherein would the singular gifts; wisdom, power, and holiness which He had imparted to Him in His human nature have been manifested?

He revealed His wisdom as He went about teaching as we read in Matthew 7:29 "For He taught them as one having authority, and not as the scribes."

His strength was apparent in His miracles. The men on the way to Emmaus said to Him, "Concerning Jesus of Nazareth, which was a Prophet mighty in deed and word before God and all the people." Luke 24:19.

Wherein did His holiness consist? In that He had no sin; neither original or actual.

Now I shall enumerate 5 points that you should remember.

Jesus Christ the Mediator is:

1st. One in essence with the Father and the Holy Ghost.

2nd. The second person in the Divine Essence.

3rd. Is begotten of the Father according to His divine nature; yet He is not less than the Father even though His name is, "God's Son".

4th. He has been ordained to the office of Mediator from eternity.

5th. He was qualified for that office in the fulness of time.

He was the true Priest after the order of Melchisedec, who was to come, because He had no father according to His human nature. He was born of the Virgin Mary.

According to His Divine nature, He had no mother.

He was a Priest but not out of the generations of Levi. As far as His priesthood is concerned He had no geneology. Paul said, "It is manifest that our Lord is generated out of Judah."

He is the Son of God from eternity, without beginning of days and in respect to His Godhead there will be no termination of life. It is clearly evident that He is the true Melchisedec, the King of Salem!

How clear it has become manifest that He had received the gift of the Holy Ghost in a very special measure in His ministration as mediator.

John the Baptist had seen this Spirit descend upon Him and remain on Him.

Solomon says in Proverbs, "Wisdom hath builded her house".

Whom did Solomon refer to here? He himself was the world's wisest king and also had built the finest house; the temple. Would Solomon be refering to himself here?

Jesus said to the jews, "The queen of the South shall rise up in the judgment with this generation, and shall condemn it: for she came from the uttermost parts of the earth to hear the wisdom of Solomon; and behold, a greater than Solomon is here." Matt. 12:42.

The Lord spoke forthrightly when He said Solomon had not the greatest wisdom; He, the eternal Son of God, the Mediator of the covenant was greater than Solomon. He alone is the supreme Wisdom.

He, then, is the supreme wisdom. Also in His Word, Christ gives testimony that besides wisdom, He received power. In Matt. 28:18 He said, "All power is given unto me in heaven and on earth."

God's people receive much power through grace. But the Mediator has not little or much power, no, He has all power.

He had to defend Himself against the Jews in respect to His holiness, too. He said, "Which of you convinceth me of sin?"

It was made manifest that He was born the holy one.

The declarations from His own mouth proved that He possessed perfect wisdom, power and holiness, not only as God in His own right, but also given by the Holy Spirit to His human nature as Mediator.

And why was it necessary that He possess the gifts of wisdom, power and holiness?

1st — He is Prophet and as such manifests His wisdom to a foolish people that are void of knowledge. They must be thoroughly taught of and through Him.

2nd — He is King having a powerless people. He must possess perfect power to be able to reign over these foolish and impotent people, protecting them from all enemies. They are entirely powerless and because they are, they are dependent upon their King.

3rd — He is a Priest representing an unholy people. He stands now as an holy, undefiled High Priest to atone for their guilt.

In His prayer He said, "And for their sakes I sanctify myself, that they also might be sanctified through the truth."

So, He stands a wise, powerful and Holy Prophet, Priest and King before a foolish, sinful and impotent people whom He teaches, helps and purifies.

His wisdom is manifest in His teachings; His power in His miracles.

Now before we close I would put a question to you: When Jesus was upon earth He often manifested His Divine power in His miracles but what would be the greatest miracle on earth since the creation?

The great creation in six days was, certainly, a mighty miracle. And — that the dead were made alive, the sick healed, the blind made to see, all were great miracles. But what is the greatest of all?

Are you not able to tell me?

Then I shall tell you by way of an incident that took place lately. I was present in a certain home where a man led in prayer. It was a long prayer in which the man told the Lord that it was such a wonder that he still lived and was now well again (he had been ill), that he still had food and drink, and that he was privileged to hear the true gospel and so forth. He related one great series of wonders after another.

When he finally said, "Amen," another man said to him, "In listening, I noticed you related so many miracles."

"Well," he answered, "isn't it a great wonder, that we are yet alive and have food?"

"Surely", said that man, "that is certain, but I believe you still haven't related the greatest wonder."

"What is that?" he asked.

"Well, man, the greatest wonder is that God converts His people who are yet on the earth, and do you know what will be even greater? That I may be one of them. It all comes down to that, man!"

But, no one will see this wonder as the greatest one except those who are truly converted. When this happens, then they begin to realize that this is true.

I knew a young man in Zeeland in whom the Lord was evidently working. He visited God's people regularly and very often called on an old man who was well versed and had much experience in spiritual matters.

Often when he was with that old man the boy would say, "O, it is such a wonder that I still live and am not yet in Hell!"

"Yes, my boy," said the old man, "It is true; It is a wonder, but, that is not enough."

The old man never dealt harshly with him, but always reminded him of his lack.

The boy came to him another time. The old man noticed that something had happened to him because he did not care to talk; he was very troubled. "Well," said the old friend, "what seems to be the trouble now?"

"Oh," the young man called out, "now it is not only a wonder that I live, but — there is an eternal wonder that I can be saved. It has been shown me by the eternal Mediator of the covenant."

The old man was very glad to hear that. He had been waiting for it.

He said, "Come my boy, sit down so we can talk awhile."

The Lord had led this boy to meditate on eternity and the fact that Jesus willingly became a surety to reconcile a guilty people with God. To him that was the greatest wonder. He was one of those known of God!

It surely is necessary that we count it a wonderful blessing that we may still have life; that is certain, but — all people live by virtue of common grace. If this remains the greatest wonder and is held so until death, it will not be well.

193

Has it, however, even once become a wonder to you that you still live? I fear that most of you still have your desires in the world. Is it not true?

The devil has something new every day with which he draws your evil heart into sin and idleness. Every day he lets you see something new in the fashion stores. He stands invisibly behind those alluring large lighted windows saying, "See how nice this would be, and how fine this is." Isn't it true, girls?

The people go about this world practically naked, many, because it is style and this has Satan's approbation.

And boys, what did you do last week when the circus was here?

Do you see that Satan uses everything to draw people further and further into idleness and to lead them away from God's Word? The people say, "Oh, what harm can that be, to see some elephants play or to see some dancing horses?" — but, do such matters take God and His Word into consideration? Listen to the way His Holy Name is profaned and observe how His day is disregarded. What idle and frivolous talk takes place and what soul-vexing music is being played.

I admonish you children to not listen to an enticing devil. He talks nice now; but soon when death comes, he will mock and torment you and say to you, "Why did you listen to me? You certainly knew that I was a liar and a murderer!

But, are there some among you with an open conscience?

Possibly it happens when you are being warned in church or catechism, that you can hardly restrain your emotions. Yet, you pursue your favorite sinful activities and stifle the voice of your conscience.

Perhaps you have thoughts which say, "Do you think I am about to concede to those fears I have so often?"

"I'll have none of that, I am too young and I want to live in the world!"

Does it ever happen that you weep and pray because of your sins when you are all by yourself at home? And then, soon after, you sin against that prayer. Isn't that what happens?

I am very sure that there are those who would seek wordliness even more if it were not for the restraint of father, mother and their own conscience. For that reason I warn you: do not fight against these admonitions; do not smother your conscience. Do not strive against the Spirit when in the way of common grace He restrains you from sinning. I am not implying that this is conversion; O no, you know that too. Conversion is a deeper experience than being stricken in conscience.

Oh, how happy I would be if it would be a saving work and you would be caught in the "net" of salvation. Even though you would struggle to be out of it you would never succeed. The Spirit of God would hold you securely in that saving work.

Your nature would constantly desire to be free of that net; always at large; continually calling out, "Still too young; much too young." But the Lord says, "That is not the way for you, my child, I would see you abased; you must learn to be submissive, always sinking and yielding."

May the time arrive soon, that the Lamb enter into your soul, conquering, in that He has conquered! May He remove all ground and support from your feet, and may you in that helplessness, discover the only Mediator of the new covenant; Jesus, that is: Savior!

> Lord, if Thou shouldst mark transgression,
> In Thy presence who shall stand?
> But with Thee there is forgiveness
> That Thy name may fear command.

Christ's Offices

Lesson 19 His Prophetic office

Before we proceed with the lesson at hand, we shall see if you have remembered something of the previous lessons.

Who created man?

Answer: The Triune God. "Let us make man."

How did God create man?

Answer: In His image which consists in knowledge, righteousness and holiness.

With which covenant did God govern man?

Answer: With the covenant of Works.

Did Adam keep that covenant?

Answer: No, He was disobedient.

What covenant did God reveal after the fall?

Answer: The covenant of Grace.

Who is the Mediator of that covenant?

Answer: The Lord Jesus Christ.

What do His names signify?

Answer: Jesus means: Savior, and Christ means: Anointed.

Who anointed the Mediator?

Answer: God the Father.

With what is He anointed?

Answer: With the Holy Spirit.

For what is He anointed?

Answer: To be Prophet, Priest and King.

Well, I notice you have remembered very well. Remember these truths always.

Now to continue, we come to the subject of the three offices of the Mediator.

We learned last week that the singular gifts of the Spirit, namely: wisdom, power and holiness, were imparted to Him in a singular way. He received:

Wisdom in His prophetical office to teach ignorant people.

Power as King to rule a helpless people, and

Holiness in His office of Priest to purify an unholy people.

Now the question is asked:

Was He typified under the Old Testament in these offices?

Answer: Yes, by anointed prophets, priests and kings.

Elijah and Elisha were anointed prophets; David and Solomon were anointed kings, and all the priests of the Old Testament were anointed to their offices.

Are there examples where one person was anointed to two or three offices?

We read about Melchisedec in Hebrews 7:1 that he was king of Salem (Jerusalem) and also a priest of the most high God.

According to God's Word, then, Melchisedec was both king and priest.

David the king is also mentioned in the New Testament as a prophet. Peter says in Acts 2:29 & 30, "Men and brethren, let me freely speak unto you of the patriarch David, etc.---Therefore being a prophet and knowing that God had sworn with an oath, etc."

David was, therefore, king and prophet simultaneously, but we cannot find examples where a person had three offices. That is peculiar to the Mediator alone.

The kings, prophets and priests of the Old Testament did not fill these offices as a surety, but only as types of Christ.

Why was it necessary for Christ to be a prophet?

Answer: To enlighten our darkened understandings.

Were we created so ignorant that it is necessary to have a prophet teach us?

No. God had created us with perfect knowledge, but in sin we lost this divine knowledge completely. Spiritual ignorance is a property of spiritual deadness.

Now I shall put another question to you. Pay close attention!

Are we spiritually dead because we are spiritually ignorant? or, are we spiritually ignorant because we are spiritually dead?

Answer: Spiritual ignorance is fruit of spiritual deadness.

That is the way it is. Ignorance is a property of spiritual death. However, ignorance is not our only tragic property. If that were so, then, spiritual death would not extend further than ignorance. No one is born with only some properties of spiritual death; no, we possess all its properties, including total ignorance, consequently, we are

198

totally dead. That is why the Mediator of the covenant must necessarily be a prophet to enlighten darkened understandings. Moses, in Deut. 18:18 predicted Christ to be raised up a prophet, — "I will raise them up a Prophet from among their brethren, like unto thee, and will put my words in His mouth; and He shall speak unto them all that I shall command Him."

When this Prophet enters into the hearts of the elect and discovers unto them their ignorance, they become aware and readily accept, through God and before Him, the fact that He had not created them ignorant. They are shown enlightened to two facts:

1. That they had had perfect knowledge and,
2. That they are now completely void of it.

They become aware that they have no knowledge. When, through grace, they accept their condemnable ignorance, there room is made for the prophetic office of the Mediator, and an ignorant person finds the way to salvation.

His light discovers their darkness, His life expels their deadness and His wisdom replaces their folly.

How do they arrive at these experiences?

Outwardly through His Word and inwardly through His Spirit.

Does Christ enlighten the elect exclusively or the whole world too?

In a certain respect He instructs others also.

Outwardly He instructs through His Word, all those who hear His Word.

This was much in evidence when He was on earth. Each and everyone who heard Him speak were instructed by

Him. But this external instruction is not effectually saving to all. It is so only to the elect. These He teaches externally through His Word and internally by His Spirit.

A good example of this is Lydia, a seller of purple, who is spoken of in Acts 16:14, "Whose heart the Lord opened, that she attended unto the things which were spoken of Paul."

From Adam to Noah, from Noah to Moses and from Moses to the coming of Christ to earth, He has always taught His people by His Word and Spirit.

Does He not use other means besides His Word?

Surely He does, because before He came upon earth, during the Old Testament times, He was a Prophet just as much as during the New. He taught His prophets throughout all ages, for they spoke through the Spirit of Christ which was in them. He uses His servants, who teach His Word, as the means in His hand whereby He discharges His prophetical office and instructs His people.

But during the three years, from His thirtieth to the thirty-third year He manifested Himself in the flesh and taught them personally.

Were Christ's teachings universally accepted? No, far from it. You should read John 9 this evening to see a clear example of how His words were despised by many Jews and how He himself was renounced as God and Mediator.

It gives the account of the man who had been born blind. Naturally, you are all acquainted with that story in the Bible. Am I correct in assuming that?

The disciples thought that the blind son or his parents had sinned more than other people, but Jesus said, "Neither hath this man sinned, nor his parents; but that the works of God should be made manifest in him."

After Jesus had spoken these words, He spit on the ground and made clay of the spittle and placed it on the eyes of the blind one. Then He told the blind man to wash his eyes in the pool of Siloam. When he returned from the pool, he could see.

Some of the Scribes and Pharisees witnessed what had taken place, and since they did not respect this Nazarene anyway, the performing of this miracle made them dreadfully angry. It was Sabbath when Jesus had done this and according to the pious Jews it was a great sin to heal on that day.

They did acknowledge that Jesus, the son of Mary, was an exceptional person. They had to because of all the miracles he had done. But now they were greatly offended. He had done this miracle on a Sabbath day and this the very religious Jews found to be terrible! Do you know another reason why they were so angry on this occasion?

They actually did acknowledge that Jesus was an exceptional man for His ability to perform the miracle of healing the sick. But to give sight to one who was born blind was going too far! It could not be any other way than that a person who could do such a miracle was more than an exceptional person. And, to acknowledge He was God, they would not do. They roared out in enmity against Him.

On a previous occasion, they had called the one who was born blind to them for questioning to determine exactly how this had taken place and now they called him again.

They said, "This man cannot be of God" (They really wanted to say he is not the Son of God) "because he keepeth not the Sabbath Day." Others said, "How can a common person do such miracles?" There came a discord amongst them. It was manifest then, when they had called the blind man the second time, how great their enmity was against Christ but they made it appear as though it was an act of the very best religion, saying to him, "Give God the praise". Ordinarily you cannot do better than to give God the honor, but, what followed? "We know that this man, (named Jesus) is a sinner."

That was the honor they were giving to God! They denied that Jesus was the Son of God.

But the blind man, by grace, thought differently about it and dared to say so.

He said, without hesitation, "If this man were not of God, He could do nothing."

At this point the "piousness" of the Pharisees came out in the open. They became furious when they heard this confession and said, "Thou was altogether born in sins, and dost thou teach us?" They cast him out of the synagogue. He was no longer allowed to stay with their religion.

But this was not so bad for the one born blind, because a little later Jesus found him and said, "Dost thou believe on the Son of God?" At first he did not know who He was but when Jesus told him, he said, "Lord, I believe." And he worshipped Him.

He was, then, by grace and trust in Christ taken up into the new congregation, even though men had thrown him out of the old synagogue. That was not such a bad result!

Do you see how little the Jews knew about the offices of Christ? Absolutely nothing. They would give God honor by circumventing Christ and that cannot be done.

The one born blind had great profit of the gifts that had been bestowed upon Christ in the consecration to His offices.

He received internal enlightenment from the Divine Spirit which showed him that Christ was the Son of God, and also experienced the Divine Power of His miracles in that he was made to see.

Does the Lord still exercise His office as Prophet even though He is no longer upon the earth in a bodily form?

O, yes. He still instructs all the elect through His Spirit internally as well as externally through His Word, which He causes His pastors and ministers to proclaim over the whole world. We shall go no further now but, if the Lord be willing and we live, we hope to continue this lesson on the offices next week.

Last week we became so involved in our lesson that I had no time to receive the answer to the question I had given you to study at home two weeks ago. We should do that now.

What was the question again?

Answer: Why is Jesus Mediator?

That is right. That is the question we gave you. Now let us hear from those of you who have given thought to it.

Each one give your answer in turn.

First answer: To reconcile God and man. "And all things are of God who hath reconciled us to Himself by Jesus Christ, and hath given to us the ministry of reconciliation."

Second answer: He has become a Mediator because He alone was able to be both God and man.

Third answer: To bring the elect to salvation. Etc. etc.

Final answer: To accomplish with crowning splendor the eternal purpose of God, that is; To glorify to the highest, God's honor, the honor of the Triune God. The reason why a certain number was elect and why Jesus became Mediator for them was to glorify God through the salvation of sinners.

Do you hear that? That is the answer I was intending.

We could say in brief: Why is Jesus Mediator?

To bring God's Honor to the highest splendor and salvation to His church.

Children, I placed this question before you to refresh your historical knowledge in the basic truths. But, I hope the Lord will show you the hidden mysteries that are to be found in that answer in an experiential way.

You are bound now hand and foot with the shackles of sin, faithfully serving the father of lies. But if the Lord should apply the teachings of His prophetical office to your soul, you would realize that it is an oppressive service you are rendering and that your soul is bound unto that inhabitant of hell eternally, if the Mediator has not paid the ransom for you.

I hope your allegiance may be turned to another King.

There are people whose lives were rough and uncouth but suddenly experienced a change.

Instead of frequenting the tavern, they attend church services and have turned from lives of sin to upright and moral lives. This is simply a change of living but not a change of heart. They still serve the same king and are captives of Satan's power even though their manner of life is different than it used to be.

These people can be likened to soldiers that are transferred from one garrison to another. They have changed troops but are still serving under the same king. In order to serve another king their present king must be conquered.

Therefore, keep this firmly in mind, boys and girls, you must make a change in your loyalties. This change is not to be in outward appearances only; from immorality to moral conduct, but you must be transferred from the realm of Satan to the kingdom of God.

You need not think there is no religion in the kingdom of Satan! O no, you just heard that in the account of the one born blind; men were so very religious wanting to give God honor but in the meantime they cursed Jesus!

It is still the same in these days. One would not be able to count the number of false religions there are in our days whose banner is hoisted in the name of God.

But I would warn you against pernicious doctrines. They will deceive your soul for eternity. So many things are called "Christian" now-a-days but it is a name without substance, an empty formation of letters; nothing more. They form "christian" football associations, they present "christian" dramas and other similar things. It is the spirit of the times which keeps creeping in, undermining and corrupting all things. Boys, I would warn you; do not desecrate the Lord's Day by attending a football game. Do not presume you will not be held accountable for desecrating the Lord's Day because the name "christian" is associated with the event.

In Psalm 73:27 we read: "For, lo, they that are far from thee shall perish; thou hast destroyed all them that go a whoring from thee." I fear you will experience one day, if and when you become an adult, that the Lord will visit our country for its mockery. Men use God's Holy name carelessly every where now-a-days, but the Lord says, "Woe unto those who take my name in vain."

The Lord Jesus said to the proud city, "And thou, Capernaum, which art exalted to heaven, shalt be thrust down to hell". The proud and lofty Netherlands will experience this also.

When the measure of the old world was full, it had to go through water. When the measure of the Canaanites was full they were destroyed by the Israelites. When the measure of the Jews was full, they were scattered over the earth.

Rutherford, one of the Scottish divines, said in one of his books, "Scotland did not pay heed to God's voice and so God owes Scotland a day of judgment." And that day of judgment came upon the church of England.

A day of judgment is due for the Netherlands too because Netherlands has broken the covenant and summoned God's wrath upon itself.

Our land was rich in truth and had many who became martyrs for the truth; rich in Divine visitations and prosperity in all areas. But it is now a country of pride, insolence and extreme wicked sins. The heroes of truth are passed away and the heroes of sin have taken their place.

Perhaps you have thoughts such as this, "Dominie, what good does it do to relate how deep the Netherlands has sunken?" I merely want to remind you while you are young and are able to store it in your memory so that, if the Lord spare you, you will see it come to pass. This is providing you may become older. Do not count on it, however.

I was visiting a man on his death bed. He was 75 years old. It was very evident that death was approaching and he realized it too. In his fading voice he said to the family gathered around his bed, "Do not wait until you become old. O, do not delay because it will fare poorly with you.

When I was a boy nearly twenty years old my soul was exercised in heavy convictions of guilt. I remember the places in church and catechism very well where I silently wept about my lost condition. I often sought out solitary places to pray. But, I overruled my conscience and would not listen to its warnings. Now I lay here, an old man, without hope for eternity and I know where I shall go. O, people, do not trample over the warnings of your conscience."

That is the admonition this old man gave in broken and hesitant speech with long intervals between words just before he passed away.

God can prevail over man, however, and what cannot be done by man can be accomplished by God's love. I hope that you may experience this to your eternal benefit.

So be it.

> Secured by Thy unfailing grace,
> In Thee they find a hiding place.
> When foes their plots devise;
> A sure retreat Thou wilt prepare,
> And keep them safely sheltered there,
> When strife of tongues shall rise,
> When strife of tongues shall rise.

Psalm 31
Psalter No. 81:2

Lesson 20

Of His Priestly Office

The subject of our lesson today is the Priestly office of the Mediator of the Covenant. We mentioned previously, that the priests of the Old Testament executed their offices as a type of the Mediator. During the Old Testament dispensation only some of the sons of Levi had the right to be priests: all those who were of the order of Aaron.

According to which order was Christ a priest?

Paul mentions in Hebrews 7 that another priest arises, not according to the order of Aaron but according to the order of Melchisedek who, like Christ had no priestly ancestry. Like Melchizedek, Christ also had no priestly ancestry. Our lesson begins with this question: "Was He also promised as a priest?"

Answer: Yes. Psalm 110:4 "Thou art a priest forever after the order of Melchizedek." David prophesied of this priesthood by an act of faith.

Immediately following this answer comes the question, "What does this intimate?"

Answer: 1st. That He alone is a priest. 2nd. That He is an everlasting priest.

Before we proceed with discussion on this subject I would interject this question; pay close attention:

What distinctions were made between the priests out of the lineage of Levi according to the order of Aaron? I mean, did they all have the same duties, or were there various ranks among them?

208

Yes, in the Old Testament times there were just common priests and high priests. The high priests had certain duties that ordinary priests were forbidden to perform, namely; to do atonement for the sins of the people by entering into the Holy of Holies on the great day of atonement. When the high priest died, his successor would receive his clothes. This is verified in Exodus 29:29, "And the holy garments of Aaron shall be his son's after him, to be anointed therein, and to be consecrated in them."

When you arrive home this evening you should take the time to read Leviticus 8 to see how solemnly these ceremonies were performed. First the high priest was washed with water, then clothed with holy garments and adorned with ornaments such as the breastplate, etc. Subsequently he was anointed with oil. All these procedures had to be carried out according to the law.

What was the difference between these priests, who were consecrated and anointed, and Christ in His priestly office?

The tribe of Levi was chosen by God to the priesthood. God directed Moses how all this should be carried out. Even though these priests were installed into their offices according to God's ordinance, they were, nevertheless, mortal men, full of infirmities with original and actual sins.

But Christ was not an ordinary Priest, no, He was the High Priest of all High Priests. Sinless and undefiled and immortal in His Divine nature. But, was He a priest in conformity to the law of Moses?

No, because he was of the lineage of Juda and not out of Levi. He was a priest of a higher order than that of the Mosaic law. In what way?

Christ was a priest with a divine oath which transcends the law.

David, under the influence of the Holy Spirit, speaks of this very clearly; "The Lord hath sworn and will not repent, Thou art a priest for ever—" Christ was, then, the great High Priest by the word of oath as the fulfillment of all the symbolic services which the priests of the Old Testament typified of Him.

God the Father appointed and qualified Him for the great work to which He had been ordained.

God's Word reveals clearly that He is the High Priest, but what are His functions in that office?

Answer: Offering sacrifice and praying.

We read in the gospels that He prayed often in His sojourn upon earth and He often assured His people He would pray for them in heaven. I have never read, however, that He offered up animals such as did the other priests.

How should that be understood?

Hellenbroek states it this way, "He offered Himself." Hebrew 9:14 "Who through the eternal Spirit offered Himself without spot to God."

When did that take place?

Generally speaking, it took place from His birth to His death. His entire life was an offering, but especially His suffering on the cross.

To whom did He offer Himself?

Answer: To His Father.

And for whom?

For all the elect and for the elect only.

There are three things involved here: 1st. The priest. 2nd. The offering. 3rd. The altar.

Any rational person can understand that these three matters are not to be separated from one another. What is a priest without desire to make an offering? And how can he offer unless he has an altar? These, therefore, are not to be separated.

Now we know that Christ as Mediator was a Priest and that He was also the offering itself. The Priest, then, offered up Himself. But what was the altar?

Jesus asked the Jews, "For whether is greater, the gift (that is, the offering) or the alter that sanctifieth the gift." The Jews believed that a man who swears by the altar is not duty bound, but whoever swears by the offering on the altar, his oath is binding. In response to that, the Lord said these words, "Ye fools and blind; for whether is greater, the gift, or the altar that sanctifieth the gift? Who so therefore shall swear by the altar, sweareth by it, and all things thereon." In this way the Lord said that the altar sanctifies the gift because it is more than the gift of the offering. The offering that He made was His human nature including both soul and body, which He yielded to the death of the cross, but the altar upon which He offered His human nature was His Divine nature. Only that nature could bear the suffering; support Him in His suffering and bring about eternal benefit upon the suffering.

We mentioned previously that His human nature, which was the same as ours, was offered, including soul and body. Can it be proved from the Bible that He also actually offered His soul?

There is no question about the body being offered up; you just recited in answer 5, "Who His own self bare our sins in His own body on the tree." 1 Peter 2:24.

Who can give proof concerning the soul?

Answer: Isaiah 53:10 "—When thou shalt make His soul an offering for sin, He shall see His seed."

211

Take notice of that. We should always prove our statements from God's Word.

So we have the Priest, the offering and the altar. But, what is the fire upon the altar on which the offering must be laid? That must also be there because an offering that is not burned cannot be considered an offering.

The fire in this case is the righteous wrath of the Father and the eternal love of Christ. These two elements comprised the great Divine fire whereupon the Divine offering of this Divine High Priest was consumed. The Father's wrath burns for satisfaction to His sacred demands and the love of the Son burns to glorify the attributes (which had been shamefully blasphemed) of the Divine Being, of whom He was also a part and in this way to satisfy for the guilt of the elect, so that they can once again enter into the favor of God.

It is clear that the fire was meant to consume the offering.

What was left of the offering when it was made in the realm of nature?

Nothing, but a handful of ashes. According to the Mosaic law these ashes were to be taken out of the camp and brought to a clean undefiled place.

What is the meaning of this?

Christ, in the divine offering, was not burned to ashes by fire as in ordinary offerings. His deceased body remained and Joseph and Nicodemus carried it out of Jerusalem and gave it an honorable burial in a new grave.

Without realizing it they did with the one great offering just as it was symbolized under the law of Moses.

Would the effects of this offering remain until this day?

I am sure of that! Paul said to the Romans (5:10) "For if, when we were enemies, we were reconciled to God by the death of his Son, much more, being reconciled, we shall be saved by His life." The real fruit of this offering is having reconciliation with God! Isn't that a blessed fruit? That is the purpose for which the Mediator became a Priest.

Do you see now the important significance of the offices the Mediator has?

He was a Prophet to enlighten their darkened understandings and a Priest to make reconciliation to God for their sins. But, for whom? For everyone?

Will everyone be partaker of these benefits? No. He has made complete satisfaction with the one offering, but only for those who are brought to salvation.

The world does not acknowledge this High Priest, nor the offering He has made, so they will never have a portion in the fruit of that offering.

Did Christ as High Priest do something other than offer Himself?

Hellenbroek indicates He does. He says He executes the office of a priest by offering and making intercession. The place where this is done is at the right hand of His Father in Heaven.

Would His prayers there be like those we pray to God?

Not at all, because the Mediator does not pray for necessities as we do. His prayers are actually an intercession. He prays only for others. What is His intercession?

Answer: That He continually presents His merits unto His Father and demands thereupon the salvation of His people.

213

Just before He entered into the garden of Gethsemane, while in the hall where they had celebrated the Passover, He uttered a precious prayer which we call, "The Intercessary Prayer". It is to be found in John 17.

The actual character of that prayer comes forth so clearly in the 24th verse, just as Hellenbroek explains: That He presents His merits unto the Father and thereupon demands the salvation of His people.

He prays in verse 24, "Father, I will that they also, whom Thou hast given Me, be with Me where I am, that they may behold My glory, which Thou hast given Me; for thou lovest Me before the foundation of the world . . . "

He said, "They, whom Thou hast given Me". At once it is evident, that He does not pray for everyone. He very specifically states in verse 9, "I pray not for the world, but for them which Thou hast given Me".

Someone asked me one time, "Dominie, is it true that Jesus prays only for the elect? Does He not pray for the whole world?"

I asked him, "Why do you ask that?"

"Well," said he, "It says in Luke 23, when Jesus went to the cross, He called out, 'Father, forgive them; for they know not what they do'. He did pray here for wicked people".

I made this reply to that man, "The fact that Christ cried these words on the cross, is not proof that He prayed for the world, but without a doubt there were Jews and Gentiles amongst them who lay under the seal of election and must still be brought to salvation."

There is no doubt about that and it was revealed to be so later, when, on Pentecost Day, Peter said, "This Jesus ye have taken, and by wicked hands have crucified and slain."

214

Surely, then, there were men converted on Pentecost Day that cooperated in the crucifixion.

Also, even if this were not true, this anguished cry was not necessarily a prayer for their salvation.

One must make a distinction between Jesus in His Mediatorial intercessory prayers and His conduct in life as an example for us to follow.

In His intercessory prayer as Mediator He, in all certainty, included no one in His prayer for salvation but His own; otherwise, it would be a contradiction of His own words, "I pray not for the world."

But He walked upon this earth as an example for us to follow, and viewing it in that way, it is possible He prayed for His enemies, even though they never were converted.

This is verified in Matt. 5:44, "But I say unto you, Love your enemies, bless them that curse you, do good to them that hate you and pray for them which despitefully use you and persecute you. That ye may be the children of your father which is in heaven; for He maketh His sun to rise on the evil and on the good."

His prayer on the cross was definitely an intercession for the elect. Even though He had prayed for the world there, it would not have been a prayer for their salvation. That is impossible. If it was true that He prayed for the salvation of persons that never finally obtained it, He would have, in that case, prayed for those for whom He had never paid the price, and the Father had never accepted the satisfaction and intercessions He had made for them.

It is impossible for either one of these conditions to exist. Hold firm, then, to this fact that Christ prayed only for those whose guilt He had assumed and for whom He had satisfied God's justice.

I shall ask yet another question: You are acquainted with the fact that the church of God is divided into two parts. The one part is on earth and is called the church Militant. The other part is in heaven and is called the church Triumphant. Christ is sitting now on the right hand of His Father praying for this church. (This is spoken of in a figurative sense; God is a Spirit and has no hands.) For what part is He praying? Is He praying for that part which is in heaven or on earth?

That ought to be an easy question, don't you think so too?

Do you see what I mean; they all say "For the Church Militant!"

It goes without saying that the Church Triumphant no longer needs intercessory prayer. It is in heaven, far above all sin, trouble, strife and misery. But that part on earth sorely needs His intercessory prayers. Paul says, "Who is even at the right hand of God, Who also maketh intercession for us".

Are His prayers only for those who belong to the church militant and consequently separated from the irreligiousness of the world and joined to the children of God? No, He prays not only for the church which is restored but also for those who are still pious or profane; for those who are disguised in their moral excellence or are disguised in their open wickedness. He prays for those who still have not been taught to know Him but whose name, nevertheless, is written in the book of life and at God's appointed time will be converted.

This is what the Lord meant when He said what is recorded in John 17:20 "Neither pray I for these alone, but for them also which shall believe on me through their word."

In using the word "These" the Lord was referring to the disciples who were standing round about Him and who already belonged to the visible church. And by the word "them" he meant those who are lying under the seal of election, but who still live in an unconverted state, and even for those who were not yet born. He prays for those also, because they belong to his inheritance.

Think what this could mean!

Boys, now you are living merrily in the world and in sin, drinking life's enjoyments in full measure as often as you can manage to do so. But if it were really true that you belong to that number whose name from eternity was written in the Lamb's Book of Life, oh, then, the Divine High Priest is even now praying for you. He was praying for you in heaven long before you were born. Even though His intercessory prayers are prayers made generally for the whole church, they are also individual intercessions.

By way of explanation; this Divine Christ would say in His office of Priest: "Father, there they are (that boy or girl) going about upon the earth. They are dead in sins and trespasses, but they are still My very own, Father, because I have shed My blood for them. I have discharged their debt and paid their ransom. They are estranged from thee in their walk of life, lost and sunken in a state of death. But now is the time of love, Father, and, being those thou hast given me I desire now to have them at My side. Oh, send that Divine Being, Thy Holy Spirit, into the heart of that boy or girl".

Their hearts are wrought upon, their complacency is gone forever. The Spirit discovers to them that they have

217

sinned against God even though they are only fourteen or fifteen years old. God's holy justice is made manifest to their heart and, fight though they may to close their minds, it is of no avail. The charging steed must perish, no matter how young he is. The Spirit works deep within the heart just as a farmer in plowing the ground, lays it open and makes it fit to receive the seed or kernels of grain.

Does that boy or girl know that the High Priest in heaven is praying for him or her?

They know nothing of that. They do not know there is a Mediator. They are involved only with a Holy God from whom they are estranged. They become sorrowful and lonely persons.

Does Christ cease praying for them when the Holy Spirit begins His work in their heart? Oh, no. He prays not only during the time of love (as it is called in Ezekiel 16) but also as they progress along the way.

Saying it in a childlike way (and yet with respect) in order to make it understandable to you, He says, then: "Father, there is a wounded soul crawling on the earth. She cannot live in the world but neither can she die in that state. She acknowledges that she has sinned against Thee and that Thou art righteous in her condemnation.

She cannot pray and ask that Thou teach her to pray. Father, I have prayed that the faith which the Holy Spirit has placed in her soul fail not. I have shed My blood for that soul."

Oh, that is the manner in which the precious Intercessor labors in His Priestly office; offering and praying.

He had to sacrifice Himself but once; that was sufficient. In His one sacrifice He made perfect satisfaction. But He will continue to pray as long as the world exists because His church will be here until the very end.

Boys and girls, don't you think that this was an especially serious lesson this afternoon? It is so necessary that your heart be instructed in these matters. Without that instruction your eternal state will be sad indeed. Any person who has never been the subject of Christ's intercessory prayers, cannot become a member of His church.

And all who are comprehended in those intercessory prayers have their names written in the Book of Life. This is not a book made of paper or parchment, but it is called a "book" in the figurative sense.

It is the eternal counsel of God in which everything is firm and sure. The Lord does not consider who your father or mother were, or whether you are rich or poor, pious or profane. Oh, no, the Lord considers only the names that are written in the Lamb's Book of Life.

Those are the people He must have, regardless of what their walk of life is upon earth, or what their circumstances were under which they were born or reared; none of these things have any bearing on the matter. Salvation is a personal matter. May each one of you discover this to be truth. It is unspeakable and wondrous to believe that our persons are remembered in the holy and precious intercessory prayers of that great High Priest!

Oh, the love of the Father, the love of the Son and the love of the Holy Spirit, eternal, incomprehensible and unchangeable! When the soul by faith may see that he is included in the eternal intercessory prayers of God's own Son, he sinks away, and, there is no bottom for a sinner, who has fallen dead at His feet.

Oh that wonder: "Thou hast prepared of Thy goodness for the poor."

But our time is almost spent and we must consider more of this question.

The question is: "Is there more than one Mediator of intercession?"

Answer: No, 1 John 2:1 "We have an advocate with the Father, Jesus Christ the righteous, and He is the propitiation for our sins."

This is the proof, then, that Christ is the only intercessor.

Now, pay attention to this: Paul says in Romans 8:26 "For we know not what we should pray for as we ought: but the Spirit itself maketh intercession for us with groanings which cannot be uttered — He maketh intercession for the saints according to the will of God".

How can we reconcile this text with the answer just given?

It states here in this text that the Holy Spirit is also an intercessor, doesn't it?

Paul does not infer here that the Holy Spirit prays for the church while in heaven but that He prays in the hearts of God's people.

God's people pray to God in and through the Holy Spirit. That is why Paul says that He maketh intercession for the saints according to the will of God.

Christ is the only Intercessor in Heaven for the church.

I hope you may become aware of both the intercessory prayer of Christ and the prayer of the Spirit in your hearts. If you may have that privilege, earth's miseries and adversities will be transcended.

I often think about a woman in Rotterdam who passed away just recently. She was twenty six years old when God converted her and she died at the age of forty. Her body had passed through so much suffering that it was but skin over bones. It was severly emaciated. She appeared to be more like eighty years old than forty. She underwent heavy trials on her sickbed too. I shall never forget what she said to me while I was visiting her. She said, "My heavenly Father permits the devil to drag His child through mud and mire up to the gate of heaven. But when we come before the very door of heaven, the Father says, 'Leave off now, that is My child, your work is all done' ".

"Oh", she exclaims, "That is truly the love of the Father".

I stood quietly listening to every word. I had never before heard anyone relate anything like the terribly severe way that this lady had to go through.

Just imagine for a moment a father standing at the doorway of his home, watching his dear child of about 4 years old (not old enough to defend itself) being knocked about and dragged through the mud by a couple of bullies. The father doesn't go over there to rescue it right away but watches quietly until his child has been dragged right in front of the doorway. Then he speaks out, "Leave my child alone now, you have gone far enough". He picks the child up and carries it into his house.

Wouldn't you say this is a hard-hearted father? In this life that would be true. But if that little child, instead of crying, says, "Father, you have shown exceptional love to me by holding off that long." Then, a strong tie of love exists between the father and his child, isn't that true?

221

You could hardly expect this situation to arise in this life but it could in the spiritual. That woman had experienced an unusual amount of misery in this life, but she had been given faith to believe that those chastening hands were kind hands, and those angry eyes were friendly eyes! She went to be with the Father eternally. The door was closed behind her shutting out her persecutor. All misery and bustling activities were shut out. Anything that is impure does not enter there.

She went to be with her Oldest Brother and that eternally! He who was her Intercessor, was so, even until death. Now, being in the Church Triumphant, she is no longer subject to the fury of the old hell hound nor her own earthly sins. The intercessory prayers of Christ are no longer needed either.

My poor children, are you still unacquainted with these matters? I hope you may come to realize what it is to be a stranger to God while you are still in your youth.

You had better not believe that you will live a life of ease when God converts you. Oh, no. When God begins His work, then other things begin to happen! Then the devil, the world and a person's flesh and blood also begin to work! They work in direct opposition to the Holy Spirit. One hears within, "I am much too young; it would be better to be converted when I am older." But as long as the Intercessor continues His prayers for that soul, nothing can hinder; the Spirit works on irresistably to the eternal salvation of that soul, even if he does not want it.

The work must proceed. The devil tries mightily to hold his prey and the vanities of the world allure and pull at young flesh, but, in the end everything must yield. Oh, the

222

blessed prayers of Him who prays for the transgressors! Oh, that has such deep significance.

What a wondrous thing that will be when such a transgressor, who has constantly rebelled may, despite it all, abide within eternally.

May it be, where by beginning to conversion a cut in the flesh, becomes so severe a wound that only God can cure it and that your own healing efforts cease in favor of God's covenantal remedy.

It could still happen because you are still in the day of grace and the Lord lives too.

May He bestow eternal mercy upon you; may that High Priest be your Intercessor for salvation.

May God bless this instruction to His honor.

So be it.

> The poor and needy He shall spare,
> And save their souls from fear;
> He shall redeem them from all wrong,
> Their life to Him is dear.

Psalter No. 194:5

Lesson 21

Concerning His Kingly Office

Our lesson this afternoon concerns the kingly office of the Mediator.

Cannot the offices of Prophet, Priest and King be considered separate entities? And, contrariwise, why are these offices of Prophet, Priest and King always mentioned together?

Answer: Because it is impossible to separate them. A distinction can be made between them as we are doing now, but they can never be separated.

Our instruction last week indicated that Christ as Prophet and Priest had been promised to the Church. Was He also promised as a King?

Yes, read Psalm 2:6 "Yet have I set my king upon my holy hill Zion."

It was not only prophesied in the Old Testament that He was to be a Mediator but His offices were foretold too.

Once again, What was Christ's work as Prophet?

Answer: To enlighten our darkened understanding.
What was His work as Priest?

Answer: To atone for our sins.

And what as King?

Answer: To reign over us, to protect and redeem us from the bondage of the devil and sin.

All of you are aware, of course, what a king is supposed to be. A king is one who reigns over a people. His orders are carried out by his subjects.

A good king must defend his land from all enemies and protect his people from all harm; he must provide for their welfare and reign in a manner that tends to their good.

Now, we could present the work of Christ in His Kingly office in a three-fold manner.

1st. The Lord Jesus, being God, is the second person in the Divine Essence and in Himself is worthy of all majesty, honor, power and glory. He is king over all and was so even before man was created. His kingdom is not only an earthly kingdom, no; listen to what David speaks of Him in 1 Chronicles 29:11, "Thine, O Lord, is the greatness and the power and the glory and the victory and the majesty; for all that is in the heaven and in the earth is thine; Thine is the kingdom, O, Lord, and thou art exalted as head above all."

It states here very plainly that His kingdom is exalted above all kingdoms. He reigns, then, universally.

2nd Christ is especially king over His Church. He reigns over it by His Word and Spirit. What proof does Hellenbroek present for this?

Answer: Psalm 43:3 "O send out Thy light and Thy truth: let them lead me; let them bring me unto thy holy hill, and to Thy tabernacles."

What do you suppose is meant when I say that Christ especially rules over His church?

There are countless numbers of "churches" and various church denominations. Are they all comprehended in this rule?

No, that is not what is intended. God has His own peculiar people amongst all the inhabitants of the earth. These belong to Him. He has gathered them by His Word and Spirit and they could be properly called "The Kingdom of

Grace". The Mediator has been established as a special King over a special people. Paul says in Ephesians 1:22, "And hath put all things under His feet, and gave Him to be the head over all things to the church."

He is not King over the church militant just for a season of time, but,

3rd. He shall be the eternal King in the kingdom of glory. He remains Shepherd and King of the redeemed church which is the church Triumphant.

Just as Hellenbroek speaks of it in question 5, He is not an earthly king, but is a spiritual and an eternal. He said this to His disciples in John 18, "My kingdom is not of this world." Also, in Luke 1:33, the angel Gabriel, in speaking of Him, said to Mary, "He shall reign over the house of Jacob forever; and of His kingdom there shall be no end."

Now I am going to ask a question which is not in our lesson, so pay attention!

Did the Kingly office of the Mediator begin at His birth here on earth? The angel told Mary that, "He shall reign". Does that mean He was not a king before coming to earth in person? No, it does not mean that; He was a king before. He is not only the eternal King in heaven and earth by virtue of creation, but also King of His church. He continually ruled and defended His church of the Old Testament and presented them with laws wherein He expressed His will to them. Now, the question might be asked, "If the Mediator is the only king of His church, is it permissable to have ministers and other office bearers to function in their respective duties?

It is true the Lord does not need servants or ministers to teach and to rule because being perfectly wise and powerful

He can do that in a most perfect way. But it has been His wisdom and desire to use means to reign over the whole world in general and His people in particualr. That is why He has placed rulers in the world under various circumstances; teaching certain persons by means of others.

Every lawful power that has been placed over us is an institution of God, but He is King over all of them.

Have you ever noticed how nicely the catechism speaks of this in its explanation of the 5th commandment? It is Lord's Day 39. Each one of you should memorize it.

Question 104: What doth God require in the 5th Commandment?

Answer: That I show all honor, love and fidelity to my father and mother and all in authority over me, and to submit myself to their good instruction and correction, with due obedience; and also patiently bear with their weaknesses and infirmities, since it pleases God to govern us by their hand.

Do you see now that we are actually governed by the King of kings? It is only that the Lord would use people as a means in His hand, through whom He governs us.

Do you suppose everyone just naturally acknowledges the Lord as their King by virtue of creation?

O, no, no one wants to admit to that.

Through sin, the first sin, we have adopted Satan as king or prince. We serve him with delight and obey him willingly.

Is the devil really a king?

He is a cursed fallen angel whom God banished to hell. That is and will be his eternal habitation. But even though the Lord stands above him in power, the Bible does say he is a mighty one and the "Power of darkness".

The Lord has never given the devil the desire of his heart, such as men have done. Being God and man, He could not sin and the evil one had no effect upon Him. He bruised the head of the serpent and triumphed over the devil in the dignity of His Kingly office.

But now, if men have willingly given themselves over to Satan and have given obeisance to him as king, how shall Christ gather a kingdom to Himself? We said earlier that no one by nature, will acknowledge Him as King. How is that going to be brought about?

That has been determined in eternity according to the holy will of the Divine Essence. The Son of God being Mediator shall shed His bood for the elect whom the Holy Spirit will snatch away from the devil. You can imagine what happens then! He just roars, and with his entire satanic power attempts to hold the prey.

But the Lord, being the superior one, can master him, conquering completely.

It is as we read in the history of Zedekiah, a wicked king who ruled Judah. When the measure of wickedness was full Nebuchadnezzar, the king of Babylon arrived on the scene. He conquered Jerusalem and captured Zedekiah. He bound him with ropes rendering him helpless. He burned the city and temple, after having robbed all the golden vessels from the house of the Lord. He then brought them to Babylon. Nebuchadnezzar murdered Zedekiah's sons while he watched and took him in custody to Babylon. These were all very dreadful acts and it was very wicked of Nebuchadnezzar to do them.

What I am trying to show you with this example is this: Originally Zedekiah was free to do what he wanted to do in his country. But when he was bound in ropes, it didn't help him one bit whether he prayed or cursed, made supplication or went into a rage; Nebuchadnezzar still went his own way and took one vessel after another out of the temple. Zedekiah never saw them again.

I have used this merely as a simple illustration. I do not mean that this story has any connection to our lesson, no, you should not think of it in that way. I only want to say: this is the way the Lord (reverently speaking) robs the devil of his vessels. The devil has used some of them for many years in the world. Some ten, twenty or thirty years and some even longer. But if it is one of the redeemed, upon His appointed time, the Lord says, "You have had enough, devil; dismount, this is my horse. It is a chosen vessel, over which I shall be King and not you."

Then the devil bellows out in spite and enmity. He is witnessing before his very eyes the vessels being "robbed" from him. He is a subject of the sovereign authority of King Jesus. Jesus has bruised Satan's head and taken the catch from him. He sits eternally now on the right hand of the Father as Prophet, Priest and King; as Priest to pray for His elect vessels and as King to conquer them.

You must not believe that Satan just willingly and voluntarily gives up his prey. O, no. Just as soon as he notices that Christ begins to apply the unction of His offices upon a soul, he tries, with all his might, to pull that soul away and conspires every way to retain them. If it is someone in their youth he says, "Did you have it so bad when you lived with the world? You had pleasure, had freedom to participate in all manner of activities, wear fashionable clothes and were companion to all sorts of desirable persons. And what do you have now? You cannot even sleep peacefully nor do what you are really eager to do. You have had to forsake all your former friends and now go around with a few of those despised poor people. They don't even know what pleasures there are in the world and are the' most stupid of all society."

That is the way the devil argues, always having something new, and, the worst of it all is, that our flesh and blood are inclined toward his point of view. Not toward God's. But, through it all, the Mediator exercises His Kingly office, personally, in the soul of such a one, until He has gained the victory.

Boys and girls, our class time is spent and we must close for today. If the Lord spare, it will be awhile before we see one another in class again. According to custom we do not hold catechism classes during the months of harvest. As a consequence, we shall not meet one another for a few weeks. I do hope and wish that all of us may be spared during this time. If we were to be called up meanwhile, could we meet God? And that could happen. Most of you live now just like the little birds you see singing so merrily in the tree. But it is possible that very soon some one would come over and shoot them out of the tree, causing them to die. If death were sent to cut off your young merry life like that, what then?

I once visited an old lady who was not feeling well. She was well enough at that time to sit in a chair. I spoke, as we usually do, with the family and with the lady herself, but it was merely casual talk.

Before I left I closed our visit with prayer, as usual, though it was only a common prayer that time.

But what happened? Exactly 45 minutes later they called me saying the lady had died very suddenly.

O, how guilty I felt at that time for having been lax in my duties. I had not talked seriously to her, making myself free from her soul.

I was the last person who had visited her. Three quarters of an hour after I had left her she stood before the High Court, summoned before the Judge of heaven and earth, and ----she could rightly accuse me of unfaithfulness. That is why, children, I must warn you each week. A person is accountable to God!

Are there among you, who have been stricken in conscience, have been given to see the blessedness of the children of God, who are aware of the drawing power of the devil and their own flesh and blood, and are trying to divert them?

May the Lord follow through to a good conclusion. May the breach and wound be made so severe that only the healing power of that blessed Mediator can make complete restoration. May He also be glorified through the working of His redeeming grace.

May the Lord spare you from sin during the summer months and preserve you in the evil times in which restraint is lacking and all manner of dangers exist.

Above all, may His gracious influence be made effectual in many hearts and bring to a conclusion the work He has already begun. May you be able to sing in truth, Psalter No. 205:8

O God, Thou art our King of old
Salvation Thou hast wrought;
In safety through the mighty sea
Our fathers thou has brought.

231

Lesson 22

Of Christ's Natures

The greatest part of the Summer is past and the Lord in His goodness has spared all of us, permitting us to attend class again.

I am curious to know how much you remember of the lessons we had before vacation began.

We shall review briefly and then continue on with further lessons in our catechism book.

There is one God in Essence and three in Persons, Father, Son and Holy Spirit.

Wherein can this God be known?

1st. In His Essence, 2nd. In His Names, 3rd. In His Attributes and 4th In His Persons.

Which one of the Divine Persons became the Mediator?

The second Person who is Jesus and Christ.

Wherein must the Mediator be known?

1st. In His names, 2nd. In His offices, 3rd. In His natures, 4th. In His states and 5th. In His benefits.

We covered the lesson on His names. "Jesus" means Saviour and "Christ" means anointed.

We also talked about His offices. To which offices was He anointed?

Answer: To the offices of Prophet, Priest and King.

Now the sequence of the lessons has brought us to the subject of His natures.

How many natures does Christ the Mediator have?

Answer: Two natures; a Divine nature and a human nature.

Who can provide a text which proves Christ has two natures?

Answer: I Tim 3:16, "And without controversy, great is the mystery of godliness; God was manifest in the flesh."

Why would the Mediator have two natures? Was that absolutely necessary?

Answer: Yes, He definitely had to have two natures.

1st. He had to be God in order to satisfy Divine justice.

2nd. He had to be man in order to suffer and die; it is impossible for deity to suffer and die.

But is the Mediator God in the fullest sense?

Answer: Yes, He is eternally one in essence with the Father and the Holy Spirit. He remains what He is; and that is God. John says it this way in 1 John 5:20 "This is the true God and eternal life."

In the fulness of time, though, He took a human nature unto Himself by being born out of the virgin Mary through the Divine operation of the Holy Spirit upon her. Galatians 4:4 speaks plainly of this saying He became a true human being, "But when the fulness of time was come, God sent forth His Son, made of a woman."

Paul wrote to Timothy about this assumption of human nature like this, "For there is one God and

233

one Mediator between God and men, the man Christ Jesus."

Be sure to keep these texts in mind. Perhaps you have thought, "Why must we verify each one of these answers with a text from Scripture?"

It will take some time to answer that. It is necessary to substantiate our answers with Scripture because there have always been errors in which the two natures of Christ are interwoven, and in which His Deity and His Human nature are not kept separate and distinct from one another.

I know very well that you shall find these things to be tiresome and, because we are spiritually dead and incapable of any spiritual good, it is impossible to understand spiritual life and those things that involve the Kingdom of God.

But even though a person is spiritually dead he is not rationally dead. So, with your rational mind, which God has given you, you should retain as much as possible the historical matters being taught you.

Christ then is: 1st. Ordained to His office of Mediator with a Divine anointing in respect to both His Divine and human natures. 2nd. Qualified to serve in His human nature.

It was not necessary to be qualified in His Divine nature.

Hellenbroek asks at this point: Of how many parts doth His human nature consist?

Answer: Of two parts; soul and body.

Should we understand that Christ's soul is actually meant to be His Deity?

No, His Deity did not take the place of His soul.
What was the reason He had to be true God?

Because the human nature alone would not be able to bear the sufferings. He must, therefore, be God to carry the human nature through the infinite wrath of God and also to bring about infinite value to His merits.

Even though His divine nature was indispensible He also had to be true man. This was necessary so that He could suffer and die. A god cannot die and since death was threatened upon sin, the Surety was required to die. This was needed to satisfy the demands of justice.

That is why the two natures of Christ were united into a single Person.

Did the human nature adopt the Divine nature? Or, the Divine the human?

Answer: The Divine nature adopted the human nature.

That is a good answer. The human nature would never have been able to adopt the Divine nature; and why not?

Because He is and remains God. But He took upon Himself that which He did not possess; a true human nature consisting of soul and body.

The human nature would never have been able to sustain the entire burden of the wrath of the Father.

But on the other hand He definitely had to be a human in order to die, because God requires that the debt be paid and punishment be meted out to the same nature in which sin had been committed and by which the law had been broken.

That is why we say, Christ in His Priestly office is not only a Mediator of intercession, that is, only praying for His church, but also is a Mediator of reconciliation, having offered a sacrifice.

What is it He offered up?

Answer: Himself.

And what was the Altar?

His Divine Nature. The Altar is more than the gift and the offering is sanctified through the Altar. So, this is precisely the way His Divine nature brought value to His suffering.

Who can give clear proof from God's Word that those two natures were indeed united in one Person, so that there were not two Persons, but only one Person with two natures?

Cannot one of you tell me? Then I shall try to explain it to you.

When Jesus was in a ship on Lake Gennesaret with His disciples, a terrible storm arose. He slept peacefully on a pillow in the stern of the ship.

It stormed so hard that the disciples became afraid. At first they just let Jesus rest, thinking the storm would let up. But, as time went on and it became worse, they finally called out to Him, "Master, carest thou not that we perish?"

They thought, "It appears the Lord cares not if we all drown."

Now, I believe firmly that (with permission of God) the devil has influence on the elements. That

Hell hound must have thought, "If I can send that little ship to the bottom of the lake with that "Great Foundation" of the church including the twelve "stones" with Him, then I shall be victorious.

You can imagine that the devil placed great priority, during those thirty-three years in which the Mediator, with His two natures, spent here upon earth, frustrating the whole work of salvation, and attempting to annihilate the Son of God or cause Him to sin.

But he was a conquered enemy, so all his rage and fury were for naught.

What is the point I am trying to emphasize with this account?

I want you to understand which of the two natures of Christ slept in the rear of that ship; the divine or the human.

Of course, it was His human nature. If it had been His Divine nature that had slept, the ship would surely have gone to the bottom of the sea. It is eternally impossible for the Deity to sleep, which includes the Father, the Son and the Holy Spirit.

The Holy One of Israel never slumbers.

Has not this Biblical account served to show that there were two natures in one Person? His human nature slept. The Bible tells us that plainly. But it also very definitely shows that He was Divine because the storm and the sea were obedient to Him.

Christ had but one body. Be sure to remember that, because there are many sects having erroneous opinions who are teaching to the contrary. When you become older you will read or hear about the Lutherans who teach: That upon the ascension, divine properties were communicated to the human nature of Christ so that His human nature became omnipresent just as His Divine nature.

Luther continued these errors of the Roman Church. The Roman church believes:

"That the two natures are associatied so closely that they blend into one another and that the human nature had been given so much worthiness and Divine power that it must be prayed to and honored as highly as is the Divine nature."

We reject these opinions on the basis of God's Word and say that Christ is to be prayed to by virtue of His Deity.

If you had paid close attention in church Sunday, you would have observed that our Confession of Faith speaks contrary to the belief of the Roman Catholics and Lutherans. We read the article concerning the two natures of Christ to the congregation. Who can recall which Article it was?

Answer: Article 19.

You have paid good attention. The confession in Article 19 speaks thus:

"We believe that by this conception, the person of the Son is inseparably united and connected with the human nature; so that there are not two Sons of God, nor two persons, but two natures united in one single person; yet, that each nature retains it own distinct properties. As then the divine nature hath always remained uncreated, without beginning of days or end of life, filling heaven and earth; so also hath the human nature not lost its properties, but remained a creature, having beginning of days, being a finite nature, and retaining all the properties of a real body."

(Notice, now how this confession is directly opposed to the Roman position.)

"And though He hath by His resurrection given immortality to the same, nevertheless, He hath not changed the reality of His human nature; forasmuch as our salvation and resurrection also depend on the reality of His body."

So then, boys and girls, remain firm in your belief to this old confession and do not be swayed by all sorts of erroneous opinions.

Pay attention now: I am going to ask you another question: If, since Jesus has two natures, couldn't we just say that He is God-man? Think about this before you answer.

I hear some saying "yes" but there are a few who shake their heads "no".

I am in accord with those who shake their heads "no". Do you know why?

Because it is in error, too. There are some liberals who teach that Christ has simply one nature and not two. They say He has a God-man nature, so that the human nature becomes divine and the divine nature becomes human.

What are the consequences of this error?

They are saying, in holding to this position, that the Son of God would have become a God-man even if the created man had not fallen. They say He, in His position as God-man, had to accomplish a bond between the Creator and the creature.

If this is reasoned out, God is degraded and man is exalted so that the two can bring about Jesus the God-man.

Think about it this way; that you never say, "Jesus is a God-man," because that word denotes a single nature. You should always say that He is God and man; two natures joined in one single Person.

Men will never understand this doctrine perfectly. It must be believed in faith. But, even so, it is not an absurd or an unreasonable doctrine.

It is a mystery far above our natural comprehension, but not adverse to it. It is a Divine mystery which causes God's children, by faith, to sink down in amazement.

I do hope and desire that each one of you may come to realize the necessity that Christ have two natures.

Hellenbroek presents an objection in our lesson: Is then His Godhead not changed into His human nature? It does say in John 1:14, "The Word was made flesh".

He answers, "No; all making is not a change of essence, Galations 3:13, 'Christ is made a curse, but not changed into a curse'."

This is a definite proof. But along with that, I would say that it is so necessary that each one of us have knowledge that He has become a curse for us.

God does not look through His fingers as is so often used in a manner of speech, similar to what a father sometimes does to his naughty child. The curse must definitely be meted out, either upon Christ or upon the sinner. If the Mediator, in His Divine and human nature, has not endured the curse for you, you must bear it yourself and that eternally. That will not be an agreeable experience.

For that reason it is such a great wonder that He was willing to take upon Himself our human nature and thereby fully sustain the curse for such execrable creatures.

Reverently speaking, He is able now, having taken on the human nature, to lay one hand upon the human party and the other upon the Divine party and as a consequence a Holy God and a cursed creature become reconciled. We have reconciliation by satisfaction.

May the Triune God impart this to you in your youth and may this serious but mysterious truth be imparted to you in an experiential way.

Lesson 23

The States of Christ and the Degrees of His Humiliation.

His Humble Birth

Our teacher asks us this afternoon: How many states must we distinguish in Christ?

Answer: Two; a state of humiliation and a state of exaltation.

What is meant by a state?

The word "state" is not to be confused with the word "condition". A person can be in a certain state and at the same time be in various "conditions".

An educated person would say the word "state" is: A lawful position which one might acquire or a phase of existence.

Is each one of us in a "state"?

Answer: Yes, we are in a state of misery.

Exactly; we all live in a state of misery. But has it always been this way? There was a man who wrote a book on the states in which men have existed. Who knows the name of that man and his book?

Answer: Thomas Boston. The name of his book is: Human Nature and its Fourfold State.

That is a good answer. Thomas Boston was a Scottish preacher. He was born in 1676 and died in 1732. He wrote various sound books.

How does he classify this fourfold state?

Answer: 1st, The State of Innocence; or Primitive Integrity in which man was created.

2nd, The State of Nature; or Entire Depravity (through the fall).

3rd, The State of Grace; or, Begun Recovery (for the elect).

4th, The Eternal State; or, State of Consummate Happiness or Misery (after death).

Are all men involved in this fourfold state in its entirety?

No, not all. God did place all men in the first state; in Adam. Men did not enter this first state by themselves; it was through God.

Man did bring himself into the second state, though; he sinned willfully. All men, without exception are in a state of misery.

But do all men come into the third state, which is the state of grace?

Man will never come into this state by himself. God brings only the elect into this state. The others remain in their state of misery during this life.

After death, when the last conversion has taken place, it will be an eternal state of bliss for the children of God, but an eternal state of misery for the others.

God leads His people into three of the four states. Man brought about his own state of misery.

Which state is it that the unconverted never enter?

In the state of grace, or, begun recovery;

consequently, neither do they come to the state of happiness.

We have, actually, diverted somewhat from our subject, because we are not studying the states of man this afternoon but the states of Christ.

We have already answered the first question, namely, that we must distinguish two states in Him: One of humiliation and one of exaltation.

Are we to view His states as being prior to His incarnation or after His incarnation? Think about this.

Answer: After His incarnation.

Right, because He could not experience humility prior to His incarnation. And the state of exaltation had to follow His humiliation.

Were both states positively necessary in the work of redemption?

Answer: Yes, He had to merit salvation in the state of humiliation and He applied it in the state of exaltation.

Now, quickly, who can tell us what the steps of His humiliation were?

Answer: 1st, His humble birth; 2nd, His suffering; 3rd, His death; 4th, His burial; 5th, His descending into hell.

His exaltation follows immediately after His humiliation, so the first step in that state is: His resurection; 2nd, His ascension into heaven; 3rd, His sitting at the right hand of God and 4th, His coming again to judge the living and the dead. Three of the four steps of His exaltation are already experienced and all of the steps of His humiliation are accomplished.

He ascended into heaven after He rose from the dead. He now sits at the right hand of God. He is praying for His people there until the appointed time comes that He shall come again on the clouds for the last judgment.

Because each step is treated separately in our catechism book we shall cease talking about these steps in a general way and spend the rest of this afternoon's session discussing the 1st step of His humiliation namely: His humble birth.

We shall inquire into the historical aspect of Jesus' birth this afternoon. The person who was born was Jesus Christ, the Mediator. We mentioned in previous lessons: He remained what He was, God. But He took upon Himself something he did not previously possess: a real human nature.

Who was His mother?

The virgin Mary; this having been prophesied in Isaiah 7:14, "Behold, a virgin shall conceive, and bear a son, and shall call His name Immanuel."

Tell me again; what does that name mean?

Immanuel signifies: God with us.

That was, surely, an appropriate name for the Mediator. He was one with the Divine Essence from all eternity with the Father and the Holy Spirit and, in that manner, came to men upon earth: God with us.

Each one of you are well acquainted with the story which you hear each year at Christmas time.

It was in the time when Caesar Augustus ruled the Roman empire.

At that time it was an amazingly large empire. It comprised not only Italy but also Greece, Asia and the Northern countries which had been conquered by the Roman army.

Palestine, then, was included in the rule of the Romans. Now Caesar desired to know how many subjects he had in his kingdom and so he issued a decree to all the territories over which he ruled, that all the inhabitants be registered.

Gaius Julius Caesar (this was the real name of Caesar Augustus) gave the order that everyone go to the city from which they had originated to be registered.

It was an exceptional leading of providence that this order be given just at this time. The virgin, who was to give birth to the Messiah, lived in Nazareth and it had been prophesied in the Old Testament that The Messiah was to be born in Bethlehem. How were these two facts going to be reconciled? Nazareth was a long distance away from Bethlehem.

If you have a map of Palestine at home, just figure out how many miles they are apart.

But, what happened there?

Mary and Joseph, the man to whom she was engaged, were both of the lineage of David and were required to go to Bethlehem to be officially recorded. You are well acquainted with the events following. There was no place for Joseph and Mary to stay, so, they found shelter in a stable.

It was exactly the time that the Messiah was to be born. It was so recorded in Luke 2: "She wrapped Him in swaddling clothes, and laid Him in a manger, because there was no room for them in the inn."

Now, you need not think that Joseph and Mary went to that stable because they were a dirty and slovenly type of people; people to whom it mattered not where they spend the night.

Absolutely not. God's Word tells us they were poor people, but they were not dirty people. God's Word never defends filthiness, but does just the opposite.

It was because of the multitude of people who assembled to be registered in Bethlehem that there was no place for them to spend the night in the inn. There was surely no one in all Bethlehem nor amongst the thousands in Palestine, who knew that the Messiah was being born in the manger. Who learned of it first?

Answer: Zacharias, Elisabeth and John the Baptist.

Zacharias and Elisabeth knew it alright because Mary, who was their cousin, had told them she was expecting. John the Baptist was born only a few months previously, consequently he was only a child; so that answer is not correct. But would Zacharias and Elisabeth have known exactly when and where the Messiah was to be born? I don't believe so.

Who was the first to know of it after the birth?

Answer: The shepherds in the field of Ephratah.

Correct. The shepherds were the first to be privileged to see Christ after His birth as a human.

It was a step of humiliation which the Son of God had to undergo to be born from a common poor virgin who was a nobody in the world, and, with all that, born in a stable.

Was it humiliation to the Mediator to have a human nature?

No, that was not the cause for His humiliation, because He took His glorified human nature with Him upon ascending into heaven and still, becoming a human was a humiliation to Him. Paul speaks of this so clearly to the Philippians in chapter 2 verse 8, "And being found in fashion as a man, He humbled Himself, and He became obedient unto death, even the death of the cross."

His humiliation consists in this, that He took upon Him the human nature with all its weaknesses, because He came in the likeness of sinful flesh; not in sin, but for sin, and has condemned sin in the flesh.

His "weaknesses" are meant to be the fact that He had hunger and thirst, He slept and had sorrow just as other men and as mentioned in verse 7, "took upon Him the form of a servant and was made in the likeness of men."

For Him to be the same in all things, (sin excepted), it was necessary to undergo the first step of humiliation which is His humble birth. This had to be in order to come up to the other steps; His suffering, death and burial. That is easily understood, isn't it?

Now Hellenbroek asks: By Whom was He conceived?

Answer: By the power of the Holy Ghost.

The Angel said to Mary, "The Holy Ghost shall come upon thee, and the power of the Highest shall overshadow thee: therefore also that holy thing which shall be born of thee shall be called the Son of God". Luke 1:35.

Why would Hellenbroek ask this question?

Each one of you are old enough to realize that everyone is born out of and by means of human beings. John the Baptist, who was appointed to be an extraordinary man (the forerunner of Christ), had not only a natural mother but also a natural father.

John was a person out of a person and by means of a person.

Was that true of the Lord Jesus too?

No, for if that were true, He would have had original sin just as all children do. He would have been conceived and born in sin, and that could not be.

That is why He was born out of a person, that is, the virgin Mary, but was not conceived by a man.

His human nature involved having a mother but no father.

The Holy Ghost came upon Mary in a way we cannot understand, and with almighty power caused her to be with child which possessed a

Divine nature as well as a human nature. We could explain it further this way: Just as the Father and the Son worked through the Holy Spirit in the creation of the world, They in like manner worked through the Holy Spirit to form the human nature of Christ.

We ought not ever to attempt comprehension of this, because we cannot understand it. We ought only to believe and marvel in this Divine mystery. As you become older you will become aware of the misunderstanding there is in the world regarding the birth of Christ.

That is why the next question asks: Was He also born of her flesh and blood?

Answer: Yes. Gal 4:4 "But when the fulness of time was come, God sent forth His Son, *made of a woman,* etc."

Hellenbroek posed this question because he knew there are people who say that Jesus used Mary's body for His birth, but that He did not acquire any of her flesh and blood and consequently not her true son. They contend that Jesus passed through Mary's body like water passes through a pipe without taking on any of its substance. Don't you ever believe this.

The Holy Spirit, in His infinite knowledge, foresaw that men would refuse to accept Christ's human nature as truth and therefore caused clear counterproof to be written in Holy Scripture concerning that denial. Did you notice that in the text of Galatians 4 which you just recited?

It does not say: "made through a woman" (like water through a pipe) no, it says, "made of a woman".

Now there could be some opposition to that. Might He not have brought His human substance (flesh and blood) from heaven?

No, He first acquired it initially from Mary. Is there someone who can give proof of that from God's Word?

The Holy Spirit directed the pen of the various writers so that not one word is more than is needed or without a meaning. It is plainly written in Luke 1:57 regarding Elizabeth, "And she brought forth a son."

But it is written of Mary in Luke 2:7. "And she brought forth HER Son. The Holy Spirit gives emphasis to that little word "her", pointing out that Jesus was Mary's own son and He had acquired from her his flesh and blood.

The old church fathers were in conflict with these errors too. This can be detected in the confession that (according to historical accounts) Bishop Athanasius authored in defence of the foundations of the truth. Athanasius was the bishop of the great and beautiful city Alexandria. It was the capital city of Egypt. He lived in the time about 300 years after Christ was upon earth.

There were very many heretics in those days who troubled the church with all sorts of false doctrines. In order to defend the established doctrine against the heretic Arius, Athanasius, in the year 333 A.D., set up a "confession of faith" in brief form.

He became the most eminent of the Greek church fathers in the 4th century and his confession continues to be used in the church. It can be found in the book called the "Doctrinal Standards" of our churches.

You ought to concentrate on and learn by heart the articles in the confession that refers to the incarnation of Christ.

Article 29. Furthermore it is necessary to everlasting salvation that we also believe rightly the incarnation of our Lord Jesus Christ. Article 30. For the right faith is that we believe and confess that our Lord Jesus Christ, the Son of God, is God and man. Article 31. God of the substance of the Father, begotten before the worlds; and man of the substance of His mother, born in the world. Article 32. Perfect God and perfect man, of a reasonable soul and human flesh subsisting. Article 33. Equal to the Father as touching His Godhead, and inferior to the Father as touching His manhood. Article 34. Who, although He is God and man, yet He is not two, but one Christ. Article 35. One, not by conversion of the Godhead into flesh, but by taking of the manhood into God. Article 36. One altogether, not by confusion of substance, but by unity of person.

I am very sure that here are some statements too difficult for you to understand, but try to remember the words; God may apply these matters to your personal understanding one day.

It is very profitable and necessary that you

become grounded in these historical truths, but, even if you were able to recite in a very nice way, who was born in Bethlehem, out of whom and through whom, when and under whose reign he was born exactly as it was, you would still not find it to be profitable for your poor soul.

What must take place?

You must obtain a personal saving knowledge of the Mediator and His humble birth. When the Lord quickens the elect sinner, that person becomes aware that there is just as little room in his heart for Jesus as there was room for Him in Bethlehem. He will also experience that life is empty without Jesus and that his soul is in an eternal state of ruin. The situation is the same, then, as it was in Bethlehem. There was no room for Him, but the event took place regardless. He was born; nothing could hinder that.

Mary must surely have thought, "How can this all be accomplished?" It seemed impossible that the prophesies would be fulfilled upon the exact time and place. The closer it came to the time the more impossible it seemed, but: everything was accomplished in its own time.

That is the experience a sinner has too. When he really accepts the fact there is no room for the Mediator in his heart, then that is the exact time that God makes room for Him there. But do you know what happens? The more urgently the Lord works to accomplish this the more strongly the sinner opposes it. This is because he is hostile to salvation by free grace. He constantly tries to make himself suitable in order to be accepted through the Mediator. Therein lies his enmity.

But it is a blessed fact that God rules man. He is the only one that can conquer his people. What is impossible for man, can be accomplished by the love of God. They must come before Him without one plea and in due time will yield all to Him. It is against man's nature to be saved by free grace, but if he is finally subdued and by grace experiences grace, it is a matter of everlasting amazement to him.

What a blessing then, for a young person or an old one, if they are no longer free to do what they are inclined to do. This is because the Lord is holding them securely.

I hope you are one of them, boys and girls. You can be sure that after we die we can no longer hear the proclamation of salvation through the Mediator but it will be too late to be saved anyway.

This is my hope: that you will find it impossible to live without Him and then it will not be necessary to die without Him.

> All glory, might and honor
> Ascribe to God on high;
> His arm protects His people
> Who on His power rely.
> Forth from Thy holy dwelling
> Thy awful glories shine;
> Thou strengthenest Thy people;
> Unending praise be Thine.

Lesson 24

Of His Suffering and Death

Our lesson today on the suffering and death of Christ is still in connection with our study on the "Mediator Of The Covenant".

This lesson is a subdivision of a general subject. Can anyone tell me what it is?

Answer: The States of the Mediator.

Correct. The Mediator is known in His names, offices, natures, states and benefits. We have learned about His two names, His three offices, His two natures and His two states in previous lessons. His states are humiliation and exaltation. Each one of His states have various steps. This afternoon we will be studying about the second and third step of His state of humiliation, namely, His suffering and death.

When you learn your questions and answers of the catechism at home, take notice of the position your lesson has within the main subject. Doing this you will keep a good connection with that which preceeded it.

The first question we have today is: Was it necessary that Christ should suffer?

Answer: Yes, it being foretold in the Old Testament. Isaiah 53:5 "But He was wounded for our transgressions, he was bruised for our iniquities: the chastisement of our peace was upon Him; and with His stripes we are healed."

Should there be distinctions made in Christ's sufferings too? Yes, we could classify them as follows: 1st, The suffering of the body. 2nd, The suffering of the soul.

Who can verify from God's Word that His soul suffered?

Answer: Matt. 26:38 "Then saith He unto them, My soul is exceeding sorrowful, even unto death; tarry here, and watch with me."

And what is there about His suffering in body?

Answer: I Peter 2:24 "Who His own self bare our sins in His own body on the tree."

What would we call the suffering in His body?

The humiliation of His birth. His humiliation began when He was born and continued until He died.

1st, It began with His humble birth in a stable. There was no other place available for Him. Instead of a crib He had to be placed in a manger.

2nd, The painful circumcision on the eighth day. This circumcision served a twofold purpose to prove that He not only was born of a woman but that He was also born under the law. Galatians 4:4.

Being the true Messiah, promised to the patriarchs, He had to have a token of Abraham's seed and consequently had to be circumcised.

3rd, He had to flee into Egypt, though very young, because men sought to kill Him.

4th, Though Joseph and Mary were honorable and decent people their simple circumstances permitted only a poor and humble bringing up for Jesus.

5th, Actually, His enemies continually heaped hatred, scorn, repudiation and persecution upon Him.

6th, At last He was arrested, beaten, mocked, blasphemed, crowned with thorns, condemned and crucified. His hands and feet were pierced with nails, which in itself is a fearful suffering, and then He endured the painful death on the cross. After His death His side was pierced.

Did not Paul have a good reason in writing to the Corinthians: "For you know the grace of our Lord Jesus Christ, that for your sakes He became poor?"

What did Paul mean when he wrote this? Jesus Christ was indeed Lord of lords and King of kings. How could Paul say Jesus was poor? Would he have meant this for His divine nature or for His human nature?

Answer: For His human nature.

That is evident enough isn't it?

This suffering of the body involves His human nature. The divinity of Christ is no more susceptible to suffering than that of the Father or the Holy Ghost.

We have considered a certain amount of the subject regarding the bodily suffering of Christ.

What was involved in the suffering of His soul?

Doesn't anyone know what that was?

Come now, you are to express yourself. There will be no harm if you answer incorrectly.

Answer: Satan tempting Him.

Another answer: In Gethsemane, where an angel strengthened Him.

There are many instances that one could use as examples of Christ's suffering in soul, but the one that involved the heaviest conflict of soul is in His bearing the full burden of the wrath of God.

The Westminister catechism speaks of it this way, "Having also conflicted with the terrors of death, and the powers of darkness felt and borne the weight of God's wrath, He laid down His life an offering for sin, enduring the painful, shameful and cursed death of the cross."

Matthew says, "He began to be sorrowful and very heavy."

Mark: "He began to be sore amazed and to be very heavy and saith unto them, 'My soul is exceeding sorrowful unto death' ".

Luke: "And he was withdrawn from them about a stone's cast, and kneeled down, and prayed, saying, Father, if thou be willing, remove this cup from me: nevertheless, not my will (His sinless though human will) but thine, be done.

And there appeared an angel unto Him from heaven, strengthening Him.

And being in an agony He prayed more earnestly: and His sweat was as it were great drops of blood falling down to the ground."

Was not that an inexpressible suffering? That was the suffering in His soul. A creature would never be able to suffer like that.

His suffering was not just an ordinary suffering of body and this agony of soul was not the strife or conflict of soul experienced by God's people. No, Christ's suffering was the suffering of a surety; a suffering of a mediator which had never been endured before nor after that time, nor ever shall be.

Was it necessary that He endure this for Himself?

No, because He has never uttered anything deceitful. He was completely sinless and undefiled. Why did He suffer then, this being the case?

Answer: He suffered in another's place.

Exactly. He suffered as Surety, that is why it is said, He suffered as a representative, a debt payer, a satisfier of justice and an acquirer of grace and eternal life. He had to undergo this suffering in soul and body, terminating in death, to stand before the Judge in the stead of a guilty people.

It is often called a substitute; a person acting in the place of another.

You are perhaps acquainted with the meaning of a surety in everyday affairs.

Someone purchases a business or a house but does not have enough money to pay the whole amount of the sale. He borrows, for example, fifteen thousand dollars from someone on which he pays interest each year. But the person from whom he borrows this money says: "I will loan you this money if you can provide a good surety; someone who is rich enough to return the amount of the loan if you do not pay." So, a third person is sought who is willing to sign before a Notary that he obligates himself to pay if the debtor does not.

Now, if the affairs of this man do not go well and is unable to pay the interest on the money he borrowed, to whom does the creditor go? To the man to whom he loaned the money, or to the surety?

Answer: to the surety.

To the surety, of course, because he had given his signature that he would pay. The debt is not demanded of the debtor but of the surety. If he does not have ready cash to pay the debt, the business or house is sold.

This is the way it was with the Mediator too, since He had given Himself as a surety and had said "I come to do thy will, O God." He was in this way responsible for the debt which had been incurred by His people.

The Judge does not require satisfaction of the elect but of their Mediator. Therefore Christ had to suffer all that there was to suffer on account of sin.

Do you understand now, that His suffering consisted in being a representative and paying a debt not His own? It was also an act of acquiring grace, because the Judge would not ever, thereafter, require payment from the elect.

The Mediator satisfied in a most perfect way and He did this all alone. The Father does not require a double satisfaction, one from the surety and another from the debtor; no, when restitution is made by the Surety the debtor is forever free.

Hellenbroek asks in question 7, "Is there an absolute atonement made by this satisfaction, or only a possibility of salvation merited?"

Answer: There is an actual, absolute and personal atonement made, 1 John 2:2, "And He is a propitiation for our sins."

He trod the "winepress" of God's wrath all alone. There was no angel or man to help Him in that work.

That is why it is so wicked of some people who say that the suffering and death of Christ merely made it possible for us to be saved and that we must receive the merits of that work by faith and in that way do something ourselves before the meritorious work of Christ can help us. The adherents to the Roman Catholic church believe in only a partial Savior, because they must do all sorts of good works themselves, offering candles and money etc. before they can expect any consideration of the merits of Christ.

But they are in error. The Mediator has made complete satisfaction for the elect. There is nothing left for them to contribute and upon God's appointed time this will be impressed upon the soul. As a consequence they will readily accept the fact that there is nothing more to add. Neither faith, nor prayers, nor good works are needed to complete the merits of Christ. These are simply fruits which flow from His meritorious work.

I shall ask a question now which is not in your regular lesson, "Why was it required that Christ suffer in both soul and body?"

Answer: Because we have sinned in both soul and body.

That is a very good answer. And since He has suffered in both soul and body, His people can be redeemed in both soul and body.

But what is in store for those who are not redeemed? They shall be condemned in soul and body, because they sinned in both.

When will that take place?

Just as soon as an unconverted person dies, his soul enters eternity and his body goes to the grave. When the Day of Judgment comes and God judges the world, all bodies shall be resurrected and rejoined with the soul, the unconverted, to enter hell. God's people, on the other hand, shall go to heaven with soul and body.

Will there not be people with both body and soul in hell before the great resurrection day?

Yes, they are there even now. We read of Korah, Dathan, and Abiram, who stood up in the camp against Moses, that the earth opened her mouth and they went down alive into hell.

These did not die the common death. Their bodies are not resting in the earth. We must believe God's Word; it speaks literally of what happened to them in Numbers 16:29-33, "If these men die the common death of all men, or, if they be visited after the visitation of all men; then the Lord hath not sent me. But if the Lord make a new thing, and the earth open her mouth, and swallow them up, with all that appertain unto them, and they go down quick into the pit; then ye shall understand that these men have provoked the Lord.---------and the ground clave asunder that was under them: And the earth opened her mouth and swallowed them up and -- they and all that appertained to them went down alive into the pit and the earth closed upon them." Was not that a dreadful happening? It is plainly written there that their body and soul is in hell.

You can prove this from Rev. 20:13 too. It states there that the sea gave up the dead which were in it; and death and hell delivered up the dead which were in them. The meaning is this: Every person that ever was born, will be resurrected again in body in the Judgment Day.

No matter where that body rests, whether buried in the earth or drowned in the sea, or having entered Hell alive, God will summon the bodies from those places.

You might be saying, "How is that possible?"

Millions of bodies, of course, have turned to dust, but the Almighty God can restore those bodies to what they were before as easily as He created Adam from a handful of dust, by merely beckoning them.

Do you believe that too?

Are there persons in heaven having both body and soul?

Answer: Yes.

And who are they?

Answer: Elijah ascended into heaven and Enoch was taken away by God, "and he was not." Did you notice what was said? Enoch and Elijah reaped, in actuality, the benefits of those sufferings Christ was yet to undergo. (And those that Christ had experienced in resolve.) He can deliver the soul of His people as easily as He can their body. In sovereign and extraordinary grace, the people of God need not wait until the Judgment Day for their bodies to be glorified.

They may enter in with body as well as soul. Those two examples are exceptions, though. In the ordinary way, according to God's Word, the soul and body of the converted and unconverted alike will be reunited for the first time at the great Judgment Day.

O, what an event that will be! The unconverted will go to eternal torment, but God's people will experience eternal bliss. They will come to salvation with a glorified body through the bodily sufferings of their oldest Brother.

They acknowledge that, righteously, they are worthy of eternal punishment, because they deliberately forsook God spiritually and corporally. For that reason, the mediatorial suffering of the Mediator is inexpressibly meaningful to them!

But, boys and girls, it is also inexpressible what it shall be to be without God spiritually and corporally. It will be a punishment of physical pain, but also of an awareness of God's absence.

I read a chapter in the book of Jeremiah

yesterday wherein he cursed the day he was born. That was a terribly sinful thing for him to do. The Lord definitely brought him into a sense of guilt for it. The prophet was in very great dejection when he did this sin. But God held him accountable and finally this sin was reconciled through the satisfaction of his Surety.

It came to my mind, when I read that, that was done by a child and servant of the Lord here upon earth when he was not close to God, and when God permitted the power of his fallen nature to rise to the surface.

But how will the unconverted fare in eternity, soon, where they are unable and unwilling to do anything else than curse God and the day of their birth, never feeling any guilt for doing so.

I thought, too, about you, children. O, what will the consequences be if Christ's suffering and death have not had an effect upon your soul?

It will be an eternal cursing and slandering of God and each other.

This morning I officiated at the burial of a child only 6 months old. It is not for us to know if that child was converted or unconverted. If it is lost, it is lost deservedly because of original sin. If it is saved, it is saved out of free grace. We may not judge.

Each one of you, though, have reached the age of discretion. When you sin, you are conscious of the fact. You are living under the means of grace in having heard our talk about the suffering of Christ. This is called common grace, and while it is a blessing, it is not sufficient for eternity.

May the appointed time come when you receive saving grace.

I wish sincerely that your precious souls may be cleansed and atoned for in the blood of Christ.

So be it.

Lesson 25

Of His Death and Burial

Before we proceed with the discussion of today's questions, I want to ask you about some of the simpler matters to make sure you have not forgotten what we had spoken about earlier.

Who was the first one on earth to speak about death?

Answer: The Lord.

Correct, and where did this take place?

Answer: In Paradise.

To whom was this spoken?

Answer: To Adam.

And in what connection did He mention this?

Answer: "In the day that thou eatest thereof thou shalt surely die."

But now another matter. Who was the first liar?

Answer: The devil.

And what was the first lie?

266

Answer: "Ye shall not surely die."

Which did man believe?

Answer: The lie.

When was that revealed?

Answer: When Adam became disobedient.

In what was it shown to be a lie?

Answer: In that Adam and all men after him die.

What, then is the real cause of death?

Answer: Sin.

Who perpetrated the sin?

Answer: Man.

Whose fault is it, consequently, that sickness, misery and death came upon us?

Answer: Our own fault.

Well, well; I can observe that all of you do not sleep in catechism class.

Now we must proceed with the questions of our lesson. You have told me that men must die for their sins, but now Hellenbroek asks, "Which death did Christ die?"

Answer: The death of the cross.

How is that possible? Did Christ sin too? Why did He die such an accursed death?

Answer: To redeem us from the curse. Gal. 3:13. "Christ hath redeemed us from the curse of the law, being made a curse for us."

All of you know in the historical sense that Christ the Mediator died for His people and quenched the wrath of God toward His elect. Our lesson this afternoon deals with the historical account of Christ's death, and we shall elaborate upon it.

Was the death of the cross foretold in the Old Testament?

Answer: Yes, in Psalm 22:16, David, being a type of Christ said, "They pierced my hands and my feet," and in verse 18, "They part my garments among them, and cast lots upon my vesture."

The manner in which men would treat the Messiah was foretold precisely.

And who was it that treated Him that way?

You are all acquainted with the fact that the Romans had rule over the Jews during the time Jesus was upon earth. Palestine was subject to the Roman governors.

Now according to God's decree, as recorded in Deuteronomy 21:23, he who is hanged upon a tree dies an accursed death and the body of the offender, whose punishment has been meted out this way, must not remain all night upon the tree. In verse 23 it states: "His body shall not remain all night upon the tree but thou shalt in any wise bury him that day; (for he that is hanged is accursed of God)".

It was a custom among the Jews to stone those who were given the death penalty, but the Romans almost always crucified the condemned. When the time appointed had arrived the Jews were desirous that Christ be crucified and Pontius Pilate surrendered Him to them for that purpose. It was an accursed death, but what was it in addition to that?

In the 2nd place the Son of God had to undergo a scornful and a painful death.

Was it absolutely necessary that He die in this accursed way?

Yes, it was. How would He have been able to free His people who lay under the three-fold curse in any other way? God permitted His death on the cross. It was necessary. There was no alternative. Paul could say in faith to the Galatians (Chapter 3), "Christ hath redeemed us from the curse of the law, being made a curse for us, for it is written, "Cursed is everyone that hangeth on a tree."

Hellenbroek is very brief in this lesson. He covers only a few points in this particular instance and proceeds with the question.

Where was Christ crucified?

Answer: On Mount Golgotha between two murderers.

And what happened on the way while men led Him to that place of crucifixion?

He had to carry His own cross while being led away by soldiers. And as they led Him away, they laid hold upon a man called Simon, a Cyrenian, coming out of the country, and on him they laid the cross, that he might bear it after Jesus.

Some interpret this to mean that the Lord Jesus carried the top of the cross and Simon came behind carrying the bottom of it. It could also be that Simon had to carry the whole thing because Jesus' body was severely wounded in the scourgings. In either case, Christ had to bear the heaviest part of the cross all alone. And, what was that? What weighed the cross down so severely that neither angels nor men could bear up under it?

Answer: The sin of His people and the righteous wrath of His Father.

Did you hear that now? That was the heaviest thing that ever had to be carried. Think about this: The Holy Son of God, in the form of a man, pure and undefiled, fastened to a cross. His holy hands and feet were pierced, He was hung between two murderers, outcasts of society. They had deprived Him of all rights.

Adam, in his state of rectitude, received from his creator: 1st, a civil right. He was a free man and possessed rights to all things here upon earth.

2nd: He possessed a church right and had free access to God.

3rd: He had been given a Divine right to bear the image of God.

But man lost his civil right, his Divine right and church right through sin. Everything is lost. Christ had to endure these losses, too, in order to return those rights to His people.

Under the permission and foreknowledge of God that it all might come to pass, men deprived Him of His citizenship. Everywhere He went they harassed Him saying He had been born "illegitimately". They did not allow Him a church right either. They threw Him out of the temple and synagogue.

They refused to acknowledge His Divine right saying: "You have heard the blashpemy, He maketh Himself God's Son." The Jews did not allow Him a place in heaven nor a place upon earth. What then?

They called out, "Crucify Him, Crucify Him. Away with Him. He claims to be God's Son!" He was brought to Calvary as one accursed, mocked and despised, beaten with a reed, and forced to wear a crown of thorns.

What happened at that time? God the Father indicated with visible signs that He observed what was taking place on Golgotha. Christ hung on the cross for six hours. The first three it remained light, but the last three it was dark.

Was it dark because it was night? No, according to our way of expressing time, He was crucified at 9 o'clock in the morning and it was dark until 3 o'clock in the afternoon. It was not only dark in Jerusalem, but, according to Matthew, "There was darkness over all the land." The sun became so obscured that its light could not be seen for three hours.

Rev. Ridderus, in his explanation of this text, says that the heathen philosophers in Egypt and throughout the world spoke of and wrote about that darkness.

Certain atheists, in opposing God's truth and His Word, say that this incident was a common eclipse of the sun which happens quite often in the Eastern countries. But Ridderus says, "A national eclipse, which occurs when the moon is between the earth and the sun, never comes about in the time of the Jewish Passover because the observance of the Passover is regulated by the full moon. Also, an ordinary darkening of the sun does not effect the whole world at the same time, and especially does not last a full three hours." Therefore, it was an extraordinary token effected from heaven by God at the time of this great event wherein the Son of God died on a cross for the sins of the elect.

But another miracle took place at that time too. Do you know what it was?

After Jesus had been silent during these dark three hours, at the ninth hour, He called out with a loud voice, "My God, My God, why have you forsaken me?"

And a bit later He cried again with a loud voice and gave up the Ghost. He had died. What happened then?

1st. The veil of the temple was torn in two from the top to the bottom.

2nd. The earth trembled.

3rd. The rocks split apart.

4th. Graves were opened.

5th. Many bodies of the saints which slept arose out of their graves.

They were awe inspiring Divine miracles, were they not?

The veil was a magnificiently embroidered curtain which separated the holy of holies. You will remember, that the temple was divided into three parts. First was the court in which all the people were allowed. Then the holy place where the priests and Levites performed their responsibilities. Beyond that was the place of the holy of holies, wherein only the High priest could enter, and that but once a year.

This rugged, expensive tapestry tore from top to bottom right through the center. Was not that a supernatural wonder?

By this the Lord intended to say that Christ by His death had taken away all partitions, and made possible a free access to the Holy of Holies through Him. We have mentioned in the worship services upon occasion that the curtain of God's virtues reached above so high that the perfect angels in heaven were not able to push it aside and it hung so low that the devils in hell also were not able to part it. No, the Divine Mediator was the only one who was able to break down the partition, that is; satisfy God's justice and make reconciliation for our sins. No longer is the oppressive guilt of the elect left unsatisfied.

These miraculous demonstrations were so majestic that the Centurion, who had charge over the 100 soldiers, guarding Jesus, became very afraid and said, "Truly, this was the Son of God."

But just before Jesus died He performed another great miracle. What was it?

Two murderers were being crucified, one on each side of Jesus. They were mean persons. One of them was a wicked mocker, taunting Jesus. Luke says he treated Jesus reproachfully saying, "If thou be Christ, save thyself and us."

This man wanted to be released from his misery. His sins did not trouble him. His only concern was to be taken off that cross.

But the other?

He was ordained to be, by free grace, the "first fruit" of the New Testament Church. He rebuked the mocker saying, "Dost not thou fear God, seeing thou art in the same condemnation? And we indeed justly; for we receive the due reward of our deeds; but this man hath done nothing amiss."

Do you notice what is contained in these words? It is this:

1st. He admonished his neighbor, "Dost thou not fear God?"

2nd. He condemned himself, accepting his guilt, "And we indeed justly."

3rd. He justified God and accepted the punishment, "We receive the due reward of our deeds."

4th. He was convinced that Jesus was without sin and undefiled, because he said, "But this man hath done nothing amiss."

5th. He acknowledged Jesus in His Deity and as King, because he prayed, "Lord, remember me when thou comest into thy kingdom."

Pilate did not have this faith because he said insultingly, "Art thou the King of the Jews?" The characteristics of saving faith were very clear here in this murderer, but it is also clear that his confession could not fulfill his needs. No, he had a need of the Saviour. That is why he said, "Lord, remember me!"

And what was the answer?

The Mediator knew He had taken this murderer to Himself in eternity to be the first-born of the New Testament Church and to take him to His

Father's House. Even here in His death He revealed His love for sinners saying, "Today thou shalt be with me in Paradise."

That must have been a momentous experience for that young man! He would no longer have a desire to be removed from that cross alive! There was a far better life prepared for him. His sun of salvation began to appear.

When He had spoken this to the murderer, He called out yet further, "Father, into Thy hands I commend My Spirit." Having said thus, He gave up the ghost.

An ordinary person bows his head after death comes and his body collapses or becomes rigid. But Christ had Divine authority over death and, only to the extent He allowed it, death had power over Him. It is for that reason He bowed His head first and then gave up the spirit.

Who can tell me where Christ's soul went after He died? Did it just hover over the face of the earth, or was His soul in the grave with His body?

No, as soon as He gave up the ghost, His soul entered into Heaven. He had said, "Today thou shalt be with Me in Paradise." His body, however, was placed in Joseph's grave. It had not yet gone to the Heavenly Paradise. What about His Divine nature; where did it go?

His Divine nature is everywhere present (omnipresent). It had not been separated from His soul nor His body.

What else took place after He had died but before

He was placed in the grave?

Men pierced His side with a spear. It was common practice amongst the Romans to break the legs of a person who was crucified before he was removed from the cross. This was to make certain he was really dead. But the Divine Being did not intend that this should happen to the Mediator. That is why it had been prophesied "A bone shall not be broken." And in order that the word would be accomplished that was spoken in Zechariah 12:10 "And they shall look upon Me whom they have pierced." His side was pierced. Blood and water gushed out of His body which served to prove He was not merely unconscious but had actually died!

The shed blood was a symbol of justification of all the sins of the Church and the water a symbol of it's sanctification.

So, He *lived* to be a surety for the Church, but He also *died* as a surety for them.

What happened after that?

When Jesus died on that Friday prior to the Easter Sabbath, Joseph of Arimathea, an honorable senator (who had not at all consented to the wicked decision of his fellows to kill Jesus), went to Pilate for permission to remove the body of Jesus from the cross.

Pilate gave his consent, so Joseph wrapped the pierced body in fine linen and laid it in a new tomb which he had hewn out of rock in his garden.

The "Rock" was interred in a rock.

Boys and girls, our lesson time is about gone. We

276

must discontinue our talk on this very serious subject.

It is my wish that you may experience in your young life how the Son of God, the eternal "Rock of life", met the devil head-on in his most secure fort, conquered and annihilated him.

He had to be entombed in order to prove that He had actually died, to show that His death was not a fictitious story.

Only by dying could He conquer in death!

It was on the cross and in the grave that He conquered the devil, sin, death and hell in order to recover His people from them!

For that reason you definitely must come to know during your life time whether He has borne the curse for you, because, if He has not done this, you must bear it yourself eternally. There is no other way!

Because of sin there is a Divine curse upon us, separating us from Christ. Everything we do or neglect to do is cursed. All our activities: worship, labors, speaking, hearing, eating, drinking, sleeping, our entire existence, outside of Christ, is cursed in God's sight. In addition, if we should die without Christ, our coffin and grave are also cursed. This means we shall curse God eternally. There is no alternative. The Lord Himself speaks of this in John 3:36, "And he that believeth not the Son shall not see life; but the wrath of God abideth on him."

So may you obtain profit in the death of the Mediator, children, and become aware of the need of finding shelter in Him from the tempest of God's justice and the flood of God's wrath.

May there be a time when you can no longer live in sin.

Would you care to see how terrible sin is in God's sight? Go, then, to Gethsemane and Golgotha and see what God's Son had to suffer on account of sin! God can not overlook any sin. The very last "penny" had to be paid toward satisfying God's justice.

In the deepest abandonment Christ cried out: " My God, My God, why hast thou forsaken me?" It was not a cry of complete despair, no, He said, "My God". But even so, these words indicate an indescribably deep suffering that Christ was able to bear in His Divine nature.

May you come to hate and forsake sin as sin, in order to be completely delivered from sin and its curse through Christ's suffering and death.

So be it.

278

Lesson 26

Of His Descending Into Hell

Last week you learned a few questions in connection with the lesson of His descending into hell. Before we enter into the questions concerning "His Satisfaction", we shall explain last week's lesson a little further.

If you had not had the advantage of learning the questions of this lesson, and I would ask: "What does Jesus' descending into hell consist of: did it involve His soul and body or just one or the other", what would be your answer:

Be careful to answer honestly. What are your thoughts in the matter?

Some are of the opinion He was not there personally, others think only His soul was there. But what does Hellenbroek say about this?

What is meant by His descending into hell?

Answer: That He suffered the agonies of hell in His soul.

When did He suffer them:

Particularly in the garden of Gethsemane, and on the cross, where He spoke out in anguish: "My soul is exceeding sorrowful, even unto death." On the cross He said, "My God, My God, why hast Thou forsaken Me?"

So He actually did suffer the agonies of hell, but He was not there personally. This is evident because even while He was dead His body was in the grave and His soul in heaven.

His descension into hell had taken place prior to His death during the suffering of His body.

Last week we had said, the sense of abandonment while in the garden was so extreme, that He had to call out, "Father, if it is possible, let this cup pass from me." The suffering of the anguish of soul was so great that His sweat was as great drops of blood.

He felt the full burden of wrath upon Him. The agonies of hell were so great that an angel of heaven came to strengthen Him, whose coming meant to say, "Keep courage, only a short time more and all will be completed and Thou, eternal Son of God, shalt have conquered all."

Yet while in the greatest anguish He cried out, "Father", and even on the cross, where God's abandonment of Him had reached its extremity, He still said, "My God."

It was not a case of hopelessness, no, one who is in despair and desperation would tend to cry out, "O God, I am forsaken; abandoned." But Christ did not express it that way. He only spoke out in distress, "My God, why hast Thou forsaken me?"

His people have earned hell as their just punishment. For that reason He had to suffer agonies of hell, to deliver them from it. He had to experience suffering of soul because we have sinned in our soul.

Never minimize the suffering of the soul of the Mediator! There is not a creature that could ever measure what was involved when the Divine Mediator cried out: "My soul is exceeding sorrowful, even unto death!"

The justice of God demands two things: Not only obedience to the law, but also suffering punishment.

His descension into hell, His death and burial were the final steps in the state of His humiliation in which He must accomplish these two matters.

On seven different occasions upon the cross He spoke certain sayings; who can recite these seven "Words of the cross?"

Many have raised their hands, come, let us hear them:

1st. "Father forgive them, for they know not what they do."

2nd. To Mary, "Woman, behold thy Son." To John, "Behold, thy mother!"

3rd. "Verily, I say unto thee, Today shalt thou be with Me in Paradise."

4th. "My God, My God, why hast Thou forsaken Me?"

5th. "I thirst."

6th. "It is finished."

7th. "Father into Thy hands I commend My Spirit."

Did all of you hear that? These are the words spoken by the Mediator while hanging on the cross. It was light for three hours and then there was darkness for three hours. At the end of the three hours of darkness the great Prince of Life called out, "I thirst." For what did He thirst? As a human with a tortured body, Christ thirsted for water; as God He thirsted for justice, and as Mediator He thirsted for the salvation of His people.

Near the end of His life as a human being, Jesus, knowing that Scripture was completely fulfilled, said, "It is finished." The entire matter of deliverance had been accomplished.

In what sense was it finished?

1st. It was finished for God the Father who required it as judge.

2nd. It was finished through the Son. The demand was made of Him as Mediator and He brought it to a satisfactory conclusion.

3rd. It was finished for the Church of God, the elect, whom it concerned and for whom it had to be finished, the debt paid and the right to eternal life wrought out.

We mentioned in the previous lesson that the murderer acknowledged that Jesus was King. He said, "Remember me when Thou comest into Thy kingdom." But the kingly authority of the Mediator is much more clearly revealed in the last words Jesus spoke upon the cross. He released His soul from His body with these words: "Father, into Thy hands I commend My Spirit."

Stephen had said, "Lord Jesus, receive my spirit."

But Christ died in a royal manner and commended His spirit, that is, his soul, into the hands of His father, where it would be kept in safety as in a treasury, from which He would take possession of it again.

The Divine Majesty was now perfectly appeased. The darkness and the earthquakes vanished. God had been satisfied through God, and God was reconciled with the church through God! Obedience had been demanded and the Mediator met those demands. It was required that the punishment for sin be sustained and the punishment for sin was sustained. It was finished! The Holy Divine head was bowed down. He gave up the ghost.

Now, I shall ask you a question; listen to me, boys:

If a person were able to live without sin continuously from his birth to eighty or one-hundred years of age, living each day sincerely, praying, reading God's Word and performing His will, should not God allow eternal life to such a person after his death?

I think it would not be necessary for Christ to suffer and die for a person who could keep from sin during his whole lifetime, would you? I see many of you are shaking your heads in disagreement with me, so you must explain to me, why Christ must necessarily die for such a person before he could receive eternal life.

Answer: A person is born with original sin. That is the reason. If it were possible for a person to live perfectly (it is impossible, naturally) all his life, then it would still not be possible to be saved.

If we, in Adam, had kept God's command, it would not have been necessary for a Mediator to have been upon earth, and we could have received eternal life for that obedience; but it is impossible now.

And do you know who are best acquainted with this matter?

Those who know this best of all are those persons who have been uncovered by the Holy Ghost sometime during their life. When a person such as this, be he young or old, is brought to a standstill in his life, and becomes aware that he has sinned, he begins to sigh, to pray, to do good works and attend church, and to live differently than he had before, and he tries in every way to become converted. Sometimes this goes along quite successfully in his opinion, until God reveals unto him where he actually stands in respect to his relationship with Adam.

O, then he becomes aware that he has not been created in the state in which he finds himself now with an evil heart, but perfect and according to God's image.

All those who are made aware of this, cry out, "even if I had never sinned from my birth, I shall be lost, and that justly, because I am inherently lost. From Adam's estate I have received nothing but sin."

All efforts and church attendance for the purpose of being saved are discontinued. The knife of God's righteousness cuts right down the middle of our own arrangements in order to dispose of them completely. Everyone must personally become an Adam in God's Holy sight. Then he becomes aware of the necessity of the Lord's suffering in anguish of soul and he sees He affected the satisfaction of God's justice all alone.

I am very sure that if this happens to anyone of you this evening, you will call out, "I am lost, and that righteously, and if I die in this condition I shall be eternally lost, and that righteously." Then a little religion and conviction won't do.

It is a great thing if a person may concur or bow before Divine justice in his life, but to embrace justice is still another matter and it is necessary for everyone to do so.

The Mediator also had to go further than the garden where He voluntarily agreed to drink of the cup. The Father did not say in Gethsemane, "It is now enough, I see you are willing." No, he had to continue to Golgotha, to the cross and to the accursed death. And because He suffered the full extent of the punishment He was able to free His own people from punishment.

Boys and girls, think about this; if the Mediator has not suffered these hellish agonies for you, it will be necessary for you to suffer them yourself eternally. What a terrible thing that will be! When the Lord Jesus died His body went to the grave and His soul went to His Father. When God's children die, their bodies also go to the grave and their soul goes to God in heaven. But what happens when an unconverted person dies? Yes, his body does go to the grave too; but his soul?

If you had to die here in this moment, or, if you should be stricken dead in an accident as you leave the catechism class, where would your precious souls go?

They cannot remain here upon earth, and are not permitted in heaven; what is there left for them?

Nothing but that dreadful place, which in God's Word is described as a habitation for devils, the "Tophet" the place for condemned people and angels.

I hope and pray that you never come there, but, O, little children, I cannot emphasize it enough that, if you die unconverted, you shall surely go there and you shall say, "The half was not told me in the catechism class."

The anguish of hell was borne by the Mediator, suffering in His soul for the sins of the elect. And, if He, who possessed a Divine and perfect human nature had to cry out, "O, My Father, if it be possible, let this cup pass from Me," what will it be for the creatures who must enter into that place?

Not one drop of favor shall fall there because God is not there. Favor exists only where God is present.

His eternal and righteous wrath shall burn upon the open conscience, which shall accuse and condemn sinners unceasingly.

Wouldn't it be worth all the world to attain the knowledge while we are still living that the

Mediator has suffered the agonies of hell for us? What do you think?

May the Lord make the priceless work of redemption in all its aspects precious to you. You are still very young, but not too young to receive a new heart. I am very sure if that may come to pass, the suffering of Christ will be worth more to you than a world full of gold.

May the Lord in His sovereign grace grant that each one of you may personally be able to give testimony of what we have been discussing.

So be it.

Lesson 27

Of His Satisfaction

We shall, with God' direction, proceed a little further this afternoon in our catechism.

We have advanced in a gradually moderate sort of way through the various steps of humiliation that the Lord suffered and come now to the purpose of this humiliation. If one would carefully consider this lesson on His humble birth, His suffering, His death, His burial and descent into hell, we could approach Rev. Hellenbroek with, "Sir, you have written a lesson each to those subjects but what are your intentions with this?"

"Wait," he would say, "I'll show you what my intentions are:

I am going to entitle my lesson:

6. Of the end of His humiliation: His satisfaction."

That is the real essence of the matter. Did you think that the Mediator experienced all these various steps in vain? No, He had a magnificent and Divine purpose in all this, and this was: His Satisfaction.

Was this satisfaction absolutely necessary?

Yes, because without it, reconciliation would be impossible. It is as I mentioned in the pulpit yesterday. By the way, who remembers what we preached about yesterday afternoon?

Answer: Lord's Day 5, question 12.

You have a good memory. What did the instructor have to say there?

He didn't ask: "Is there any salvation for me?"

No, his question is - -

"Is there no way by which we may escape that punishment, and, be again received into favor?"

And his answer is not, "Just believe in the Lord Jesus and everything will be allright, no, far from it. The Heidelberg instructor sends his bared sword right down the middle, and says, "God will have His justice satisfied."

Casper Olevianus and Zacharias Ursinus didn't do like men in our time usually do, namely, immediately present the Lord Jesus, but they gave precedence to the truth that God's righteousness must be satisfied.

Hellenbroek is, then, not so far in error after all to write one whole lesson in the catechism book on "Satisfaction".

That is why he asks in the first question: "Hath Christ by His humiliation also satisfied divine justice?"

Answer: Yes, Isaiah 53:4, "Surely He hath borne our grief and carried our sorrows; yet we did esteem Him stricken, smitten of God and afflicted." It is very clear in this text that He made satisfaction, but *wherein* does this satisfaction consist?

Answer: It consists in two parts: (1) In obeying the law; (2) In suffering punishment. Neither one of these is effective without the other; both had to take place. Obedience to the law was as necessary as suffering punishment in making satisfaction. Paul speaks of this in Romans 5:19, "For as by one man's disobedience many were made sinners, so by the obedience of one shall many be made righteous."

Likewise suffering punishment was as necessary as obedience to the law. It also had a place in making satisfaction. Isaiah 53:5 "But He was wounded for our transgressions; He was bruised for our iniquities; the chastisement of our peace was upon Him; and with His stripes we are healed."

Even so, suffering punishment in itself was not enough to make satisfaction. Suffering punishment can serve to free His people of punishment but gives no right to eternal life. Eternal life was promised only by keeping of the law. "Do this, and thou shalt live." Luke 10:28. He, consequently, had to do both; keep the law perfectly and suffer punishment.

289

Could it be demonstrated at all that God the Father acquitted Christ upon His having been obedient to the whole law?

Christ actually accomplished that in Gethsemane but was still not acquitted. Satisfaction had not been perfected; there was more to be accomplished. He would soon bring complete satisfaction upon the cross. He suffered punishment to the highest degree, because He loved His own, and He loved them to the end. He died and was entombed in a cave dug into a rock; this being sealed by a huge stone, while guards stood at watch all around it.

But did He remain in the grave? No, death and the grave were not able to keep Him. Why not?

Well, He had accomplished both parts of the satisfaction perfectly, and if He had remained in the grave it would have indicated that only half of the work had been done.

The resurrection was proof that the satisfaction had been accepted by God the Father. If the Father had not accepted this, the Son would not have been declared free and He would not have raised Him from the dead. Later, when you go about in the world always listen:

1st. Whether men teach our total depravity in Adam, as is Biblical, but also; 2nd, whether men are genuinely sound in both aspects of the satisfaction of Christ. Don't believe anyone who would say, we can do with less and that we need not preach the strict necessity of His satisfaction.

Hellenbroek was convinced of it. He asks in the

6th question: "Was satisfaction necessary?" His answer is, "Yes, (1) By reason of God's justice, which admits of no remission of sins without punishment or satisfaction, (2) by reason of his truth, having thus expressly declared Himself.

We were taught in the lesson on God's attributes that righteousness is God Himself. When that Divine Righteousness was offended by man's sin, God Himself was also offended. It is just as impossible for a Holy God to let sin go unpunished as it is for Him to sin. If He were to forgive sins without punishment, or overlook sin, so to speak, He would deny His righteousness which is the same as denying Himself and that is eternally impossible.

There is a peculiar question in our lesson. I refer to the 7th question:

Is there an absolute atonement made by this satisfaction, or only a possibility of salvation merited? His answer is not doubtful, but very firm: "There is an actual, absolute and personal atonement made, I John 2:2 "And He is a propitiation for our sins."

Who can prove that?

Answer: 2 Cor. 5:19, "God was in Christ, reconciling the world unto Himself, not imputing their trespasses unto them." Paul doesn't say: "God, in Christ, has possibly been reconciled!" No, He was satisfied completely and definitely.

Why would Hellenbroek have asked this question?

Because, even in those times, there were people who taught that man had fallen but had retained a free will, nevertheless.

It is true, they say, that Jesus came upon earth to suffer and die. Jesus has, in so doing, opened a way that everyone can be saved. But salvation is determined by the free will of man himself. It is his own fault if he does not make use of that which the Lord Jesus made possible.

In other words, the application of the work of redemption is the responsibility of man; he can accept or reject it. Hellenbroek was aware too, of this doctrine taught by Socinius, and for that reason asked this question.

But, boys and girls, please be warned, it is a cursed speculation or theory of his, because it salvages something for man and belittles the work of the Mediator.

What does it salvage for man?

A free will to accept the merits of Christ.

And in what way do these Socinians discredit Christ? They show him to be an incomplete, impersonal and imperfect Savior; one who is not absolute.

Christ not merely makes possible but has earned salvation in its entirety for His own, knowing each one by name.

Would Christ have made satisfaction for everyone?

No, only for the elect. Be careful, then, that you do not believe in false doctrines such as these. It is a difficult natter sometimes for some people to prove from the Bible that Christ had not died for everyone. For example, 2 Cor. 5:15 reads, "And that He died for all!" and the text just mentioned, "God was in Christ reconciling the world unto Himself."

How is this properly understood?

When you become older you must read the exposition of Lord's Day 7 by Dr. Comrie. He handles this matter in great detail. This is what he says about it:

"Since there are many evidences that all men are not saved, would anyone dare to propose that Christ shed His precious blood for those who are now in condemnation? Would He have died in vain for all these people or are His merits, for some of them, worthless? No one would be so foolish as to think that God is not mighty enough to redeem them who had been redeemed by the blood of Christ. There is but one conclusion to make from this erroneous doctrine; and that is, God punishes some people twice for the same sin: first He punishes Christ who had died for a certain person and then again punishes the person himself by condemning him."

It is evident enough that Christ did not die for everyone for if He had all men would be saved.

But how are those texts to be understood that say that Christ died for all people?

It is very easy to explain. Where it reads in Titus 2:11, "For the grace of God that bringeth salvation hath appeared to all men," does not say, "Is applied or accepted by all men."

Well then, it has appeared or been published to all men, because God has commanded the gospel to be preached to the whole world. And where it is written, "And all things are of God, who hath reconciled us to Himself by Jesus Christ," it is very plain that it means the world of the elect.

Out of incomprehensible, sovereign love, He has chosen a determinate number, of whom He often speaks in His Word and for whom a ransom had been delivered. The angel spoke of these to Joseph concerning Mary in Matt. 1:21, "And she shall bring forth a son, and thou shalt call His name Jesus; for He shall save His people (thus not all people) from their sins."

In John 10:11 He calls them "His sheep." And in Acts 20 they are referred to as the "church of God." God's Word often makes a clear distinction between people and people. Even the Lord Jesus says in John 17:9, "I pray for them; I pray not for the world, but for them which Thou hast given Me."

What is the result of this satisfaction for them? What are the benefits of it?

1st. God is now reconciled with the elect sinner.

2nd. The sinner receives the right to life.

These are the two consequences.

Being reconciled is not the same as having a right to eternal life. I hope you understand the difference.

A typical example from life can make it easy to understand that Christ's satisfaction consists of two distinct parts.

Take this case: There is a person who once was extremely rich but because of certain circumstances became utterly poor, and not only poor, but in addition had an amazing amount of debt. It was so bad that his creditors eventually had to bring him to court and since he had nothing with which to pay, he was committed to prison.

There he sat, without a single ray of hope of ever being released, because he had nothing with which he could satisfy those to whom he owed money. But what happened? Along came a very rich man, who loved the debtor. Without the poor man knowing it, his great debt was paid. As a consequence, of course, the judge could no longer keep him in prison. All his debts were wiped away and he was a free man.

What is he considered now, in his circumstance of discharge, standing outside of prison? A free man and one completely free of debt. This is true, but what other fact is to be considered?

He is still very poor, having not one penny on which to live or to look forward to for support. If that rich friend gave him no second sum of money with which to buy bread, he would still perish in spite of the fact that he has no debts. There is no question about that, is there?

That is the way it is in Christ's work of satisfaction, too. We were promised eternal life upon our keeping the law, otherwise we can have no part in it. When we sinned, eternal life expired for us. It could not be given to us because we had broken the law. Instead, we now receive punishment for the act of sin.

Do you understand now that there are two circumstances involved? If the Mediator had suffered punishment only for sin that had been committed, God the Father (reverently speaking) could not condemn the elect to eternal punishment, because the punishment had been borne by their Surety and God's righteousness would allow it to be punished but once. They need not inhabit hell, then, after they die.

But could God allow them to come to heaven? No, not there either, because eternal life (in heaven) was promised only upon obedience to the law. It would be contrary to His righteousness to take them into heaven.

What is the result of this? They cannot go to hell because punishment had already been borne, but they cannot go to heaven either because the law had not been satisfied. Was it necessary, then when they died, to hover about between heaven, hell and the earth? That is impossible because God's Word speaks of only two places, hell or heaven. That is why Christ had to suffer punishment; to free them of punishment; but He also, secondly, had to fulfill the law in order to return eternal bliss unto them. Just as in our example, the rich man, besides paying the debt, must also give a second amount of money so that the poor man could have the necessities of life.

Our lesson finishes with the question: Has everyone grounds to believe that Christ has satisfied for him?

Answer: No, but only those who accept Christ as the meriting, working, effecting, and exemplary cause of their spiritual life.

What is really the essential fact in all this for us, children?

That we have every detail of this instruction applied spiritually to our souls by the Holy Spirit.

Our lesson time is about gone and we must bring our instruction to a close. Perhaps while you were memorizing these long questions and answers this week, you said to yourself, "What a boring lesson this week. It is a good thing the lesson is much shorter next week." This is about what you thought, isn't it?

Don't try to make yourself more pious than you are. The Lord is able to see within our hearts anyway! However, what a blessing it would be if the satisfaction of Christ became the most valuable possession we could have in this world. It is the only way through which God can accept us.

You are 12, 13, 14 years of age and even older, but has not sin become a burden to you? Perhaps your thoughts are: "Dominie, we are not that old yet!"

I once spoke to a boy who was 10 years old when God converted him.

My words to him were something like this, "My boy, you are but 10 years old, that is still so very young; wouldn't you desire to participate in worldly pleasures for a few more years?"

"Oh, no," he said, "It was not my desire then and still is not. I realized I had lived without God for 10

297

years and had sinned against Him. It had been ten years too long."

I am sure if this happened to you, you would have expressed the same feelings.

Last week when we discussed the agonies that will be experienced in hell we said, "We mentioned that if you should die unconverted you will then agree I had not exaggerated at all." In words of human limitations I want to give you an impression how fearful a lot that will be. If, by way of an example, you were in hell for five minutes you would call out, "It is impossible to remain here," and yet it will be for eternity. It is impossible to bear and yet the full weight of God's wrath must be borne. There will be the unquenched anger, the eternal despair, without one moment's relief in company with other wretched creatures and devils. There God will be cursed with a cursed body and soul.

Oh, we are but a candle light in a small part of God's church here upon earth in these dark days, but children, I must not neglect to warn you each week. We fail in our duty too much as it is.

The Lord expects us to be a guard over your soul, but he shall require an account from us too, how we have dealt with your souls.

I stand before you now and look at you, and you look at me, but soon we shall stand before God's judgment seat. Would you dare to look at the Lord in the condition in which you are now? No, that would be impossible, but then it shall be as in Luke

30, "--mountains, fall on us; and to the hills, cover us!" But then it will be too late. Then those who stand on His left side will be swept away by His consuming wrath. "Before their face the people shall be much pained; all faces shall gather blackness." Joel 2:6. Everything shall stand still and rigid because of the exceeding wrath of the Almighty.

Oh, then you will not laugh and mock, boys! You will not be concerned about pretty clothes or "going out", young ladies!

Just as there will be no sorrow and pain among those standing on His right hand, there will be no joy or gladness for the others.

Last week our lesson brought to our attention that the Mediator hung upon the cross for three hours. The whole earth quaked as if in delivery when the great King of heaven and earth went to that cursed tree, defied the agonies of hell and subjected Himself to death.

And we, who are deserving of eternal darkness are yet permitted here in the light of day. Wouldn't it be just and righteous if He removed all light from us? Light as we experience it each day, spiritual light and eternal light? God's people particularly can and are privileged to enjoy the light of day and the world in general and are allowed to partake of this benefit of Christ only because Christ subjected Himself to darkness.

Hasn't the fact, that you opened your eyes in the morning, beholding the light of a new day, been a wonderful experience to you, boys and girls?

It is only because of the merits of Christ in behalf of His elect that there is not absence of light eternally for soul and body. The benefits that the unconverted share now will last only to death and then it will become and continue to be darkness eternally. It shall be and remain to be light eternally without a shadow of darkness anymore for the despised and mocked people of God.

May the Lord bless these truths, which have been spoken in much weakness to the salvation of your precious immortal souls.

Psalter No. 67:1

 Lord, to me Thy ways make known,
  Guide in truth and teach Thou me;
 Thou my Savior art alone,
  All the day I wait for Thee.

Lesson 28

Of His Resurrection

The 1st Step in His Exaltation

Having studied the state of Christ's humiliation, we now enter the lessons on the state of Christ's exaltation. How many steps are there in this state to which we must give our attention?

Answer: 4 steps: 1st, His resurrection from the dead. 2nd, His ascension to heaven,; 3rd, His sitting at the right hand of the Father; 4th, His coming again to judge the world.

We have studied and are to be discussing this afternoon the first step, namely, His resurrection.

We can read of several resurrections in God's Word. Who can recall a few of them? We shall proceed leisurely in our lesson today enumerating some of them, beginning with those in the Old Testament.

1st. We read of a resurrection of a community. When Israel was carried away to Babylon because of her sins and apostasy, she was, by way of speaking, buried alive in that strange land. But upon the appointed time the Lord spoke these words in Ezekiel 37:12 - "Behold, O My people, I will open your graves, and cause you to come up out of your graves, and bring you into the land of Israel."

This actually took place. The Israelites had served strange gods many years, but then experienced a reformation, as in the time of King Josiah. This is understood to be a communal or ecclesiastical resurrection.

2nd. In the Old Testament there are recordings of extraordinary (very unusual) resurrections. Elijah and Elisha, as means in God's hands, were used to resurrect to life some who had died.

We read in the New Testament that God raised some people from the dead through Jesus Christ and His disciples.

3rd. There is a spiritual resurrection, as when a person is converted. Because of man's first disobedience he is involved in a three-fold death. He must be brought from this dead state to a new life. This is a spiritual resurrection.

4th. When the appointed time arrives, at the last day, there will be a universal resurrection. Everyone who has died since Adam's time, shall by God's power and at His command be made alive again. This is called the great or last resurrection in the day of judgment. Anyone can read of these resurrections in God's Word, so you see I am not telling you fictitious stories.

But, are we considering in our lesson today the resurrection of the son of the widow of Zarephath?

Answer: No.

About the resurrection of Lazarus?

Answer: No.

About the resurrection to take place on the day of judgment?

No, not about that one either. Is there another one besides those we have mentioned?

Yes, there is still a:

5th: A resurrection of a Surety.

If this resurrection had not taken place which had first been Divinely decreed in eternity and performed at the appointed time, these other resurrections would never have taken place. The resurrection of the Mediator (as Surety) is the foundation or basis of all the other resurrections.

The first question in our lesson is: Was the resurrection of Christ necessary?

Answer: Yes, it was foretold in Psalm 16:10, where David, led by the Spirit, prophesied of the Messiah: "For thou wilt not leave my soul in hell; neither wilt thou suffer thine Holy One to see corruption."

In the first place, Christ had to be raised from the dead that the prophesy of the Scripture be fulfilled. But was there still another reason why He must be raised from the dead? What advantage would there be in His resurrection? Actually, I gave a very brief answer to this question last week. I would like to find out whether you took notice of it.

It was definitely necessary that He die on the cross. If He had not, He could not have satisfied His Father's justice. But what necessity would there be for His resurrection? He had already called out, "It is finished."

The Apostle Paul gives a very distinct answer to this question for us in Romans 4:25, where he says,

303

"Who was delivered for our offences, and was raised again for our justification."

For what reason had He died?

Answer: For the sins of His people.

But why was it necessary for Him to be "raised"? Just as the Father expressed satisfaction in the work of His Son by the resurrection, at the same time this satisfaction (of His justice) made it possible for the elect to be justified or set free. That is why it is written, "Raised again for our justification," which is to say, "that we may be justifed."

If the Mediator had remained in the grave how could the Church have known that their sins had been requited? There would not have been any evidence that their debt of sin had been paid. The eleven disciples, the women, and the men from Emmaus would have been in a state of discouragement until death. They had actually seen the corpse of Jesus being carried to the grave and consequently all their hope in Him had been for nought. But, He is alive and has risen from the grave.

"For in that He died, He died unto sin once: but in that He liveth, He liveth unto God!"

Peter said in effect, that it is impossible that He could be kept from death. Christ destroyed death and completely conquered it by dying and rising from the dead.

And what else has He conquered by His resurrection? Is someone able to tell me?

1st. The devil who was His prime enemy.

2nd. Sin which was the reason for His death.

3rd. Death itself which is the result of sin.

4th. The world which loves sin.

5th. Hell, the habitation of the devil.

We could list many more but remember these as the principal ones.

The resurrection of Christ is the grand proof that God the Father's justice was satisfied, because if it had not been, He would not have ever been raised from the grave.

We mentioned last week (but are now repeating in order to imprint it upon your memory) that: In eternity Christ concurred in the need for the Father's satisfaction. It is written, --"Lo, I come---I delight to do thy will, O My God." He submitted to that justice in Gethsemane: "Not as I will, but as Thou wilt." But the judge would not release Christ in His concurrence or submission to that justice. Performance was required to bring it to its fulfillment. He had to "empty the cup" completely.

He then became obedient even to the extent of dying, yes, the death of the cross. He died under the Holy justice of the Father.

Do you suppose that the Father would have raised Him from death if He was then yet not satisfied?

Definitely not. You can be sure of that. The judge could not be content in accepting only a part of the work. But now that He was satisfied and could require no more righteousness (speaking reverently now) it would have been unrighteous if the

Surety (Christ) had not been discharged of His obligation. For that reason He had been "raised again for our justification."

Now we shall consider the second question:

What certainty have we that He is risen?

Answer: Ist. The testimony of angels and watchmen; 2nd, The numerous appearances of the Lord Jesus to the women and the disciples.

There were two types of people when Jesus was upon earth, just as there are today.

There were people who were enemies of Jesus (just as we are now by nature) and there were also a few who, by grace, were loyal to Him.

When He was placed in the tomb, the hostile Jews sealed the boulder into the opening of the tomb and set watchmen for positive security. People would be inclined to think, "The events in the life of Jesus the Nazarene upon this earth are definitely ended."

In spite of the fact, that the hostile Jews and watchmen were glad to be rid of Him, there were a few who sorrowed in the loss of Him. There were a few women, who, very early in the morning after the Sabbath, went to the cemetery of Joseph, the place of the new grave. The gospel says, "And very early in the morning the first day of the week, they came unto the sepulchre at the rising of the sun." It was that early.

While they were going the day began to dawn, and when they arrived at the tomb the sun was above the horizon.

Why were these women so hasty to get to the grave of Jesus? Well, in the Eastern countries it was the custom to anoint the bodies of their beloved deceased with all sorts of spices which gave the bodies a pleasant odor and checked the process of decay. It was for this reason that these women prepared ointments from all sorts of spices in order to anoint the body of Jesus. As soon as the Sabbath was past they went to the garden to perform this service.

But were these women not aware of the fact that the Jews had placed, and even sealed, a huge stone in the opening of the tomb? Did they not know that watchmen were on duty there?

If they did know about all this, it has never been recorded, but Mark does say that they said among themselves, "Who shall roll us away the stone from the door of the sepulchre?" Perhaps in love and zeal in the early morning hours, they had not thought about that matter, but now the difficulty worried them as they journeyed along! It was no small matter for these feeble women. This was beyond the ability of these women to roll away such a large heavy piece of rock! Mark, in indicating the basis for the concern they had, follows with, "For it was very great."

But what was the first thing at which they marveled? "---and when they looked, they saw that the stone was rolled away."

They must have expressed wonder to one another, saying, "How is that possible?"

307

They were not puzzled with it very long, however, because when they arrived at the tomb they saw the angel who explained all these matters for them. That must have been a surprise! There was no stone, no watchmen, but neither was Jesus there.

The angel said to them, "Be not affrighted, ye seek Jesus of Nazareth, which was cruficied; He is risen; He is not here: behold the place where they laid Him."

That is the manner in which the angel spoke and even much more. He said that they should hurry back and tell His disciples that He was going into Galilee and that they would see Him there.

You can imagine these women must have been surprised, It is recorded that they quickly ran to tell the disciples, trembling with amazement.

And what about the watchmen? O, as soon as the angel descended there, they fled immediately. The watchmen were not at all interested in Jesus and would have nothing to do with a holy angel from heaven. They were terribly frightened and as soon as they recovered from their terror, ran away from there as fast as they could.

The angels spoke not a word to the watchmen. There was no concern for them at all. The interest of the angels was in those who came to see the grave, in those who felt the loss of Jesus and who thought they could not live without Him, and therefore, came to seek Him, even if He were dead.

O, how glad these women were! They had come to

anoint the body of Jesus, but now, instead, were being told that He was alive again. What a marvelous day this was for them.

But do you suppose the disciples and the others who also loved Jesus (but had remained in Jerusalem) actually believed what the women told them?

Not all. We have just mentioned that there were two kinds of people in Jerusalem, but now there were two kinds of reports there in those days, too. First there was the story originating from the Jewish Sanhedrin. What was that rumor? Well, they said, "That Jesus of Nazareth, the son of Mary, was certainly an exceptional person, in that He performed all kinds of miracles, healed the sick, etc.

But, He was, nevertheless, an impious person because He said He is the Son of God and the King of the Jews. Now, that is blasphemous. Only the Messiah who is still to come can be God's Son and our king. In order to purge Israel of this wickedness, as we are commanded by the law of Moses to do, we have condemned this Nazarene to death by crucifixion. This we managed to have done by Pilate. When we were sure that He was dead they put Him in the grave.

Since He still had many loyal followers, all strange, despicable, ignorant Galileans, we placed a guard of Roman soldiers around about His grave for security. We remembered what this seducer had told us earlier about rising from the dead. This is impossible for anyone to do, of course, but His disciples could remove His body from the grave and try to make us believe that He has risen.

These are the arrangements we made for security. But what happened in spite of all this?

The clumsy Roman soldiers slept all night instead of watching, and now it is just as we expected. The disciples came quietly to the grave and removed His body from the grave. The disciples are now spreading abroad that he has risen.

Now, you can imagine this rumor spread like wild fire through Jerusalem, because you remember the watchmen were paid off in money to tell this lie.

But, the same day another story was being published abroad. This originated from the women who had been at the empty grave very early in the morning and had received the message from the angels.

Even the men from Emmaus related this story to Jesus saying, "Yea, and certain women also of our company made us astonished, which were early at the sepulchre; and when they found not his body, they came saying, that they had also seen a vision of angels, which said that He was alive!"

Apparently this rumor had spread quite a distance.

But the men from Emmaus and the other disciples were experiencing the same as the queen of Sheba had.

There was a rumor being spread abroad concerning King Solomon in his days, too. It spread so far that the queen of Sheba heard of it. But the queen was not satisfied with just hearing this rumor, so she personally went to determine how much truth there was to it.

Well, she was agreeably surprised, she said, "The half had not been told her."

There were some people in Jerusalem who were not satisfied with rumors, either. 1st: They could not believe the rumor that Christ had not risen, but secondly, even less could they believe the rumor He had risen. They needed the certainty that He was risen as much as the certainty that He had died. O, those poor, despised people were well aware that they could not find salvation in a mere rumor. They had to have the Author of salvation Himself!

It did not remain a rumor though, no, for He made His appearance five times that first day to various people. They could not live without Jesus and they need not live without Him either, for He had appeared in person to Peter, the man who had fallen so deeply. The gladdened disciples were able to report to the men of Emmaus, "The Lord is risen and has been seen by Simon."

Who can tell me how many times Jesus made appearance after His resurrection?

Answer: "Three times" (another) "five times."

Both of you have given a wrong answer. Doesn't anyone know it? Then we shall try to make a list of them together.

1st. He made an appearance to Mary at the grave.

2nd. To the four women.

3rd. To Simon Peter.

4th. To the two men of Emmaus.

5th. To the ten disciples in the absence of Thomas. (These five took place on the first day)

6th. To all the disciples with Thomas present eight days later.

7th. To the seven disciples at the Sea of Tiberias.

8th. To eleven disciples on a mountain in Galilee.

9th. To 500 brethren all at one time.

10th. To James.

11th. To the eleven disciples on the Mount of Olives when He ascended into Heaven.

We have all these witnesses that He has truly risen. He had died and was buried in His human nature. He also was raised up in His human nature. However, if He had not possessed a divine nature it would have been impossible. His two natures always remained untied so that even in death there could be no separation.

His body was sinless in death and it was sinless in His resurrection. And now it was not only sinless, but also immortal, death having power over Him no more. He was raised in a glorified body that is immortal and incorruptible and at the same time it was a visible body. It was not a spirit alone as the disciples had feared when they first saw Him. They thought to have seen a ghost because they knew not yet of the mysteries of His death and resurrection. But Jesus dealt with this shortcoming and asked, "Do you have any food to eat?" They then gave Him a piece of broiled fish and of a honey comb. He took and ate it before their very eyes, saying "Thus it is written, and thus it behooved Christ to suffer, and to rise from the dead the third day."

Then He opened their understanding that they might understand the Scriptures.

This opening of their hearts and minds was so necessary that they might understand God's Word. That must have been a wonderful experience for those people!

But now, we must proceed further in our lesson.

Hellenbroek closes this lesson with the question, "Who are the partakers of Christ's resurrection?"

Answer: Those who know Christ and the power of His resurrection. Phil 3:10: "That I may know Him, and the power of His resurrection and the fellowship of His sufferings, being made conformable unto His death."

And Paul says in another place, "--was delivered for our offences, and was raised again for our justification."

He comprehends, in this word "our" all the elect (himself included). But he excludes, on the other hand, the whole world. He means to say there, "Christ is raised from the dead for those for whom He made satisfaction and for whom He had died. Only for those who have been raised with and in Him and who have been absolved of all guilt and punishment by the Father.

This last question is, of itself, an application of our lesson. By nature all of us lie in death and death lies in us. That is evident enough, isn't it? But do you remain so undisturbed in the knowledge of it, without being filled with fear because of it?

While here in life you may be spared from committing gross and evil sins by common grace or restraining grace, but that shall cease in death. God's beloved people, young and old alike, have a tendency, too, to commit sins in abundance but the Lord prevents them from doing them. They cannot do as they please but are invisibly restrained. God preserves them here in His strength and soon when in heaven they will have no more desire to sin. Nothing unclean can enter there. Only that which is pure in Christ shall enter in through Christ.

But, from the opposite point of view, there will be no common grace in hell to hinder sin. And you need not expect that consciences will be inactive there, no, they shall be even more lively than they were ever here. Do you attempt to put these things aside and say to yourself, "I want to be free to do what I want to do?" Does it go that far? O, you can be very sure that will not be agreeable to you. Read I Samuel 24 this evening. You will read there how Saul was in humble submission because David had spared his life. He said, "My Son, you are more righteous than I. You can go home in peace. I shall never harm you." But, a few days later he had forgotten everything he had said and pursued David again in hotter pursuit than before; even to his own death. That is the way it goes, from bad to worse when you override your conscience. It goes from bad to worse, from one thing to another, just so long until you sink away in complete hardness. And then. . .? You sink away into eternal perdition!

O, think about this. Do not smother your speaking conscience by continuing in sin.

We have been speaking about the resurrection day and, if we have already died, you and I will be included there.

And, then, will you be on the left hand of that great judge?

Then you will see the Mediator of whom we have spoken, in His glorified and immortal body coming to judge and making the separation. But you certainly will not be at ease there as you are now sitting before me.

May the Lord graciously deliver your poor soul from the spiritual deadness in which you lie and give to you the assurance that you share in the resurrection of Christ. That would be the only comfort in life and death.

So be it.

Lesson 29

Of His Ascension and Sitting
at the Right Hand of God

Jesus remained upon earth for 40 days after His resurrection. His presence here was more clearly to establish the certainty of His resurrection and, secondly, to further instruct His disciples in certain matters.

Who can bring proof from God's Word that these are the reasons?

Answer: Acts 1:3, "To whom He shewed Himself alive" and "speaking of the things pertaining to the Kingdom of God."

Who can make a comparison with an example from the Old Testament?

The temple had a vestibule into which all the people (undefiled) were permitted to enter. Then there was a holy room into which only the priests were allowed and, thirdly, there was a holy of holy sanctuary where only the High priest was permitted to enter and then only once each year.

So, then, the three years the Lord Jesus traveled about upon this earth were as though He was in the vestibule being easily seen by all the people. But the forty days after His resurrection and prior to His ascension, He walked about as it were, in the Holy Place. None of His enemies, Jews or Gentiles, saw Him during that time. He showed Himself eleven times to His people as a visible proof that He had truly risen. It was no longer necessary that He show Himself to the world. They had not believed in Him prior to His death and so under these circumstances they would no longer be able to see Him. He had said previously, "--and the world seeth me no more." Further, the watchmen at His grave were living proof of that.

But now the appointed time for the second step in His exaltation was there, namely, His ascension into heaven. This was as if He, the Great Highpriest, should unaccompanied, enter the holy of holies.

Was this foretold in the Old Testament too?

Answer: Yes, in Psalm 68:18, "Thou has ascended on high, thou hast led captivity captive; thou hast received gifts for men, yea, for the rebellious also, that the Lord God might dwell among them!"

Paul wrote, Eph. 4:10 "He that ascended up far above all heavens." What does he mean by this?

You know that we commonly speak of three heavens: the heaven of clouds, the heaven of stars and the heaven of heavens. The heaven of heavens is said to be the eternal habitation of God and it is there that the Son of God ascended. That is why it is said, "He ascended up far above all heavens, namely: the heaven of clouds and the heaven of stars.

Hellenbroek asks: Did any witnesses attend His ascension?

Answer: Yes, angels and the disciples of the Savior, Acts 1.

Answer: From the Mount of Olives, outside of Jerusalem.

Jesus had chosen the eleven disciples to be witnesses of His entire work as Mediator, even to the very last step. Luke reports of this, "And He led them out as far as to Bethany, and He lifted up His hands, and blessed them. And it came to pass, while He blessed them, He was departed from them, and carried up into heaven." "A cloud received Him out of their sight," Acts 1:9.

They did not see Him anymore.

And what happened then? Did the disciples hurry away?

No, something else happened right then. Luke describes it in the Acts of the Apostles: "And while they looked stedfastly toward heaven as He went up, behold, two men stood by them in white apparel; Which also said: "Ye men of Galilee, why stand ye gazing up into heaven? This same Jesus, which is taken up from you into heaven, shall so come in like manner as ye have seen Him go into heaven."

What kind of men would that have been who were wearing white clothes?

Answer: Angels.

And where did these angels come from?

They had not been on the Mount of Olives as the disciples were, but came directly out of heaven to the place from where the Mediator had ascended. They had come as messengers to instruct and comfort the disciples who stood there in amazement. They wanted to say, in other words, "This Jesus, whom you have now seen ascend with a glorified body, shall return by and by with that same glorified body upon the clouds of heaven and every eye shall see Him."

Had Christ ascended into heaven with the same nature as that in which He had been resurrected? What are your thoughts about that?

Yes, He died and was raised up again in His human nature, and also ascended into heaven in His human nature. It is not as though this human nature was without His divine nature in all this, that is impossible. His deity has not a body and consequently cannot be seen.

Hellenbroek now asks:

Is not His human nature become omnipresent by His ascension?

His answer is: "No, Matt. 26:11, Ye have the poor always with you but Me ye have not always."

The Lord meant with these words, that He would be with them for only a short time in His human nature. That is a proof that He, in His human nature, was not omnipresent.

Now, possibly one would ask himself, "What was the purpose of this ascension?" Since everything had now been accomplished, the Lord Jesus had been restored to life again by the Father by virtue of having secured His satisfaction and He Himself arose from the grave. Could He not remain here upon earth as a human being?

Our lesson says not. Ascension was necessary:

1st. In order that he might rule as King,

2nd. To intercede in prayer - 3rd, to gather His own people there in heaven around Himself.

One who is to be a king over a nation must first be crowned. No one can rule as king over a land without the official coronation.

Would the Mediator have been crowned too? What a coronation He had! By faith Solomon saw Him in His service as it were and consequently speaks of it in the Song of Solomon 3:11 - "Go forth, O ye daughter of Zion, and behold King Solomon with the crown wherewith his mother crowned him in the day of his espousals, and in the day of the gladness of his heart."

He does not have himself in mind here, but he means the more eminent Solomon whom he believed in faith would surely come. He envisioned the ascension of Christ into heaven as the golden coronation of the Son of God as Mediator. A King who had conquered all enemies; He was supreme ruler over all.

And with what was He crowned?

First He was crowned with the iron crown designating might. (This is only a manner of speaking.)

Is this according to God's Word?

Yes, for He says Himself in Matt. 28:18, "All power is given unto me in heaven and in earth."

2nd. He was crowned with the silver crown of grace. John says in John 1:16, "And of His fulness have all we received, and grace for grace."

320

3rd. He is crowned with the golden crown of lordship. Hebrews 2:9 — "crowned with glory and honor."

These are proofs from God's Word that He ascended into heaven to reign as the officially crowned King. Not only in grace over His people, but also as complete master over all His enemies, the devil, sin and death. The revelation of the Son of God was made in this way to show He would subdue the work of the devil. He would break it down and bring it to nought for time, spiritually and eternally.

For what else was His ascension into heaven needed? Not only to reign as King, but secondly, to intercede in prayer.

Under the old dispensation, on the annual Day of Atonement, the Highpriest entered into the Holy of Holies with the blood of reconciliation to perform his duties there. When this Highpriest was behind the veil with the incense and the blood of the bullock and the blood of the goat, the priests, in the holy place, listened for the sound of the little golden bells that were fastened to the hem of the Highpriest's robe.

Why would they do that?

Well, the tinkling of the bells indicated to them that the Highpriest was actively sprinkling the blood of reconciliation upon the mercy seat; that he was not asleep or dead but working actively in his holy employment. This is clearly explained in Exodus 28:33-35, "And beneath upon the hem of it thou shalt make pomegranates of blue and of purple - and of scarlet round about the hem thereof; and bells of gold between them round about; a golden bell and a pomegranate upon the hem of the robe round about. And it shall be upon Aaron to minister; and his sound shall be heard when he goeth in unto the holy place before the Lord and when he cometh out, that he die not."

These were prefigurations and types of Christ, the Great Highpriest, Who would once enter into the heavenly kingdom with His own blood, shed personally.

And has He entered in, there to be inactive at the Father's right hand? No, but to be occupied as intercessor for His people. Now, they, who are waiting in the holy vestibule, can listen and perceive how the Holy Highpriest is diligently active presenting them to the Father in His work of reconciliation.

What had the disciples received while waiting in Jerusalem those ten days after His entrance into the holy of holies? Well, then the confirmation of the reconciliation was made clearly evident, that is, the Holy Ghost fell upon them as a pledge or proof that the Father received the sacrifice from the High priest and was completely satisfied.

O, this is the portion of God's people; a Highpriest, sitting on God's right hand, rendering thanks, praying and serving. He is and remains peace for such a people who had no desire for peace but who declared war upon God. He has conquered all these rebels and now reigns as king over them.

Just as I have so often made mention to you from Revelation 6; when the Lamb had opened the first seal, there was a voice which said, "Come and see." And what did John see? "And I saw, and behold a white horse; and He that sat on him had a bow; and a crown was given unto Him; and He went forth conquering, and to conquer."

Who would that have been?

That was the crowned Mediator, Who rode on the white horse representing his Gospel with the bow of His Word and Spirit in His hand, wherewith He went out to conquer, His people to eternal life and His enemies to death. He had been given the crown, that magnificent crown on which every one of the elect shall be a jewel.

Who can comfort themselves with Christ's ascension?

Answer: Those who are risen with Christ, Col. 3:1, "If ye then be risen with Christ seek those things which are above, where Christ sitteth on the right hand of God."

Was Christ's sitting at God's Right Hand also foretold?

Yes, Psalm 110:1, "The Lord said unto my Lord, Sit Thou at My Right Hand."

Wouldn't this be figuratively speaking?

God is a spirit. He has no body. But this is expressed in human words which present to us the glory and worthiness the Son of God has in heaven. We read that Stephen saw Jesus standing at the right hand of God.

We must understand His sitting at the right hand of God, as being elevated in power and magnificence.

All God's children shall behold Him so sooner or later.

Even though Paul, before his conversion, had not known Jesus, he saw Him now in the engravings (scar marks) of His Mediatorship, glistening in Holy brightness, as a result he wrote in Hebrews 2:9 & 17; "But we see Jesus, who was made a little lower than the angels for the suffering of death, crowned with glory and honor; that He by the grace of God should taste death for every man (namely those that are known of Him). "Wherefore in all things it behooved Him to be made like unto His brethren, that He might be a merciful and faithful Highpriest in things pertaining to God (and why?) - to make reconciliation for the sins of the people."

Everything having been brought to perfection, death reigns no more over Him. The Father never exalted anyone so highly as He exalted Christ. This is not in respect to His Godhead because, in that, He is equal to the Father and the Holy Ghost and could not be exalted to a higher degree.

But as Mediator, with a glorified, immortal human nature, there is this reference, "For unto which of the angels said He at anytime Thou art My son?"

Would there be still more profit in this glorification, the third step in His state of exaltation?

324

There is not a little, or much, profit in this, but, everything is comprehended in it! David saw, by faith, the great profit in the ascension of the Mediator and His sitting at God's right hand and expressed himself accordingly in Psalm 68:18, "Thou hast ascended on high, (this is the deed, but now he continues, telling about the profit of it). Thou hast led captivity captive; Thou hast received gifts for men." For which men? For good, trusting men who have accepted Jesus as their Savior? Wait a minute, he hasn't finished -- "Yea, for the rebellious also, that the Lord God might dwell among them!"

That is a very significant statement! What does He do there that makes His ascension and sitting at God's right hand so profitable? We already pointed out, 1st, He reigns there as King, 2nd, He prays as the Intercessor. We have spoken somewhat of that, but now, 3rd, He receives His people unto Himself.

His people -- They are those who want nothing to do with Him; rebellious, stubborn, inherently disobedient people who heap guilt upon guilt. They are those who shall live with him there eternally.

Does not the profit in this matter overshadow all else?

Paul, too, had experience in this; he said, "When we were enemies we were reconciled with God." All God's people shall personally come to accept the fact that they as stubborn creatures have been gathered in and saved. Then they are no longer enemies or stubborn ones, no, but by free grace they become fellow-citizens with the saints, and of the household of God.

By nature they are enemies, just as all other people are, but, where lies the difference between them and the worldlings?

That they lose their enmity. What a terrible thing that will be to be born as an enemy of God, to continue as an enemy in this life, but then; to die as an enemy and to so continue throughout eternity as an enemy without ever once yielding to the Lord.

And what makes it so sad that a person is born an enemy? That he himself suffers great harm? Would that be the chief reason?

It seems no one has an answer.

The fact is that we were not created as enemies. And yet we were born as enemies -- what is the intervening cause? O, sin came between, the horrible wilful sin against God which has ruined everything.

It is my true desire that this evening you, through the working of the Holy Spirit, come to accept the fact you are a wilful stubborn sinner.

What are you thinking now? Are you really eager to be saved? I see most of you nodding "yes".

So, if I understand, if the Lord would come in your hearts He wouldn't encounter much resistance?

I am convinced, if it should come to pass, that you would say, "Well, I thought that I was eager to be saved, but now I feel a great enmity in my heart." Augustine had also become acquainted with his depraved nature.

Have you ever heard about this man Augustine? He was born on Nov. 13, in the year 354 A.D. in Tagaste, a city in North Africa. His father's name was Patricius and his mother's, Monica. His mother was a sincere Christian. His father was a heathen most of his life but it seems he became a Christian at his old age.

Augustine was a very wicked boy who shunned the many admonishments of his mother. He was aware inwardly of his doings and, though he tried, he could not stifle his conscience, even with all kinds of gross sins. For years Monica privately struggled and prayed for the conversion of her son. It appeared that her prayers were of no avail until he was thirteen years old. Augustine drank up sin as though it were water, dismissing all warnings of conscience and people. Later, after the Lord had converted him, (and that did take place in a very effectual way), he wrote a book about his life. In those writings he says:

"I very well knew it would be better to lay down my weapons and surrender to God, but I loved sin so much that it was impossible to free my self from it. It was just like a person, waking up in the morning, whose mind tells him it is time to rise up for work and he agrees with that, but, in the meantime, the desire to sleep is so strong, that he stays in bed. And, so, he does what he himself disapproves of.

O, God, Thou said to me, 'Wherefore, He saith, Awake, thou that sleepest and arise from the dead,' and --- I was not able to answer. I knew He spoke the truth and I was convinced of that truth.

Nevertheless, my heart inclined toward the misery of sin and as with sleepy voice I answered, 'Wait a minute, give me a moment more, allow me yet a short while,' but alas, that moment came not to an end, and that 'wait a short while' lasted a long time. The law of sin reigned in my soul and I would never have been delivered from this body of death had not Thou, O, eternal God done it for me in Christ Jesus Thy Son."

That is the way Augustine related it. He wanted to be converted, but not right away. He wanted to enjoy a short time in worldliness and to live in sin before conversion.

Boys and girls, are there some of you, too, who secretly feel that way?

May Christ in His kingly office draw back His bow and shoot forth the arrow of His Word and Spirit into your heart, wounding you spiritually and removing the contentment you have in the world. Augustine stood against this for thirty two years but finally the warrior was conquered.

I hope you are not able to resist it that long a time. O, how precious is the time the Lord gives us!

Once, when the last sand of time has been poured through the hourglass and it becomes eternity for ever, the crowned Mediator will return on the clouds to take His vanquished people to His right hand side. He shall present them to the Father without spot or wrinkle and the Father's anger will no longer be roused against them nor will He rebuke them anymore, because there shall not one spot be found upon their soul, no, cleansed perfectly in the blood of the Lamb.

They will remain at His right hand eternally, no longer as enemies or rebellious people but as the redeemed of the Lord, and they shall live in eternal bliss.

O, children, children, may you become aware of your poverty in these things while you are young and still not acquainted with this glorified Immanuel. He is so worthy of all your love.

May the Lord, in free grace, gain the victory in your hearts, in order that He may be glorified, not alone in you, but also through you.

So be it.

Lesson 30

Effectual Calling

Last week we ended our lesson series on the States of the Mediator, and today we shall begin the lesson dealing with the fruits or benefits that flow from them. The first question, accordingly, is: To what end is Christ thus exalted?

Answer: To apply His benefits unto us.

Question: How may the benefits of Christ be distinguished?

Answer: Into two kinds: (1) benefits in this life; (2) benefits after this life.

From whom do these benefits come? Not from the devil. He does not have one benefit, and would not give them if he had. We cannot receive them from angels either. From whom then?

From Christ.

What benefits are they that Hellenbroek is speaking about?

They are the benefits that Christ obtained for the elect through His active and passive obedience.

Hellenbroek divides these into two parts: 1st., benefits in this life. 2nd., benefits after this life.

Principally, the benefits in this life are: calling, justification and sanctification.

Those conferred in the life to come are: Resurrection, final judgment and eternal life.

All these benefits were earned for the church, but was it sufficient that they had been earned? Could God's people be saved on the basis of these merited or procured benefits? Yes, salvation is theirs upon these grounds, but what must take place?

The merits, which had been acquired for them, must now be applied.

Whose work would it be of the Divine Persons, to apply these benefits? If you were observant when studying your catechism lesson, you would have determined which Person that was in the very first answer.

Christ is also exalted to apply the benefits that He had acquired. Who but He is most qualified to do that work! And by what means does He do it?

Christ applies these benefits through His Word and Spirit.

The Holy Spirit, Who proceeds from the Father and the Son, comes now to testify of Him. It is through this Holy Spirit, that Christ applies the benefits.

What is to be observed in this matter?

That it is a work of a Triune God. The Father is the moving cause of this work from eternity. That is the foundation of it all. The Son is the meritorious cause; He acquired it. The Holy Spirit is the applier; He works it out and makes application.

And who receives all this?

Answer: Only those for whom it had been procured, for those who by nature are unwilling, stubborn, dead sinners but--elect.

How can the elect receive all these benefits; must they appropriate them to themselves? Absolutely not. The first benefit in this time state is: the calling. It is next to election in importance, and succeeds.

Are we able to say that all men are called?

No, alas, there have been millions of people who have died upon earth and thousands still living unto whom the external call of the gospel has never come.

Whole generations of heathen and all sorts of uncivilized people have never had the external proclamation of a Savior made to them. But to the extent that the gospel is preached, the external call is universal.

I have been speaking of an external call. Is there then another kind of call besides an external?

Answer: Yes, the calling is two-fold, an external and an internal calling.

By what means does the external calling come to us?

It takes place exclusively through God's Word. The internal calling is brought about by Word and Spirit.

Is there a place in God's Word which states that all those called externally are not necessarily given an internal call?

Answer: Matt. 20:16, "For many be called, but few chosen." This text speaks of the external call. Would you think both kinds of calling are from God or just the internal?

332

Both callings come from God, but the internal is the only saving call.

Has there always been an external call? Yes, this was evident in common grace immediately after the fall, but it was not present everywhere in the world as it is now.

Scripture tells us of two generations from Adam to Noah; the descendants of Cain and the descendants of Seth. The descendants of Cain had sunken very deeply in sin and had spread themselves over all the earth. The true children of God and the external call were to be found solely among the children of Seth.

It was different from Noah to beyond the time of Christ, up to Pentecost. There were three principle sets of descendants in the world. The descendants of Shem, Ham and Japheth. The descendants of Ham were the black people. Those of Japheth were the heathen, and among them were but few and exceptional instances where the internal call had its effect. The descendants of Shem then were those from whom God chose His peculiar people, the Jews, the family of Abraham. But now, since Pentecost, the Gospel must be preached everywhere in the world and consequently the external call is far more universal than it was under the Old Testament.

Is the external call absolutely ineffective to salvation? and why?

Because, though the external call declares the Gospel, it cannot bring men to a saving knowledge of Christ. Without Him there can be no salvation.

It is my intention on this afternoon to ask you many questions, so you could also ask me how I know and prove from God's Word that the external call is not sufficient.

Answer: Paul says, "So then neither is he that planteth anything, neither he that watereth; but God that giveth the increase." I Cor. 3:7. How must this be understood?

It is very simple. The Lord uses His Apostles or ministers here on earth, calling the people through them to conversion. But Paul says, even if we plant and water, it is to no avail unless God Himself gives the increase. The Lord must work with His Spirit inwardly in those who are called outwardly. Without this it will not be to salvation.

Now perhaps there are among you who are privately thinking, if external callings are not sufficient by themselves and the elect alone are called inwardly, to what avail is it even if I do my ordinary obligations. I might just as well omit them.

So, would these be your thoughts?

Listen to me a moment. Then I shall give you three things to consider.

I have here three boys (just as an example). The first boy says, "O, why should I worry about church attendance, the minister, the catechism, the Bible and the Sunday? If I am not elect I wouldn't get to heaven if I sat in church all week. And if I am elect, well, then God will search me out and convert me. I'll go peacefully along my own way!

But the second boy has other thoughts and speaks to the first one:

334

"No, John, I don't agree with you in that. I am of believing parents, was baptized and brought up in a Christian home. I go to catechism and attend church regularly. Soon I shall make confession of faith and partake of communion. I am a child of the covenant. If I don't sin myself out of the covenant, I shall go to heaven when I die. I wouldn't think of neglecting the means."

That's the way Hendrick reasoned with John. A third companion was listening without comment. They turned to him and said, "Well, Pete, what are your thoughts about this?

Pete says, "I don't agree with either one of you. I also have been born of Christian parents and obey my father and mother in all they ask of me as far as catechism and church attendance goes. I know positively, however, in spite of all this, that I am unconverted and something else must happen before I can go to heaven. I am without God in this world and my sin has never been reconciled."

Be honest with yourself now. Which of these three boys would men find it best to follow? The first one despises the means and external calls. The second is converted by the external calls; he finds them sufficient. The third doesn't despise them but finds them insufficient too. Which one would you choose?

Someone answered, "The last." Is there another who thinks otherwise?

No one. So all of you find the last boy is correct? Think about it then later when you become older when you do just as John, the first boy, despising and neglecting all the means. You will have passed sentence upon yourself here in this consistory room. Because now, at least, you acknowledge that we may not despise the external call.

Even if you forget what you have said here, the Lord shall not forget.

Are not the external means to be acknowledged and respected? If they are, I shall ask you one more question : Do you appreciate them too? I don't think many of you dare to say "yes."

What a wretched creature man has become through the fall! Even at the very least we have no right to life because our rightful place is in hell. But now we may not only live but are being called externally too. And all this is the result of the fact that Christ shed His blood upon this earth and because all the elect are not yet gathered in. Does the Lord deserve that we should sin against Him continuously? Do you thus requite the Lord? He has done nothing but good and we have done nothing but evil.

I know without a doubt that if you accept this, it will not be easy for you to sin anymore.

We are all agreed that the external call is extremely important but ---- is it sufficient for salvation?

No. It is not. Hellenbroek asks: What, then must be added to it?

Answer: The internal call as in Lydia, Acts 16:14, "Whose heart the Lord opened, that she

336

attended unto the things which were spoken by Paul." The internal call is clearly established in these few words. It states so emphatically that this woman "attended unto". In our ordinary natural state we pay no attention to the Word of God. And in Lydia's case too, it was not the external call which bore fruit or that caused her to "Attend to the things spoken by Paul."

How did it come about then?

It states, "--Whose heart the Lord opened, that she attended unto ..." It was, then, brought about by the Holy Ghost.

Before this happened, Lydia had been called externally. This is stated in Acts 16:14, saying in effect that she worshipped God before she heard Paul. She was an elect vessel and, as such, the Lord opened her heart. It was then that the Lord called her internally.

Does it state, word for word, in the Bible that only the elect are called internally?

Yes, Paul says in Romans 8:30, "Moreover whom He did predestinate, (that is the elect) them He also called": Internal calling is meant here, because it follows "and whom He called, them He also justified, etc."

What is actually comprehended in this internal call?

Answer: It is an efficacious change of the whole man, namely, his understanding, will, affections and conversation.

Now we come to the next question of the lesson.

337

Who can recite the answer in its entirety?

Answer: The understanding is darkened, the will is perverse, the affections irregular, and the conversation is sinful. Eph. 4:18. "Having the understanding darkened, being alienated from the life of God, etc." Romans 8:7. "Because the carnal mind is enmity against God: for it is not subject to the law of God, neither indeed can be." Titus 3:3. "For we ourselves also were sometimes foolish, disobedient, deceived, serving divers lusts and pleasures, living in malice and envy, hateful and hating one another."

All these texts are presented to show what a person is by nature. What do they become by effectual calling?

Answer: The understanding is enlightened to know God in His all-sufficiency; Jesus in His preciousness, and himself in his damnable condition, I Cor. 2:12, 13. The will is changed to serve and glorify God. Romans 7:15. The affections are purified to hate sin, and on the other hand to love God as the supreme good, and to desire holiness, etc. Romans 6:19. And the conversation is sanctified.

Do you notice in this answer, that the internal call goes to a greater depth than a mere external "change"?

Why is it not sufficient for a person to be merely changed?

Pay close attention. You know that we all, personally, stand guilty before God in our relationship with Adam. Each one, then, lies in a state of death wherein we have brought ourselves, but from which we can never free ourselves.

Even if a person accomplished a great change in his life; from being a rascal to being a decent person; from living in the world to frequenting the church services, he still, despite all his change, remains in his state of death, with Adam as his covenant head. He will not, despite all this, be reconciled to God so long as he remains in Adam. What is necessary then?

A person must experience a change: being transposed from his covenant head Adam to a better covenant head Christ. In other words, from death to life. This can take place only in a person who experiences the internal call. Those called externally are sometimes changed but those called internally are renewed. This is the difference you should always remember.

We must proceed now with our lesson. Here comes a peculiar question:

Is the internal calling efficacious?

Answer: Yes, it hath an irresistible power.

This is an answer of great significance. What is its explanation?

Efficacious implies that resistance is encountered; would that be true in the internal call?

That you can believe! In the first place by the devil. Secondly, by the world, but, worst of all, by man himself! Do not these make for powerful opposition? Or do you suppose the devil does not care if a person is called internally?

If the devil got his way or was the master, don't think there ever would be a man converted! He is the original and everlasting enemy of God. Because this is so, he hates everything that glorifies God and cannot tolerate any of His works. The world is also a bitter enemy of God. Jesus said Himself, "He who would be a friend of the world is called an enemy of God." Consequently, as long as you love the world and its enjoyments with heart and soul, you can be sure that you are an enemy of God; that is certain! If the internal calling is irresistible, wouldn't it have been that way when God created the world? God created everything by an omnipotent act of a simple will without cooperation of the created. Isn't that true of people now, too?

I see many agree in this. Do not get caught up in this because it is just the opposite.

It is true, the world was created by the Almighty Power of God and it takes the same power to renew a man. The world did not cooperate in its being created nor did man, but did the world oppose or resist? No, it did not. It was as clay in the hand of the Potter. But is that so with man too? It is far from it. Man's nature is in opposition to God; never passive under God. That is why it is necessary that the internal call be irresistible. Otherwise man could never be overcome. Now all is accomplished in God's appointed time and the most powerful opposers must submit. All are thoroughly subdued. Satan's head is crushed, the power of the world is taken away, and the person becomes a conquered enemy. But all of this must be accomplished in the soul with submission.

Now I shall ask yet another question: We said earlier that a man always opposes and is never passive when the Lord calls internally or converts him. But, now that a person is conquered, will he cooperate and no longer oppose?

Be careful. Do not give an incorrect answer to this. If it was true that the elect cooperated after receiving the inward call - the merits of Christ would be worthless, because then He would be only a partial and not a complete Savior. Never speak or think of this being true! It is unspeakable the errors that would flow out of this. No, cooperation before and after the call is totally impossible. But do you know what does take place? God makes those with whom He is laboring passive. That is Scriptural. His people shall be willing in the day of His power. Psalm 110.

Isn't that a miracle? The Lord does not delay when He encounters resistance, no, because if that were so, no one would be saved. He proceeds irresistibly and changes children of the devil into children of God, impious wretches into inhabitants of heaven, adversaries into supporters, and enemies are reconciled to God!

More takes place than an external persuasion as Hellenbroek puts it; it is an inward inclining of the will. God does not compel a person, but He makes him willing.

341

In the universal call there is an external persuasion but the inward call of God is not only a knocking and calling through His Word and by His servants, or speaking to the conscience, because then it would be as Jesus says, "How often would I have gathered thy children together, even as a hen gathereth her chickens under her wings, and ye would not! No, with those who are savingly called it goes beyond that.

I shall try to make clear to you with an example in nature showing that the external call is merely superficial persuasion. For example: I see a blind man heading directly for a ditch and so I say to him, "Sir, I want to warn you, walk in another direction. If you continue in this direction you will fall into the water." I do nothing beyond this but continue walking, leaving this man to his fate. What help is that to the blind man? He could go in another direction but then he might walk over a precipice

He is blind and doesn't know which direction he must go. In what way could I have really helped him? If I had taken him by the hand and led him to a place of safety.

Now, this is but a feeble example in life but it brings out the principle. In the external call man receives a warning to avoid the dangerous paths and is pointed to the good way to go.

But man, though rational, is spiritually blind, yes, even spiritually dead. His reasoning powers come short of ability to use the well meant council. He is admonished, though, and made aware of the great peril. He can not exonerate himself by saying he had not been warned.

But God lays hold on those whom He has purposed to save, and not only admonishes them but leads them in another direction. Internally He inclines their will and mind. He does not compel them with force but with love; they have an inclination within themselves to cry out, "Draw me and I shall run after Thee."

He leads them by an irresistible power. Paul was well acquainted with this, because he had been overpowered himself. He says: "For it is God which worketh in you both to will and to do of His good pleasure." In one place he calls it a "creation". Ephesians 2:10, "For we are His workmanship, created in Christ Jesus unto good works." All the good that they desire, is brought about through God, and all the good works they perform they perform through God. This is because they become recipients of the beginnings of a Godly nature. With this nature they have no desire or ability to sin. Sometimes this work performed upon them is called a "drawing."

Jesus says in John 6:44, "No man can come to me, except the Father which hath sent me draw him."

And so that is it. We can not go further into this matter. It is time now for the following catechism class. What should we add further to this lesson?

I hope that one day the Lord may be your Applier. All of you live under the external call and admit that we must recognize the authority of it, but also that it, in itself, is not sufficient.

May the Lord draw you from within before your young lives are cut off; that He may draw you, work in you irresistibly and efficaciously to His honor and to the salvation of your souls.

> His truth unchanged shall ever stand
> He saves from strong oppressions hand.
> In Him the sad a helper find
> He feeds the poor and heals the blind.

Psalter No. 401, st. 3

Lesson 31

The Church

In previous lessons, we were taught that the chief benefits obtained by Christ were: Calling, Justification and Sanctification.

Just last week our studies were centered upon "The calling", but now would you not think Hellenbroek in error to immediately follow up with a lesson on "The Church"?

Absolutely not; Hellenbroek knew very well what he was doing. His reasoning was: First, I shall make clear upon whom these benefits are bestowed and wherein Christ is the Benefactor. That is why he now asks: Doth Christ also gather a church by this calling?

Answer: Yes.

This is a very short answer, but all of you must understand that it is the internal call intended here and by the "church" is meant the true living church. Last week we mentioned briefly the fact that the external call was not always much in evidence in the world. We read there was a great difference between the descendants of Seth and the descendants of Cain. The Bible says of Cain that he went out from the presence of the Lord, and dwelt in the land of Nod, on the east of Eden.

In saying that he "went out from the presence of the Lord" is meant that he departed from the external means of grace and withdrew himself from the external call.

He was never called with the internal call since we cannot find where Cain was converted to God. He was never a member of the living invisible church; and he withdrew himself from the visible.

If we read God's Word with attention we often notice very dark terrifying examples related, over against those that are (by grace) as bright shining lights. Saul was such a depressing example. The Lord spoke to Samuel saying, "How long wilt thou mourn for Saul, seeing I have rejected him?" That was a dreadful saying! Just as Cain, Saul was rejected because of his sins and henceforth lived under the curse.

We said the external call was not in exercise among the descendants of Cain. What are the conclusions to be made of this?

That the church was not to be found among them.

Where was the church, then, in that time?

Answer: Among the descendants of Seth. In Genesis 4:26 we find, "And to Seth, to him also there was born a son; and he called his name Enos; then began men to call upon the name of the Lord."

Thus we see the Lord had His church for the most part among the descendants of Seth who were referred to as "Children of God" in contrast to the others who were referred to as the "children of men".

Nevertheless, when the sons of God married with the daughters of the world and became conformed to the world, the Lord pronounced judgment upon them. This eventually came to pass.

But where do you suppose the church upon earth existed after the world experienced the flood?

I mentioned before that the church consists of three parts. Who remembers?

Answer: The church triumphant in heaven, the church militant upon earth, and the ungathered part of the elect who still live unconverted.

Be sure to remember that. But are we to believe there are three churches?

No, it is but two or three parts of one and the same church. Song of Solomon 6:9, "My Dove, my undefiled is but one."

What was the situation during the flood?

Well, then the Lord preserved His church in the ark. Do not be misled to think that all those eight persons constituted the church; no, because it was revealed later that Ham was among them.

346

The church is constantly preserved in Christ. It has always been manifest that the Lord takes care of His own.

It is evident that the church from Noah to Pentecost was for the most part with the descendants of Shem. There were a few exceptions and they were those brought out from the heathens.

Who can mention a few of these exceptions from the Old Testament?

Answer: Rahab, the woman of Jericho — Ruth, the Moabite.

Correct, and there are others, too, if we were to be precise.

Now it is asked: "Is there always a church?"

Answer: Yes, Matt. 16:18, "The gates of Hell shall not prevail against it."

But is it always visible?

Far from it! God's Word testifies of the fact that the church on earth can be almost or completely invisible when subjected to persecution. It is there nevertheless, just as in the days of Elijah. He thought in his great discouragement to be the only one left, but there were yet seven thousand in Israel who had not yet bowed their knees before Baal. It means that they belonged to the living church.

Was it prophesied in the Old Testament that a time would come when the church would not be solely under the descendants of Shem?

Yes, this had been prophesied more than once by the prophets. We read, for example, in Isaiah 54:2,

347

"Enlarge the place of thy tent and let them stretch forth the curtains of thine habitation; spare not, lengthen thy cords, and strengthen thy stakes."

What would be the reason for that? Listen to what it says in verse 3, "For thou shalt break forth on thy right hand and on thy left; and thy seed shall inherit the Gentiles." The meaning of these words is plain enough. When a person is converted by God, even at its very beginning, he becomes a stranger upon the earth. David speaks of it in Psalm 120, "Woe is me, that I sojourn in Mesech." A person, being a stranger somewhere on a journey, does not put forth much effort to become established because it is only temporary. It is just as if the Lord says to His people, "Don't pound the stakes of your tent too deeply in the ground and don't fasten your tent securely, because this is not your permanent home anyway."

It would be a (spiritually) profitable life for God's people if they always lived as though at a moments notice, they would be required to leave here. The children of Israel had to live that way in the wilderness. Each evening they set up their tents somewhere and pounded the stakes in, but never very securely, because every morning they were required to go further. This was the situation until they arrived in Canaan.

When the Lord says, "Do not set your stakes too securely," it refers to the day by day living of God's people.

But here in Isaiah it is just the other way around,

"—Strengthen thy stakes, lengthen thy cords - enlarge the place of thy tent."

You are all aware of the fact that people in the Eastern countries make much use of tents instead of permanent houses. The tents were secured to the ground with long iron stakes. Who was that woman who took such a pin, or tent stake, and pounded it through the head of a man, with a hammer?

Answer: She did that with a stake of her tent. Of course there were curtains in and round about these tents and these curtains and cords were sized according to the space of the tents.

The Lord was speaking to the Jews in a figure of speech as if he would say; "Up to this point of time I have had my church mainly confined to this small land of Canaan. But the time is coming that not only Jews but also Gentiles will be included. Japheth shall come and dwell in the tents of Shem!"

Noah, in faith, had prophesied that this would occur; "God shall enlarge Japheth, and He shall dwell in the tents of Shem" - Gen. 9:27.

The Jews would just have to reckon with the fact that the Gentiles would be added to the church militant. But when the time appointed came and the Messiah entered upon earth and the Gentiles truly rose from darkness to light, the Jews would not accept it. They accused Paul of defiling the temple where he had been with an Ephesian. However, it was the "fulness of the Gentiles" and that people who had remained in darkness entered into the light of God's Word.

The Lord established a part of the church militant among them.

Now the question comes: Who is at the head of the church?

Answer: Jesus Christ. Eph. 5:23, Christ is the head of the church. Men might possibly ask: Why does Hellenbroek ask something so obvious? Who else but the Lord Jesus could be the head of the church?

That question might seem superfluous to us, but you must not forget that Hellenbroek lived from 1658 to 1731; in a time when the forces of the Reformation were being fiercely resisted.

Is not the Pope of Rome the head of the church?

For this he merely gives a very short answer, he says, "No, he is the antichrist."

You are all aware that the word "anti" means "against". The antichrist then, is against Christ. Hellenbroek dares to speak out in freedom that the Pope, with all his religion, good works and Christ-worshiping, is finally a servant of Satan; in opposition to Christ. He shall substantiate his answer with Holy Scripture and says; "How do we know?"

Because everything foretold of the anti-christ is fulfilled in him.

And now he speaks of what Paul says of the anti-christ in 2 Thes. 2. The time we have set aside for catechism is far too short to go into detail. We would need at least a day to elaborate on the errors of the Roman catholic church. Perhaps we shall have the opportunity later to do it.

At any rate, they fail to acknowledge Christ as the sole Head of the church. They even dare to be wickedly disrespectful to say; Christ is the Head of the church in Heaven, the Head of the church triumphant, but the Pope is the head of the part upon earth, that he is Christ's deputy, a substitute for Peter.

Do you know what text they misuse for this? It is Matt. 16:18 - "Thou art Peter, and upon this rock I will build my church and the gates of hell shall not prevail against it."

It is clear that the Lord meant it was upon the confession that Peter had just made, ("Thou art the Christ, the Son of the living God.") that He would build His church, that is, upon Christ her only Head and Foundation. But what do these poor people misinterpret this to mean?

The catechism book used to teach their children speaks out clearly (In question 136 of the Roman Catholic catechism book):

Is not Christ Himself the preeminent in the Holy church?

Answer: Christ is the invisible head of the Holy church, but Peter was His visible representative.

Question 137: Who is the successor of Holy Peter?

Answer: The Pope of Rome.

Question 138: What is the Pope of Rome?

Answer: The Pope of Rome is the representative of Christ on earth and the lawful successor of the

351

Holy Peter upon whom Christ built His church."

This is what the Roman Catholics teach their children.

I would say our time is too limited to elaborate further in this matter, but they do say explicitly that the church has two heads: Christ, they say, is head of the part of the church in heaven and the pope is head of the part upon earth.

We cannot find that in God's Word at all. Besides that, explain to us how it is possible for a child to be born upon earth that is normal in life and conduct except that it has two heads? Would not that be a monster? Everyone would say that there is one head too many. How then can the church have two heads? It is a repudiation of Christ and nothing more than filthy pride of that sect to place a sinful man as representative of Christ - as though the power of the Son of God was insufficient!

But we shall not continue with this subject. Actually, the devil is a leader too and in a certain sense a lawful head of all sinners. We have of our own free will chosen him as our leader and we faithfully do his bidding. But does he remain the leader of everyone?

No, he does not. As early as Paradise, he was told he would lose his prey. "--He shall bruise your head--." The Lord Jesus said in one of His parables - "No man can enter into a strong man's house and spoil his goods except he will first bind the strong man; and then he will spoil his house." Why did the Lord say that?

Well, the wicked Jews said that He cast out devils solely by the power of the devil, that He had not the power to do it himself but derived his power from Beelzebub, the prince of the devils. They were not about to acknowledge Christ as the Head of the Church!

But the Lord, knowing their thoughts, in affect said to them, "Don't you understand how impossible it is? How could I break down the work of the devil and deliver a person from him unless I had authority over all devils and had power over them?"

That is why He would say: "I have conquered and bound the devil and for that reason can enter his house and spoil his goods. I can pluck sinners out of his claws, convert them unto Me, and let those who were bound to go eternally free." Isaiah speaks of it like this in Chapter 49:24, "Shall the prey be taken from the mighty (the devil) or the lawful captive delivered?"

Each one of us has become prisoners of Satan in our fall in Paradise, so in a certain sense he has a lawful right to rule over us. But what follows in this chapter?

"Even the captive of the mighty shall be taken away, and the prey of the terrible shall be delivered." Isaiah 49:25. All this is possible because the Blessed Mediator is the Head of His Church!

The church militant is so called because those who are "delivered" have a constant strife with the devil, the world and their own flesh! You need not think the devil is not aware of the fact that a part of his prisoners has been released. No, he roars in rage about this and will terrify them as much as possible.

Before we go further I will ask a question not in our text book. When it speaks of the universal church, (the church upon earth, in other words) does it mean those who have been brought to conversion? Is that what constitutes the visible church on earth?

No, we should never present it that way. There is a difference between confessing members and living members of the church. There will always be confessing members who take part with the living members. That will be so until death separates them forever. The Lord makes this clear to us in His parable of the wheat and the tares.

Matt. 13:24 - The kingdom of heaven is likened unto a man which sowed good seed in his field; but while men slept, his enemy came and sowed tares among the wheat and went his way. But when the blade was sprung up, and brought forth fruit, then appeared the tares also — The servants said unto the householder 'Wilt thou then that we go and gather them up?' But he said, "Nay; lest while ye gather up the tares, ye root up also the wheat with them, let both now grow together until the harvest and in time of harvest I will say to the reapers, 'Gather ye together first the tares, and bind them in bundles to burn them; but gather the wheat into my barn.' "

Thus it is with the visible church upon earth. It is inevitable that there be a certain amount of dead confessing members who belong to the visible church in an outward sense, but actually are the weeds among the wheat. But it is impossible to separate them now. It is as though the Lord would say, "Let both grow together until the harvest. I shall know then what is weed and what is wheat."

The great harvest is likened to the judgment day; at that time the angels will be sent out as reapers to separate all that have lived with the visible church, but are not actually members of Christ's body and shall keep them eternally separate from God and the true church.

The angels will know all the elect, they will not mistake them for any other but those who had been internally called. These they will put, as wheat, into the "barn".

But we must proceed in order to explain each question briefly.

What are the marks of the true church?

Answer: The pure preaching of God's Word, the proper administration of the sacraments, and ecclesiastical excommunication or discipline.

How can we determine from God's Word that these three matters are inseparable?

Answer: The Lord Jesus enjoined all three upon the apostles and left them as a command.

1. Regarding the pure preaching of the Word, He said in Matt. 28:19, "Go ye therefore, and teach all nations----"

2. That which regards Holy Baptism follows in the same text: "Baptizing them in the name of the

Father, and of the Son, and of the Holy Ghost." He speaks in reference to the Holy Supper in Luke 22, "This do in remembrance of Me."

3. He speaks regarding church discipline in Matt. 18:18, "Verily I say unto you, whatsoever ye shall bind on earth shall be bound in heaven; and whatsoever ye shall loose on earth shall be loosed in heaven."

When you become involved in the world later on, always remember this, that the true church of Christ is known when these three evidences are in exercise.

Sometime much is taught and preached, but if proper exercising of discipline and faithful administration of the sacraments is neglected it is incomplete. In times of spiritual declension and persecution it cannot always be openly exercised, nevertheless, those who belong to the living church will remain steadfast in these three matters.

Now Hellenbroek lists three questions in succession that need very little explanation; they are self explanatory; they are:

Is not the antiquity a mark of the church?

Answer: No, for Satan's kingdom is also old.

Is multitude of men a mark?

Answer: No, Christ's Church is little flock.

Is not prosperity in this world a mark?

Answer: No, John 16:33 - "In the world ye shall have tribulations."

These questions refer to the church of Rome. The fact that their church is very old and extensive

356

makes no impression on Hellenbroek. He says, "Satan's kingdom is also old and Christ's Church is a little flock." Besides that, the church of Rome is not really the oldest. In the early days the congregation of the Lord was always called the "Catholic Church". The word "Catholic" means "universal", in other words, the "universal church".

The first Christians, those immediately after the time of the apostles, were taught and confessed the same doctrine that we confess now. .

But little by little it died and superstition and worship of saints took its place. It came so far in the 5th century that the Bishop of Rome was recognized as. the sovereign of the whole church, and eventually was named the pope of Rome.

They began to call themselves Roman Catholics because the city of Rome was the capital.

There were a few among them that were not in accord with the majority, who deviated from the teachings of Christ. They found it impossible to continue in the old church.

The Roman Catholics being in the majority possessed great power. They condemned the church of Christ as being a handful of opinionated obstinates; they continually annoyed and persecuted them wherever they were.

As far as you are able, you should read carefully the history of the 1st century after Christ. You would see that the true church was continually persecuted and was but a small flock as compared to the large majority who held to all sorts of errors.

The time is spent and we must conclude. Our lesson closes with the question: "Is it enough to be an outward member of the church?"

Answer: No, we must examine ourselves to know whether we are a living member thereof. This is the point we are faced with continually, children.

Each one of you is a member of the visible, universal church, but might there be one among you who has assurance of being a living member of the church Militant?

You attend church and catechism. Each one of you has been baptized, but, have you ever inquired of your father or mother about your baptism? Have they ever discussed with you the fact that you are being reared in the church here on earth but, that being what it may, is insufficient for salvation? With all this you are set apart from the world of blind heathens, but even so, you live as a heathen in the sight of God and being an enemy must become reconciled with Him.

They, with whom God has dealings, will have no satisfaction in the fact that they belong to the external church. Their heart is changed. They realize their estrangement from God. They are no longer satisfied in the world nor do they find satisfaction in their duties. An earnest inquiry must take place between God and their soul. Everything in the world is examined; the good things but mostly evil things, maybe a few profitable matters but mostly unprofitable. But who makes an earnest examination whether he has good prospect for eternity and how he shall once appear before God?

Now, it is impossible that a person in his natural state can make this examination of himself in the correct sense.

This is because he does it out of self interest. We cannot have true grief about our separation from God without God's work within us. Men can make it look like the true work, but it is not genuine. Should we then live as though everything is well?

Absolutely not. The Lord shall then righteously say, "Because I have called and ye refused; I have stretched out my hand, and no man regarded; But ye have set at nought all My counsel and would none of My reproof" ---what now? "I also will laugh at your calamity; I will mock when your fear cometh, etc." Prov. 1:24-26.

May the triune God call you with His internal call and give you, in His House and within His walls, a place and a name better than of sons and of daughters. That is my wish and prayer for you.

So be it.

Heathen lands and hostile peoples,
Soon shall come the Lord to know;
Nations born again in Zion shall the
Lord's salvation show;
God Almighty shall on Zion strength bestow.
When the Lord shall count the nations,
Sons and daughters He shall see,
Born to endless life in Zion
And their joyful song shall be "Blessed Zion,
All our fountains are in thee."

Lesson 32

On Justification

Our next lesson deals with Justification. We saw last week in our lesson on the church that Christ is its sole head, just as a body can have but one head.

As long as the head is intact there is no danger for the body. Just as when you see a man swimming, there is no concern about the body if you can see his head. It is the same in the case of the church, too. Even if the body with all its members (the church upon earth) is beneath the waters of oppression, it will not drown. This is because its Head, Christ, cannot be separated from that body and it is impossible that Christ be submerged beneath the waves of oppression.

That is why Paul said, "For the husband is the head of the wife, even as Christ is the head of the church; and He is the Savior of the body."

Do you understand this now? Paul would say: the whole body of the church is kept from harm by its Head and the Head will never be separated from the body of the church. What are your thoughts about this; does the world exist for the sake of the church or the church for the sake of the world?

I would say this is an easy question. It is certain that the whole world with all its wickedness is preserved in and through the long-suffering of God. This is to the end that the elect, which is dispersed among the inhabitants of the world, shall be gathered in.

That is why the world exists. The elect are the "buoys" by which worldlings are kept afloat. The day that God gathers in all the "buoys", the others will sink irretrievably away.

It is not the government with its military power that carries and shelters the nation, O no, it is the fact that there are still children of God living in our country that have been converted or are to be brought in that God upholds our nation even until now.

This pitiful world ought to realize that it still exists because there is a poor and despised group of people in its midst. The Lord will soon gather them to Himself but, until then, they stand as a bulwark round about the world.

The Lord referred to this in a parable. He said, "The kingdom of heaven is like unto leaven, which a woman took, and hid in three measures of meal, till the whole was leavened." This is the shortest parable of the whole Bible, consisting of but one text. What was the Lord saying with this parable?

The three measures of meal are the three generations from which the whole world is populated, namely; Shem, Ham and Japheth. When the Word of God has been preached to all those generations and all the elect have been gathered in, it is as the leaven (yeast) which the woman hid in

361

three measures of meal and waited until the whole was leavened. It is in that way the Lord waits until the appointed time, until all, who have been called according to His eternal purpose, are called with His internal call and gathered in.

When a house is being built here, you see all sorts of piles, planks and scaffolds. The scaffolds rise so high you can hardly see the house. But when all is completed, the scaffolding and all other such things are removed from the site, leaving the finished home.

That is the way it is with the visible church on earth, too. All the so-called confessing members are merely used as scaffolding for the building of a house. God uses them for various purposes but ultimately it is the finished building that remains standing. Hellenbroek closes his lesson on the church very appropriately with the question: Is it enough to be an outward member of the church? And the answer: No, we must examine ourselves whether we are a living member thereof.

We have strayed completely from our lesson. We must not continue with the lesson on the church, but speak on justification.

The first question is: Are the internally called also justified?

Answer: Yes, Romans 8:30, "Whom He called, them He also justified."

What is it to be justified?

Answer: It is to be acquitted from guilt and punishment and to be entitled to eternal life. The benefit succeeding election is the calling and one succeeding the calling is justification.

What is the opposite of righteous? Unrighteous or wicked, of course. Now you enumerate who and what are justified. Do it slowly and with thought.

1. The Divine Essence is justified.

2. Each person of the Divine Essence in particular is justified.

3. All the fore-ordained angels are justified.

4. The complete creation as it was created by God is justified. And do you know who was justified in particular?

5. Adam in the state of righteousness. He was the first to receive an innate righteousness from God. But in addition he also had a righteousness in respect to the law. God had bestowed upon him the law of love to which he could be obedient by virtue of the righteousness created within him.

Can we still obtain eternal life through keeping the law?

No, that has been terminated. Why?

The law is still the same and the Lord is still the same; what then has changed?

Adam lost, not only his innate, inherent righteousness (and ours in him), but also the will and the power to keep the law. So it is impossible to become righteous now through keeping the law. That is why the apostle teaches in Romans 8:3, "For what the law could not do, in that it was weak, (why?) through the flesh, God sending His own Son in the likeness of sinful flesh, etc."

Through sin, then, two things became impossible:
1. That man can satisfy any demands made upon him, and 2. that man can become righteous through keeping the law.

But even if this is so, are not the same demands made of us that had been made of Adam?

Yes, the demands have not been lessened.

One thing more though, and be sure to express the feeling of your heart in this: Is it the perfect right of a righteous God to demand from someone, something which is impossible to accomplish?

Answer: Yes, God is always righteous.

Yes, this is easily said, but how can I explain it?

Let us just suppose that there is a man to whom I owe one thousand dollars. I am fully aware that I have this debt and acknowledge that this man is just in his demand. Time slips by and I have not been able to obtain money for paying off or even diminishing that debt. How long can these two situations exist, namely, my indebtedness and this man's demand to pay?

Well, if I never pay, it would last forever. Nothing can help this situation.

If I come with excuses and say, "It is impossible to pay, I am totally unable, so would you nullify the fact you have a just demand on me? Anyone with a sound mind would refuse to do this, especially when it is the debtor's own fault he cannot pay.

Mankind, therefore, shall remain in the state into which he has fallen; eternally guilty while the Lord requires His just demands. Not one creature born from fallen mankind could conceive of a way that the law can make him righteous again and he can be released from the demands upon him.

What men and angels could not conceive of, the Lord could, with the result that Christ from eternity with His whole heart became surety and satisfied the demands perfectly;

1st., for the church universal, but also,

2nd., for each elect in particular.

What has been made possible by this? We can be pronounced justified by a righteous God and acquitted from sin. What is this justification: Answer: Receiving freedom from guilt and punishment, and being entitled to eternal life.

Is there any difference between justification and sanctification?

Answer: Yes, (1) Justification is an act without, but sanctification within us. (2) Justification removes the guilt, and sanctification the pollution of sin, (3) The act of justification is complete, but sanctification, during this life is not complete.

Scripture speaks of the act of justification as a pronouncement of acquital as is done in the court of justice.

Are the three Divine Persons involved in this matter?

Answer: Yes, the Father represents the person of a judge. The Son is the Intercessor and Mediator for whose sake we are justified. The Holy Ghost gives us knowledge of our justification and seals it unto us.

These are very momentous questions and answers. We shall endeavor to say something of each of them in an uncomplicated way. God's Word uses the example of a court of justice in everyday life. What do we have here?

1. A judge. 2. A defendant. 3. An advocate. 4. A court recorder. 5. Witnesses.

How should this be explained?

We said previously, an elect sinner can be justified only through Christ. Not that he is declared to be righteous in himself, or that righteousness is poured upon him, no, but a time appears in his life when the Lord makes him know that he lies eternally justified in Christ.

I do not say that all elect are dealt with in equal clarity in this. The Lord is free in all His doings. But for those, whose time is at hand, there will be a feeling in their heart of being separated from God. There will be a court of tribunal set up in their consciences, where God the Father stands as judge, and the elect as an accused defendant. But who are the witnesses?

There are three witnesses testifying against the sinner. They are the law, the devil and his own conscience. We read of such a sentencing in Zechariah 3:3. Joshua stood before the Lord in filthy garments and Satan stood at his right hand. Why? To oppose him; that is, to accuse him.

The second, the law, is setting forth its complaints demanding obedience and requiring that punishment be meted out.

The third, his own conscience, stands there as accuser, saying; "All things are true; then and then you did this and that."

There stands the pitiful sinner. What is left for him to do? This is no place for him to speak out. He stands there as the Publican with penitent feet that dare not go further. With penitent eyes, that he dares not lift up. With penitent hands which he smites upon his guilty breast.

A speechless condemned sinner, who, being charged and accused, stands before a righteous Judge. What shall he do but stand in silence? He shall consider the Judge to be perfectly just in every way, sanctions the sentence pronounced upon him, and accepts his guilt and God's justice.

If the sinner justifies the Judge in the sentence pronounced upon him what shall the judge do then?

Then God justifies the sinner.

Not because the sinner justified God! No, that is impossible, but it always precedes it.

When all the witnesses have pronounced their accusations and the sinner has accepted them, the Lord (figuratively speaking) stands up and says to the devil: "The Lord rebuke thee, O Satan, yes the Lord rebuke thee. Your head has been bruised long ago, and I shall retrieve my captives."

He says to the law, "Has not My Son accomplished the whole law?" Did He not say, "I delight to do Thy will, O my God; yea, Thy law is within My heart." There is nothing more required of this sinner. The conscience too is pacified in the satisfaction of the Mediator. Hence the mouths of all witnesses are stopped. The Judge shall point out His Son to all the witnesses saying, "He was Surety for Him."

We see seven points in this subject of justification, all of which are mentioned in our lesson. Give good attention:

1. The sinner becomes aware of this in the court of his conscience.

2. The defendant in this court, being accused and acquitted is the elect.

3. The Judge, who gives the verdict of acquittal, is God the Father.

4. The witnesses who oppose the sinner and are his accusers are: the devil, the law and the conscience.

5. The person for whose sake the sinner is set free, and who is his Surety, is the Son of God, Jesus Christ.

6. The great recorder in the court of justice is the Holy Ghost. He assures the acquitted of his justification and sets His seal on him.

7. But now if all this has taken place, how can the sinner accept it?

The imputed righteousness of Christ becomes an imparted righteousness for him. By free grace it is imputed and imparted, but is that sufficient?

The sinner will have no profit of all this if he does not accept this righteousness by faith.

The eighth, then, is faith which is a hand or instrument whereby the sinner receives the merits of Christ.

368

Hellenbroek substantiates this with John 1:12, "But as many as received Him, to them gave He the power to become the sons of God, even to them that believe on His Name."

Be careful that you do not understand this to mean that justification is the result of our faith. The essential point of the matter is the imputed righteousness of Christ. This is accepted by faith by the sinner.

Just as everybody even before birth lies condemnable before God in Adam just so, all elect, from eternity, lie righteous before God in Christ. However, they first become aware of this, in the court of their conscience, in justification. It is for this reason that all who are declared free, by virtue of eternal election, shall become free indeed during this life.

Earlier in the lesson we pointed out five who were to be considered "righteous". Who remembers who they were?

Answer:

1. The righteousness of Essence. The entire Divine Essence is righteous.

2. The righteousness of each person, each of the three Divine Persons singly.

3. The righteousness of creation, respecting the entire creation.

4. Those who are comprehended in the elect angels.

5. Those who are comprehended in Adam as covenant head.

369

But now I would like to add to this list. Try to remember them.

6. There is also a righteous demand of the holy Divine law, before as well as after the fall.

7. There is an eternal righteousness in the Divine tribunal. Comrie refers to it as a righteousness before faith in contra-distinction to a righteousness by faith which comes later.

8. There is an acquired righteousness, which Christ acquired during His active and passive obedience.

9. There is the imputed righteousness which is imputed to the elect for Christ's sake.

10. There is the gift of righteousness, which Hellenbroek refers to in question 18: Who imputes (righteousness) to us?

Answer: God, by a gracious gift.

11. That righteousness becomes an accepted righteousness which the justified sinner accepts unto himself by saving faith.

12. There is a righteousness of confidence, that is to say, as soon as God's people are presented the essence of faith there is at the same time, with that essence of faith, a fruit which might be called confidence. Before the new birth there is no ability to believe. But that life of trust which flows out of the gift of life is an active reliance bringing to the conscious mind the imputed righteousness of Christ.

These points of doctrine are difficult for children to understand and intellectual knowledge of all this is insufficient to salvation but you will have no harm in knowing about these things.

To justify is the opposite of condemning.

Consequently, if we are not accepted by God in Christ as righteous (free from guilt) we remain condemned.

Now I do not say that all elect are immediately estabished in the knowledge of this, but they can be established in this knowledge and must not deny it. Hellenbroek said, "Can we be assured of our justification?" Answer, Yes, Romans 5:1, "Therefore being justified by faith, we have peace with God, through our Lord Jesus Christ." And in Romans 8:16 he says, "The Spirit itself beareth witness with our spirit, that we are the children of God."

O boys and girls, never forget how necessary it is that the merits of Christ become our possession. We can only be one or the other; righteous before God or condemned.

Wouldn't you think that to be the most wonderful occurance; to be made righteous in Christ by God? Then we are at peace with everything. Peace with the Triune God, peace with death, peace with the grave, peace with the heaviest oppressions. But do you know with what a child of God never has peace, even though he is aware of his righteousness in Christ? He cannot be at peace with himself. He is in conflict with sin, in conflict with Satan and with everything that is contrary to God. And the more of that peace in Christ he has with God, the greater the conflict he has with everything outside of God. That is the way it should be in the very heart. Truthfully now, have you ever spent a moment of your life in thought about the necessity of being righteous in Christ or otherwise remaining eternally damned?

By nature we are all lost, but then you shall be eternally lost. It is such a great step to take from this life into eternity.

I believe you would give more thought about a long journey you should make here on earth than about this one to eternity; am I not correct?

For example, if your father had plans to take you on a trip to India or America, I know you would think about it all day long and perhaps nights too. Mainly, you would think about three things:

1st. About your departure here.

2nd. About the trip itself, the passage.

3rd. About the arrival in that strange land.

First about the departing here, boy, that will be an experience; family, friends, and neighbors! Visiting places that are familiar and dear to us - don't you think so, too?

Then the journey over the ocean; what that will be like in that huge ocean liner!

But at last the arrival. It will be impossible to mentally conceive of how that will be in that distant land. I am sure your mind would be busy every day with these thoughts. And I am not saying that there is anything wrong with that. Of course not, you may think about those things without fear.

But now you stand before a far more important journey than to another part of the world, or it is more correct to say, you are on this journey. Just as soon as one is born, he begins this journey to eternity. Nothing is more sure than the fact that every creature will arrive sooner or later.

The question may well be asked: How shall we arrive? As those who are damned or those who are justified?

You sit here now, quietly laughing or talking with one another, as if it is boring. Be sure though that it is not with me you have to do but with a righteous God. And if your thoughts are about your being before His tribunal, you surely won't laugh. The Lord is still knocking on the door of your heart with all manner of callings but you continually refuse to listen. May the Lord assemble with you in the court of your conscience while in this time state and acquit you of guilt and punishment on the merits of Christ.

And, if there are some who can no longer live as they have or as they would have liked to live, may the Lord give you no rest until you may say from experience, "It is God who justifies, who is it that condemns? It is Christ who died for me, yea, rather sits on the right hand of the Father, and Who also prays for us."

May the Lord take away all the supports upon which you put your trust and prevent any satisfaction in duties or religion. They are perilous. May you experience it as the poet sings of it in Psalm 73:

In glory thou only my portion shall be.
On earth for none other, I long but for Thee.
My flesh and heart falter, but God is my stay
The strength of my spirit, my portion for aye.

Lesson 33

Of Faith

The last question in our previous lesson was:

How then doth faith operate in this matter? And the answer was: As a hand or instrument, whereby we receive the merits of Christ.

The lesson this afternoon begins immediately on this subject by asking: How many kinds of faith are there?

It appears that all faith cannot be considered to be true faith because what is the answer?

Four kinds: historical, temporary, miraculous and a saving faith. We shall first recite the questions in their order and then speak briefly of each one.

What is a historical faith?

Answer: A bare assent to known truth.

Is this not a good faith?

Answer: Yes, it is necessary, but not sufficient. James 2:19, "Thou believest that there is one God; thou dost well; the devils also believe and tremble."

What is a temporary faith?

Answer: An assent to and profession of the truth

374

for a time and with some external satisfaction. This is shown to be true from the parable of the sower to which we shall give more attention just a little later.

What is the faith of miracles?

Answer: A strong persuasion that a miracle will be performed by or on us.

Are not these three kinds of faith of a saving nature?

No, I Cor. 12:2, "Though I have all faith, so that I could remove mountains and have not charity, I am nothing. (All kinds other than true saving faith are meant here.)

In how many things does saving faith consist?

Answer: In three: knowledge, assent and trust. An implied faith without knowledge is not sufficient. It is written, "This is life eternal that they might know thee." John 17:3.

Even if men have intimate trust and great faith, without knowledge of God and Christ, it is not true faith.

In the parable of the sower the differences are made apparent: There was but one sower, and he had but one kind of seed with him but what is it that made the difference? The different kinds of ground upon which he sowed. Some of the seed fell by the way side. The Lord's explanation of this to the disciples was, "When any one heareth the word of the kingdom, and understandeth it not, then cometh the wicked one, and catcheth away that which was sown in his heart."

Temporary faith is likened to the seed that fell upon stoney places. They sprouted immediately but because they had no deepness of earth to sprout roots, they withered away quickly. Man, by nature, has a stoney heart that is unsusceptable to the Divine seed. Even if the seed falls in such a heart, between the rocks of conscience, throughout which there are crevices and cracks, it may become troubled under the preaching of the Word or other means but it passes swiftly away.

The Lord Jesus said, "And anon with joy receiveth it." That is just the opposite of that in true saving faith, because there sadness and dejection comes in first, then, in time, joy.

What is necessary then? That all the stones be taken out of the field and it be made into a fertile land. Then it is capable of receiving seed that can bring forth fruit.

Miraculous faith is even less saving. There are many accounts of miracles in God's Word that were not unto salvation for the person upon whom the miracles happened. Who can name some of them?

Answer: The nine lepers whom Jesus had cured but had not returned to give thanks.

That is one; who can give another?

Answer: Of the man in Bethesda who had an infirmity for 38 years.

That is also an example of a person upon whom a miracle was performed, but who had not saving faith. The Lord said to him when He healed him, "Sin no more, lest a worse thing come unto thee."

There are people, even in our time, upon whom or through whom miracles are performed, but, even so, they remain unconverted.

It happened this way with a woman in Zeeland. She appeared to be a nice religious person who faithfully attended church services but was unconverted. She had always been a healthy woman and had borne fourteen children. But one day she became completely insane without any previous indication something was wrong. It was a fearful situation; she wanted to murder her 5 month old child by butchering it. She had been so badly and suddenly seized upon by this thing that she did nothing but yell and shout. Naturally, the doctor was brought in immediately. He ordered her to be put into an institution because there seemed nothing he could do for her.

Her husband and children had to agree. But one child felt so terrible about their mother leaving and asked the doctor if they might try confining her to a small room to be cared for by her husband and sons and if it remained the same after one week, she would be brought to the institution.

Permission was given for this. Their minister and an elder were soon there to visit this family. As soon as they entered the little room in which this woman was, she seemed to become possessed of the devil. She acted very wild and called out, "Away with you. You are all deceivers."

The minister spoke to the elder saying, "Shall we pray?"

The woman screamed, "No, do not pray, I do not want it, away with you." She pulled hair from her head.

Then the minister said, "It appears this woman is completely possessed of the devil. Let us go away. She will soon attack us."

But the elder said, "No, we shall not go away yet, you must offer prayer, dominie, otherwise the devil will laugh and say, 'Look at this will you? I am the winner; they have hurried away.' You must sit down calmly and her husband and I will stand by her to make sure she does you no harm."

In the meantime the woman was fearfully wild, but the minister began to pray and what do you supposed happened?

He no sooner had said a few words and the woman slumped down as though she had died. The minister said, "Amen", the woman opened her eyes and was better; considerably better. She remained weak for a little while but was no longer sick. The Lord was willing to do this miracle upon the petition of His child and servant, but the woman, even so, was not converted at that time. It was miraculous faith applied to her.

This has actually happened in Zeeland.

Up to now we have explained what faith is not and now we shall see what it is.

Our lesson has this question: "In how many things does saving faith consist?"

Answer: In three: knowledge, assent and trust.

We have said before that historical faith is a bare

378

assent to known truth. This does not involve the proper sanctified knowledge, assent, and, even less, trust as is in saving faith. The person who gives this faith is God and the person who receives it is the elect. The time he receives it is when God searches him out and instills life within him. Now we see three essentials in this faith:

1. The grace of faith.
2. The action of faith.
3. The degrees of faith.

Which of these three appears first?

The grace of faith, of course. Out of that flows the exercise of faith; then come the degrees of faith.

Always remember to keep these in their proper order because they are often taken out of turn. Some persons try to exercise faith before faith is even imparted.

This cannot, in reality, be done, no more than a dead man can walk. Nevertheless, men place the exercise of historical faith or temporary faith ahead of the action of true saving faith.

Some claim, too, that there are degrees or steps toward faith as well as in faith. These are Pelagians. Do not believe any of these errors.

God Himself imparts faith in the soul first. Then, by grace, through that imparted faith, they can believe. That is plain enough, isn't it? How can I make use of a tool before I have it in my possession?

If now the soul has received faith, does it exercise faith for its own benefit or toward God?

This action is always toward the Lord. Genuine

action flows out of God and returns to God.

Hellenbroek says, "It is that deed of the soul whereby she heartily wills and desires, not alone that the promises of the Gospel be true in themselves, but whereby she also, with submissive affection longs for and actually accepts the Lord Jesus as the only cause of her salvation, accompanied with a denial of herself and all other things or persons."

There are also lawful deeds which have no origin in the Holy Spirit but flow from a disturbed conscience. These do not take place to come to know Christ, but to be free of hell and to go to heaven. Only the deeds or actions of true saving faith flow toward God, not seeking its own salvation or escape of punishment, no, true faith allows only God a place in the heart. It also admits its own guilt.

The degrees of faith are indicated according to the deeds of faith. They see (to further explain the meaning of this), at the very beginning, a necessity to be in Christ. Then a strong desire to be redeemed in Christ. This is what is called the action and the degrees in the essence of faith.

First God touches the soul in its state of deadness, making it alive and granting within it the essence of faith, and in the strength of this the soul, in turn, takes hold of Christ. But if the Holy Spirit continues, He cuts off the soul from Adam and teaches the sinner the true justifying act of faith. Denying all else, the sinner appropriates the Mediator through faith as the only way to reconciliation.

In this way he comes to the quitessence of faith. What is the fruit of this justifying act of faith?

Hellenbroek answers: "The special and certain application of the promises of the Gospel and the Lord Jesus personally to every believer." Paul experienced this and spoke of it in Gal. 2:20, "I am crucified with Christ, nevertheless I live; yet not I, but Christ liveth in me; and the life which I now live in the flesh I live by the faith of the Son of God who loved me."

Is this effect always present in God's people? "No," says he, "believers are often tossed about by the temptations of Satan and the seductions of the flesh which they must always sincerely withstand." They can be assured of the sincerity of their faith; it is Scriptural, because Paul writes, "For I know Whom I have believed, and am persuaded that He is able to keep that which I have committed unto Him against that day." 2 Tim. 1:12.

Also, they must take a stand according to this because they are admonished, "Examine yourselves whether ye be in the faith; prove your own selves. Know ye not your own selves, how that Jesus Christ is in you." 2 Cor. 13:5.

You must not misconstrue this to mean that a person can just naturally exercise faith. That is not the meaning of this text. Hellenbroek speaks here of God's living (spiritually alive) children who have received saving grace and in whom the essence of faith has been granted. They can stand in the strength of this newly given life, assured of the genuiness of their faith.

And this examination is certainly necessary because hypocritical faith can appear to be very similar. But do you know where the deficiency is?

Many people lay hold of Christ before the Holy Spirit has ever laid hold of them. Herein lies the great difference between conversion and conversion. Let us take an example: Two boys come under conviction, one comes under the common operation of the Spirit. He becomes deeply moved by a sermon or a death in the family and becomes aware that his life as it is, is not good. This boy says, "I see now my behavior and my life fall far short. If I should die in this state I shall go to hell."

He now changes his ways and lives a different life. Instead of attending worldly amusements he keeps company with God's people, etc.

If you see the change taken place in the behavior of this boy, you would say, "Something wonderful has taken place, well, well, what a change! It is not the same boy anymore." This lasts for a time and then this boy receives a text or a Psalter verse in his thoughts while at prayer or while in some anxiety. This gives him much encouragement and he believes that God has begun the good work in him. He is now confident that all will end well. He rests in these as his conversion.

But the other boy is also convinced that his life has not been good. But, through the saving work of the Spirit, he sees not only that his life has been wrong, but that he himself is corrupt. He discovers that God had created him good and upright and now

382

discovers that through sin he is completely cut off from Him. He discovers also that he not only is living without God, but actually is living at enmity with Him. This boy also takes on another way of life. The main concern of this new life is not to avoid punishment, no, even though just punishment is not a small matter to him, his main concern is more with God's holy demands than with the punishment he should receive. He becomes aware and admits that he has offended God's virtues.

He realizes that he must be reconciled with God. Without that there is no rest in his soul. These are not brought about by a text or Psalter verse entering the thoughts. I do not say that the Lord does not give a bit of refreshment or instruction through His Word. That is another matter. But He does not give security in these.

What is now the difference between these boys?

The one works, with himself in view in all things, to avoid punishment, but the other works through God unto God. The first frees himself with the Truth without ever having been freed through the Truth. The first boy gradually becomes secure and converted in all that has transpired in his life. But the person in whom saving faith has been granted, becomes more and more aware of his sins and his miserable condition and cannot save himself with the Truth and the possibility there is in it.

Thousands of people have stranded upon a reef in this matter. They believe they are prepared to die and think that God has made them ready, but they have made themselves ready in a rash sort of belief.

No, true saving faith causes the soul not only to know that he lies condemned before God, but also to know who God is and that His justice must be satisfied.

I do not say that every child of God can speak about this equally well. The Lord gives one person more gifts to distinguish one thing from another than another person but, they all shall be taught this in a greater or lesser degree. This is indispensible to salvation. "He that cometh to God must believe that He is" said Paul (Hebrews 11:6). By this he means not only believe that He exists, but also who He is in all His attributes. The Holy Spirit teaches this to a sinner through saving faith.

But now our time is almost gone. We must end this lesson.

It is the last time this year that we shall meet with another in Catechism class.

If the Lord will and we live, next week will come Christmas Day and then New Year's Day. Have any of you ever reflected upon how important Christmas is? It is written in the Bible, "For everyone that exalteth himself shall be abased; and he that humbleth himself shall be exalted" (Luke 18:14). Now this is applicable to each one of us in this life, but do you know where it had even more significance?

Adam was established in a very high position. God had placed Him there in creation. Yet he wanted to be even greater than he was. He wanted to elevate himself but was debased to an unspeakable degree through sin. Everyone understands this.

On the other hand, Christ was as God - equal with the Father and the Holy Ghost, and took upon Himself the form of a servant in His Mediatorship. He humbled Himself to become man from this extremely high state, being even God Himself. No one can humble himself as Christ humbled Himself, but can anyone ever be exalted to the degree He was? The Lord exalted Him above all brethren and said, "Sit thou at My Right hand." Adam desired to exalt himself to that position but was abased. Christ, however, abased Himself and was exalted. We commemorate this abasement at Christmas time.

It is a custom nowadays for people to erect a Christmas tree in Sunday school, churches and in homes complete with lights and decorated with all sorts of pretty things, and think that this belongs to Christmas. But I caution you, boys and girls, do not participate in this kind of ungodliness because it is heathen idolatry. Is it necessary to celebrate the precious commemoration of the birth of the Mediator in this pagan way? It is horrible to do so. Be sure that you do not go along with such things even though the whole world does it.

Even though your parents or others in whose home you live think it is not objectionable, you must still not do it. I do not mean by this to invite you to disobedience, no, I merely say: if you do not participate in such sins, it is not disobedience.

I know of one little four-year-old boy whose father and mother had no scruples. Once they went to the fair and took this little fellow along with them. But when he saw the bustle and commotion in that village, what do you suppose he did? All of a sudden he pulled his hands loose from his parent's and ran as fast as he could out of that village. The mother and father stared at him in surprise; you can imagine. But they had to go find him, though, because he was much too young to be unattended. And where do you think he had gone?

Just outside of that village was a marshy field with much reeds and ditches which were dry in summertime. They found their little boy in one of those dry ditches on his knees and they heard him fervently praying, saying that he was unconverted and could not go to that fair and asked if the Lord would give him a new heart.

When the parents heard that, they had not the courage or desire anymore to go to the fair. It made them ashamed. Quietly they went back home with their little boy. This points out how declining sinful activities is not disobedience.

I hope that you too may be burdened with sin and that seed being sown may no longer fall on a stony heart, but in a quickened heart as in well prepared soil. All sorts of thorns and weeds may grow up but they can never choke out that saving faith.

Perhaps there are some amongst us here who can relate to that little boy, who also occasionally seek out a hidden place to call upon the Lord. May the Lord discover you more and more to Himself and to yourself.

May He, by the Holy Spirit working in you, cause you to personally take hold of the merits of Christ by saving faith, that you may be privileged to say also, "For by grace are ye saved through faith; and that not of yourselves it is the gift of God."

May the Lord do this for His Name's sake.

Lesson 34

Of Sanctification and good works

Hellenbroek asks in the lesson on the effectual calling, "To what end is Christ thus exalted?"

Answer: To apply His benefits to us.

What are the benefits bestowed in this life?

Answer: They are calling, justification, and sanctification.

We have seen that the calling is the first benefit in this life and that there are two kinds of calling. The outward call only occurs through God's Word. The inward call takes place through Word and Spirit in the heart of the elect and it alone is soul-saving.

After the inward call the second benefit, justification is applied. This is an acquital of guilt and punishment and a bestowing of the right to eternal life.

Now, there are two kinds of sins: original and actual. And what were we taught regarding original sins? Into how many parts are they divided?

Answer: Into two parts—inherited guilt, 2nd—inherited pollution.

Inherited guilt is the guilt of the first sin. This is chargeable to us in Adam before we are born. But inherited pollution is the inbred corruption which we inherit from our parents.

Hellenbroek explains that justification is an act that takes place outside of man and it takes away the guilt of sin.

But sanctification takes place within a person and effects the pollution of sin.

Justification takes place in completeness, because it is an aquittal of the sinner for Christ's sake in the court of the conscience where the First Person is Judge, the Second Person is Surety and the Third, the Holy Spirit, places His seal upon the entire work. The mouth of witnesses are stopped and the accused accepts the acquittal by faith. That is a complete work.

This was just a brief recapitulation. But this afternoon Hellenbroek deals with the lesson on Sanctification.

He puts the question: Are those who are justified also sanctified?

Answer: Yes, both go together. I Cor. 1:30, "But of Him ye are in Christ Jesus, who of God is made unto us wisdom, righteousness, sanctification and redemption."

What is sanctification?

Answer: A renewing of the whole man.

Is it not only a change in the outward actions?

Answer: No, but also of the inward man.

Does an external change also flow from it?

Answer: Yes, in all the conduct. I Thess. 5:23, "And the very God of peace sanctify you wholly; and I pray God your whole spirit and soul and body be preserved blameless unto the coming of our Lord Jesus Christ."

This renewing of the inward man is the work of the Holy Spirit, Who works in the heart of the elect to take away the pollution of sin and to destroy the clinging corruption in its nature. Even though a child of God is acquitted of all guilt and can never ever be condemned, but contrariwise becomes a new creature in respect to his state. His nature, though, is still corrupt. Sins of all sorts, in thoughts, words, and deeds cleave unto him daily.

The Lord desires that this ever clinging corruption becomes progressively brought to nothing immediately after the guilt is removed in justification. Paul wrote often of this mortification of sins in believers. But sanctification is never perfected in this life, even in the most advanced believers. That is why he says in Philippians 3:12, "Not as though I had already attained, either were already perfect;

389

but I follow after, if that I may apprehend that for which also I am apprehended of Christ Jesus."

Paul did not mean in this text he "followed after" whether his sins had still to be forgiven, no, that had taken place; of that he was sure. But, he felt himself still imperfect in sanctification. That is why he "followed after" (or was concerned) that he become increasingly sanctified, "Till we come (as he says in Ephesians 4:13) in the unity of the faith, and of the knowledge of the Son of God, unto a perfect man unto the measure of the stature of the fulness of Christ." It is plain here that Paul is speaking not of justification, but of sanctification. He begins the chapter by saying, "I therefore the prisoner of the Lord, beseech you that ye walk worthy of the vocation wherewith ye are called with all lowliness and meekness, etc."

The apostle strongly urged the fulfillment by faith of sanctification after the calling and justification, "For the perfecting of the saints, for the work of the ministry, for the edifying of the body of Christ," as he says in verse 12.

Is sanctification present in all believers in equal measure?

No, it has its various degrees; in one more and in another less. It is also changeable and subject to increase and decrease in the self same person, (Question 9). Would it be possible, then, that a child of God be entirely without sanctification, or if he had possessed it, later could lose all of it?

No, that is impossible, where the grace of God has

once been, there it remains. There is no apostasy of saints.

Who can give me an example to prove that there is no apostasy of saints?

Answer: I Peter 1:5, "Who are kept by the power of God through faith" and unto what? "Unto salvation already to be revealed in the last time."

Can we cite instances from God s Word that show sanctification in a believer to be more at one time than another?

Yes, that is clearly obvious in saints of the Bible. When David had fallen into sin by numbering the people, etc. there was not much exercise of sanctification to be seen in his daily life. So it was with Noah when he was drunken and with Peter when he denied his Lord. Various persons could be mentioned to prove that the saints are subject to continual increase and decrease in the exercise of sanctification. This was true in Hezekiah's case too. He had no lively exercise of sanctification when he allowed the messengers of Babylon to see all his treasures. It was then that pride should have been mortified instead of nourished.

How do God's people advance in sanctification?

Answer: By removing all inward and outward hindrances through grace of the Holy Spirit, depending upon Jesus' power in using all means toward advancement.

Now I am going to ask you something, the answer of which, you will not find in your lesson. This is a difficult lesson to comprehend, but do try to listen atttentively.

If sanctification is merely imperfect in the saints and at times they fall into outward sins, can we consider that to be genuine sanctification? Can such a thing be?

Yes, even if it is here in part and imperfect, it is still the genuine nature of sanctification. All the elect are perfectly righteous in Christ their Head and likewise are they perfectly holy in their Head Christ Jesus. They are as free from the pollution of sin in Him as they are from the guilt of sin. Yet they must endure the indwelling corruption as a vexing power till the day of their death. The daily decreasing of sins and the increasing mortification of the old man is a matter that takes place here only in part. The difference lies in this:

1st. What God's people are before God in Christ Jesus, or,

2nd. What they actually and personally experience in practice here in this life.

Even if one would reach the highest step of sanctification here by means of the Holy Spirit, the unfolding of it and the complete removal of the inherent corruption and the succeeding glorification shall be in heaven.

God's people will not only be freed from the condemning power that is, the strength of sin, but also from the vexing power which is the deed of sin. So, not only freed from the body of sin but also from the body of death.

It was very evident that Paul knew the difference between these two; he spoke of it in Romans 7:24

392

"O wretched man that I am! Who shall deliver me from the body of this death?"

He longed for the perfection in sanctification which only exists in glorification.

Faith will no longer be necessary there because it will be a perfect beholding. Hope also will have no place because it is a matter of eternal possession. But love shall continue without end. Love never perishes and is superior to all.

But we should now continue a bit further in our lesson. Hellenbroek follows up the lesson on sanctification with some questions about good works, asking, "What are the fruits of faith and sanctification?"

Answer: Good works. James 2:18 "Show me thy faith without thy works, and I will show thee my faith by my works."

What are good works?

Answer: Deeds that are performed: (1) of faith; (2) according to the law of God. (3) to the glory of God.

Prove that they must proceed from faith.

Answer: Hebrews 11:6 "without faith it is impossible to please God."

Prove that they must be performed according to the law of God.

Answer: Matt. 15:9 "In vain they do worship me, teaching for doctrines the commandments of men."

Prove that they must be directed to God's glory.

Answer: I Cor. 10:31 "Whether therefore ye eat or drink, or whatsoever ye do, do all to the glory of God."

393

You have memorized these answers but what are your thoughts on this subject. Do good works precede, so that men arrive at faith and sanctification through good works? Or, can they not do good works without faith?

I shall take an example from nature: Imagine a beautiful tree in a garden laden with fine fruit. Must that tree bear fruit in order to be considered a tree?

Or does it bear fruit because it is a tree? It bears fruit because it is a tree, isn't that so?

There can never be fruit before the tree exists. Likewise good works cannot take place without faith and sanctification. Yet there are people who say that good works precede faith. They say, "A person should do all he can to become a Christian. One comes to faith through good works." It is our stand, based upon God's Word, God's people do good works because they are Christians. Do you see what a great difference there is between these two views?

It can be no other way than that those savingly called, justified and sanctified must and shall do good works. The Lord Jesus says in Matt. 5:16, "Let your light so shine before men, that they may see your good works, and glorify your Father which is in heaven."

Good works of men can never merit heaven; only the accomplishments of Christ have done that.

Another point is that even the best of good works is still imperfect. Isaiah does not say "All our unrighteousnesses are as filthy rags" but "all our righteousnesses are as filthy rags."

Doing good works is very different from being converted. God's children are inclined to do them, 1st. To glorify God, 2nd, To edify their neighbor, 3rd. To assure themselves of their faith. Their whole purpose is to glorify God.

Why is it that one cannot do good works without faith?

Answer: The Lord says, "Make the tree good and his fruit good."

Did you get the idea here? That is the main thing; without making the tree good there can no good fruit come from it.

And who is that good tree?

Adam, an elect, or someone else?

Come now, give us your thoughts about this. Adam in the state of righteousness is symbolized as the vine. He was the head of the covenant of works and the whole human race. All creatures were comprehended in him as the branches. This is the way it was in the state of righteousness but since his fall and being the head of the covenant discontinued, all persons as branches have, consequently, sprung out of the now corrupted vine. Does fruit grow on these branches? And what kind of fruit? Yes it does, it is sin. Sin, death, grief and misery are the fruits that continually come forth on the branches of the corrupted vine.

Do at the same time some good fruits spring out of that same evil vine? That is impossible.

Where do they come from then?

Answer: There is a good vine too!

O,---and what vine is that then?

Answer: Jesus said, "I am the true vine, and my Father is the husbandman. Every branch in me — that beareth fruit, he purgeth it, that it may bring forth more fruit!"

Do you hear that? There is also a good vine.

But now how is it possible that these evil branches bring forth fruit through the good vine? You would say this is an impossibility wouldn't you?

It is, too, considering it from a natural sense, because even if there was a bad tree set next to a good tree for over a hundred years the fruit of it would still be as bad as if it had been growing among other bad trees. What must take place for the fruit to be good?

You are all still very young but most of you live in the country where you certainly must have heard of grafting.

If a farmer or some other person has a wild apple or pear tree in his orchard he notices it grows much faster than a domestic tree. Generally the branches become large and there are many leaves. The farmer says to himself, "It is a very nice tree but what good does it do me." The fruit of it is so bitter one cannot eat it. Do you know what I shall do? I shall graft into that tree." At a certain time of the year he removes a young sprig from a good fruit tree and grafts it into the wild trunk from which all its own branches have been removed. Then he binds the sprig to that trunk securely and smears a grafting wax around the graft. Soon the good branch knits itself into the wild trunk securely, grows other branches from itself, producing good fruit.

This is an example from nature. Paul uses it to illustrate to the Romans but he says that in the spiritual sense it is "contrary to nature." Do you know why?

In nature the logical thing to do is to graft good branches into a wild trunk. But spiritually the only way is that a bad branch (out of Adam's "trunk") is grafted into a good trunk (Christ). This is just the opposite. That is why he says, "contrary to nature".

All the elect are condemnable in their old trunk Adam. They are cut off of their covenant head and grafted into the good Branch, Christ, to grow into the Vine and become one with it. By the strength of the good Branch they can now bring forth good fruit. Is not the text: "---make the tree good, and his fruit good---" become applicable? After the ingrafting they can do good works, fruits of the uniting with Christ. That is why Paul said there is not glorying for the ingrafted branches (because they were evil). The branch does not support the trunk or root but the trunk or root the branch. That good root is Christ and He receives the glory of the fruits (good works). This tree will never decay as had happened to Adam. Consequently, the fruit grown from this good tree can be none other than good fruit.

What is the one necessary thing?

The Lord Jesus explained this in John 15, "Abide in me and I in you. As the branch cannot bear fruit of itself, except it abide in the vine no more can ye, except ye abide in Me. I am the vine, ye are the branches. He that abideth in Me and I in him, the same bringeth forth much fruit; for without Me ye can do nothing --- Herein is My Father glorified that ye bear much fruit; so shall ye be My disciples."

So what do we see here?

The church can do no good works in faith and sanctification only in and through Christ, not doing them to merit but to express thankfulness, as fruit of their faith.

And who is the Husbandman that harvests these fruits, which grow on the vine through the branches?

That is God the Father, He Himself will pick the fruit in which He is glorified. We can only bear forth fruit unto death: out of the old trunk Adam, but in contrast to that there is written, "He that abideth in me, and I in him, the same bringeth forth much fruit; for without me ye can do nothing."

When Joshua and Caleb with ten companions went to spy on Canaan, they returned with some fruit of Canaan. This they did to show the Israelites how fruitful the land was to which they were journeying.

What kinds did they bring back?

Answer: Grapes, pomegranates and figs.

And how did they carry the grapes? In a piece of paper or a little basket like we usually do? No, we read in Numbers 13, "And they came unto the brook of Eschol, and cut down from thence a branch with one cluster of grapes, and they bare it between two upon a staff." Just think about that! The word "Eschol" means "grape" so a person could say instead of the "valley of Eshcol", the valley of grapes". You can find in some commentators that the grapes become so large there that a boy of 10 or 12 years old could hide behind a bunch without being seen.

Whether that is true, I do not know. I have never been there, but, I do want to comment on something else in respect to those grapes and in connection with our lesson.

Two men brought this cluster of grapes to Joshua by hanging it from a pole. The pole was carried upon their shoulders so that the cluster was between them. These men walked one behind the other and consequently one man walked ahead of the cluster and the other behind. The man in the rear walked the whole way looking at these magnificent grapes, that is certain. But the man in the front did not see them; he just carried them behind him.

What am I trying to bring out with this? Simple enough. It happens in spiritual life that a child of God must carry much spiritual fruit, through grace in Christ. In the beginning he will be very glad and in his amazement will not understand the privilege befallen him to carry fruit in Christ and for Christ.

He is like the second carrier. He will be looking upon those fruits in continual astonishment. It will be a pleasant sort of life to be privileged to carry much good fruits.

But there are other children of God that are just like the first carrier. They carry the fruits just as well as the one in the rear, but they no longer have an interest in them as such. They carry the fruit behind them. They no longer feel a sense of saving value in them and now their inward eye is on the Vine upon which the fruit has grown. It is a greater gift of grace than was bestowed on the "carrier" at the rear, because good works no longer have the preeminence, but he still is privileged to carry them. He is growing on the vine with the fruit behind him, knowing Christ as the Trunk and the Father as the Husbandman.

These are matters, perhaps, too deep for you to understand but you have received rational minds from God so try to remember these relevant historical accounts. May the Lord apply its meaning to your soul.

Do not be misled by this piece and do not be deceived by others who would try to make you think that all good works have Divine approbation. A sinner can carry fruit, that is, do good works only in Christ. The Father looks upon them only as fruits of thankfulness because they have been sanctified by the merits of His Son.

But now if I say that only these can be to the glory of God, may you go about this life as though nothing matters?

Absolutely not! There is none other name under

heaven given among men, whereby we must be saved, but that name was given, so no one can ever say there was no opportunity to be saved.

The time is about spent and this is the way the days and the years hasten on. This is the first time we have been together in this new year and who can say whether we shall still be here when the year has ended. The Lord removed one from our midst in the past year. Whose turn will it be this year?

A certain old man once said, "A person runs the mail post haste to eternity." He meant by this that as quickly as a postman hurries the mail from one place to another, in this manner does a person hasten to his eternal ruin.

O, boys and girls, may the Lord open your eyes to see not only where you are going but also where you came from. (This is pure and good from the Holy Hands of God).

May He cut you off of the old trunk and graft you into the new vine to be embodied in Christ (or incorporated in Christ) to be one with Him producing fruits of thankfulness in sanctification.

By nature we give evidence in our deeds saying, "Depart from us; for we desire not the knowledge of Thy ways." Even so by grace He can draw you unto Himself and place you with those who have a desire for Him, giving them an inheritance which endures eternally.

May God bless the truth unto salvation of your souls.

So be it.

Lesson 35

Of the Law of God
and of Prayer

The first question asked us this afternoon is, "How many laws has God given to Israel?"

Answer: Three; 1st, the moral law; 2nd, the civil law; 3rd. the ceremonial law.

Before we discuss the questions I want you to explain something to me. I read in my Bible that Noah had three sons, Shem, Ham and Japheth. Ham was cursed for his sin. Japheth's descendants were idol worshippers. But it was from Shem that God called Abraham, making him father of the faithful, and from his descendants the Messiah was to come.

Abraham became the father of Isaac and Isaac fathered two sons, Jacob and Esau. Esau was a reprobate. God spoke of this Himself, saying, "Jacob have I loved and Esau have I hated."

Further on Abraham, Isaac and Jacob were referred to as the three patriarchs from whom came the numerous Jews, the unique people of the Lord separated from all other people of the earth. Now Hellenbroek refers to them in his question as "Israel".

Why does he use that name?

Answer: God changed Jacob's name to Israel.

O, now I remember, Jacob received a new name.

Who knows what the name Jacob means?

Now, the meaning of that name is not so nice. A boy named Jacob need not be arrogant because it means - pusher, heel nipper, or crafty one. Saying it in a plain way, deceiver.

Ledeboer mentions it in his verses:

As long as Jacob remains Jacob
Jacob goes to hell,
But if Jacob becomes Israel first
Then it is with Jacob well.

When did that happen? When he left Laban with his wives and children, he came upon Esau on the way and this frightened him. Of course all of you are acquainted with what happened there. The night prior to his expected meeting with Esau he remained in seclusion on the one side of the Brook Jabbok. A man wrestled with him and said, "Thy name shall be called no more Jacob, but Israel, etc." Later on Jacob could give a good account how he received his new name.

Jacob called the name of that place Peniel. Peniel means "Face of God." He said, "For I have seen God face to face and my life is preserved."

Jacob had to tell what his name was first though and thus acknowledge that he was a deceiver before he received a new name. But when he did this by the grace of God, he received a name which contains the letters "el" which are also in God's name. El is also God's name which means; the Mighty God. Eli means; My God; Elijah means; whose God is Jehovah. There are many names in the Bible which are prefixed with the letters "el" such as Elihu (My God is He) Elisheba (God is her oath) Eliakim (Who God sets up) Elisha (God is my salvation) etc.

The name Israel means "prince of God." This is how this name makes its appearance in the Bible and from that point forward all the families of Abraham, Isaac and Jacob would be called Israelites. Jacob lived in Canaan and his sons lived in Egypt. Was the law given in Egypt or in Canaan?

Answer: Neither in Egypt or Canaan.

Well, where was it given then?

Answer: In the wilderness upon Mount Sinai which lies between Egypt and Canaan.

What does the name Sinai mean?

No one knows the answer: Sinai means, "God's mountain" or "Jehovah's Thornbush."

Now we shall attempt to briefly describe the natures of these three kinds of law.

1. They speak of the "moral law". Which law is meant here?

The law of the ten commandments. This is the law we are governed by too. This law shall stand as long as the world exists and shall remain in the consciences of the unconverted eternally. Hellenbroek could rightly say that it is an everlasting law. He substantiates this from Matt. 5:17, "Think not that I am come to destroy the law, or the prophets; I am not come to destroy, but to fulfill. For verily I say unto you, till heaven and earth pass, one jot or one tittle shall in no wise pass from the law, till all be fulfilled."

The "jot" is the very smallest Greek letter there is and is used for an example of a very tiny thing.

A "tittle" is a small mark in the Hebrew writing.

The Lord Jesus meant that even the least of this law cannot be set aside, but the smallest particle shall be dealt with as God had intended it when it was given upon Mount Sinai.

Unto whom had God given this law before any others? God gave the law in the form we now have it to Moses for Israel. It had ten commandments engraven upon two tablets of stone. And how did this take place? Each one of you know the account given of this, it is not necessary for me to relate this.

God gave the commandments to Moses when he was on the top of the mountain. Moses had stayed there for 40 days and nights. The children of Israel became impatient waiting for him and compelled Aaron to make a golden calf. When Moses returned and saw that, he threw the tables down, breaking them against the mountain. What was the reason for doing that; was there something wrong with the law? No, the law was perfect and the One who had given the law was perfect, but it was being made evident that the commandments were broken by the sins of the people.

Was this the first time that man broke God's law? Where had this taken place before?

Answer: In Paradise.

God had given His commandments there in the hearts of man for the very first time and what was the real content of it?

The Lord Jesus Himself explained it; 1st, To love God above all else and, 2nd, To love our neighbor as ourself. On these two commandments hang all the law and the prophets.

What was the requirement then; little obedience, much obedience or perfect obedience? The last one, certainly. And God created man so he could perform it.

When the law was broken in Paradise, could they live further without the law?

I should say not! Breaking of the law did not take away the lawful requirement any more than a person is free from a debt because he is unable to pay. That would be very easy, wouldn't it? It is only logical that the law remains in force even after breaking it. Immediately after Moses broke the first stone tables against the mountain the Lord spoke to him saying, "Hew thee two tables of stone like unto the first; and I will write upon these tables the words that were in the first tables, which thou breakest." After Moses had prepared the stone tables, he carried them up the mountain again and God gave him the second time the same words He had spoken to him the first time.

As I had mentioned previously, these words were parts of three different types of law. Besides the ten commandments which were written upon the tables, the Lord gave a civil law in which were instructions how the men in Israel should deal with murderers, thieves, whores or those who profane the Sabbaths.

The law of the ceremonies were the third type.

These were precepts for the different sacrificial offerings and purifications the Israelites had to adhere to. Altogether they were a very lengthy set of laws which had to be observed in the strictest sense.

The latter two laws, the civil and the laws of the ceremonies, terminated upon Christ's death. The sacrificial offerings were symbolic of Christ's sacrifice, so when He came they no longer had to be observed. They had been fulfilled.

Our Heidelberg Catechism asks, "Whence knowest thou thy misery?

Answer: Out of the law of God.

Which of these three laws are meant here? Can we rightly see our misery in the ceremonial or civil laws?

We could see our miserable state in part of them. If we witnessed a thief or a murderer being put in jail we certainly would see something of our misery. In the state of righteousness, before the fall, there were no laws against stealing or murdering needed. There was no sin.

And what was the meaning behind the sacrifices and purifications? If there had been no sin there had been no impurity. If there had been no guilt there would be no sacrificial offerings necessary. Both of these law types, in some measure, reveal the misery of man, but not completely.

When I am outdoors and the sun is shining I can see a likeness of myself in a shadow on the ground.

The sun makes it possible to see a figure of myself similar to that seen in still water. But can I see in the shadow or reflection whether I am dirty or clean? No, the shadow or reflection is not that clear. We need a mirror to see that. And do you know what that represents?

Reverently speaking, the moral law of the ten commandments is a clear mirror in the hand of the Holy Spirit in which He shows man his complete misery. And where does he see that? In the first table of the law with its four commandments and in the second table with its six commandments. These two tables comprehend the absolute, perfect demands of God.

What is the general meaning of the first table?

Answer: To love God above all else.

And the second table?

Answer: Our neighbor as ourselves.

That is the contents of the Divine demand. I am not saying man of the post fall era can fulfill God's commands, no, we shall see that presently. I am merely saying the Lord had so created us to be able to fulfill it, and that His demand remains the same and this was confirmed in the giving of the law upon Mount Sinai.

Does not the law of the ten commandments show our total depravity and our impotence in that we cannot keep even one of those commandments? There is no mirror in the whole world that reflects so exactly our image as does the decalogue.

The catechism speaks of it thus: "Man has robbed

himself and all his descendants of these gifts (of the ability to keep the law) by yielding to the devil and his own willful disobedience.

We could say it this way too. When we had the ability to accomplish the whole law we were unwilling and now we are neither able nor willing. No man in his natural state has the ability to desire or the ability to accomplish it. It no longer exists.

But how does man respond? Does he accept this situation? Without grace, never. He always tries to use his inability as an excuse. He does not say, "I am unwilling, but I am unable." Without saying so he places the blame on the Lord for requiring something from him that is impossible to perform.

I made it plain to you by examples in our previous lessons. If a person owes ten thousand dollars to someone and actually had it in his possession to make payment but recklessly gambled it away, would the creditor say, "Mr. So and so, you once had the ability to pay me, but now you are entirely unable, so I shall just release you from this obligation?" Even if the man were jailed for his debt, the obligation to pay remains until it has really been paid. Nothing is deducted.

If he never pays, well, then he never is released from his debt and furthermore the debt becomes his children's when he dies.

This is the situation in respect to the moral law and unless another kept that law for us the claim shall accompany us into death and condemnation. It will burn upon our consciences eternally without respite. The men who wrote the catechism were strongly convinced on this point. They said in question 10, "Will God suffer such disobedience and rebellion to go unpunished?

Answer: By no means; but He is terribly displeased with our original as well as actual sins; and will punish them in His just judgment temporally and eternally, as he hath declared, "Cursed is everyone that continueth not in all things, which are written in the book of the law to do them."

What is then absolutely necessary?

Since through our obstinacy we have become impotent and the obligation lies upon us undiminished, another must satisfy that law for us. Otherwise we shall remain eternally indebted, set off as a transgressor and punished. Now, because of our miserable state as related to us by the law, we need a Mediator. The children of God will surely experience this before anything else because the Holy Spirit will point out the law to them. They will no longer say, "I can do nothing about it", but will sincerely acknowledge that they stand guilty of breaking every commandment in thought, words and deeds.

When God sought Adam, (Adam did not seek God) He found him in his unrighteousness and at enmity with Him because he struck God vindictively concerning His own creation saying, "The woman whom Thou gavest to be with me." When God first confronts His children they are all like that. I visited in a home one time where two small boys began quarreling. One said, "You did it." The other called out, "It is not so, it is your fault." In anger they began hitting and pushing one another. When I saw this taking place, I said, "Both of you come over here to me and I'll tell you something. I want you to listen closely."

"Once upon a time two men went to the temple, one was a Pharisee and the other a Publican. The Pharisee stood in the front of the temple thanking God that he was such a good man. But the Publican stayed in the background smiting upon the chest. (I did not say upon whose chest). Now you must tell me whose chest the man smote?

One of the boys said, "Upon his own chest."

I said, "Correct, and you should do that too." Neither did the Publican say to the Pharisee, "You did it." No, he evidently had done it himself because he called out, "God be merciful to me a sinner."

This is what the Holy Spirit does to all His people, showing them they have transgressed the whole law. Justly they lie under the curse and wrath of God. Like the Publican they possess penitent feet which cause them to stay at the rear of the temple, penitent eyes which they dare not raise, and penitent hands which they use to smite their own guilty selves. But what else do they have?

Most important they have a penitent heart which confesses they are sinners, and what follows in the story? "This man went down to his house justified rather than the other."

411

Was he justified because he admitted and confessed his guilt? No, absolutely not. This impossible.

We have been taught that justification takes place not because of faith but through faith. The Pharisee justified himself but the Publican was justified by God for Christ's sake.

But now if a person becomes thoroughly convinced that he cannot perform even one commandment and that one must be justified by Christ, doesn't it seem there is nothing more to do? Hellenbroek teaches us differently on the basis of God's Word. He asks, "When we see our impotence out of the law, to what must it excite us?"

Answer: To prayer. Psalm 119:4-5, "Lord, Thou hast commanded us to keep Thy precepts diligently. O that my ways were directed to keep Thy statutes!"

What happens when God's people become aware of their unwillingness and their inability to do the requirements of the law? Then God's law becomes the burden of their prayer. It is not a matter of indifference with them. We see that in the prayer of David and so it is with all God's people.

Prayer is necessary because God has commanded us to use it as a means of obtaining what we need. This applies not only to our bodily needs but also to our spiritual necessities.

Now in regard to the catechism lesson on the law I want to present yet another thought.

It is said that the first table is directed toward loving God above all else and then our neighbor as ourselves. The Lord is then given the preeminence here. But who is meant by "our neighbor".

Answer: All people.

Yes, by virtue of creation all people are our neighbors. God made the whole human race out of one blood. Can a person, out of necessity, set aside the obedience to the first table in order to fulfill the second? In normal circumstances we may not do that. Everyone should seek God's honor above his own life and of course also above that of our neighbor.

We read in Luke 9, that the Lord said to someone, "Follow me." But He said, "Lord, suffer me first to go and bury my father." Jesus said unto him, "Let the dead bury the dead; but go thou and preach the kingdom of God."

It is plain to be seen here that this man had to neglect the second table to fulfill the first.

It was not a sinful desire to bury his father, but Jesus wanted him to place his obedience to Him above the duty to his father and assign the work to someone else.

In this case the man had to set aside the second table in order to fulfill the first. The Lord demanded that he love God more than anything else.

I do not say that we can prefer God's honor in our natural state, I merely say that it is our obligation to do so. In the way of grace, though, God's people are called upon to choose one or the other.

He is called upon to decrease in himself even to suffering or death rather than decrease God's honor by doing a sin.

There can be special cases though in time of need, where he, figuratively speaking, must set the first table aside for a moment in order to fulfill the second. For example, if I am walking to church on Sunday I am fulfilling in an outward sense the first table of the law, "Remember the Sabbath Day to keep it holy," etc. But if I pass by a pasture and notice a cow or horse stuck in a ditch, must I still continue on to church fulfilling the first table of the law and have no concern for the second (love thy neighbor as yourself)?

Absolutely not. It is, in a circumstance such as this, my obligation first to fulfill the second table by helping my neighbor rescue his cattle.

But do you know when it would be wrong to help my neighbor?

When I would sin against the first table to do it.

This is just a look at a very small part of these very important matters. Boys and girls, you are obliged to do the requirements of the law, too. There are people living in this world for whom the Mediator said, "Lo, I come,——I delight to do Thy will, O My God; yea, Thy law is within my heart."

He takes over the obligations resting upon the elect and fulfills them in their place. He terminated the service of the shadows or types, because He was both the Priest and the Sacrificial Lamb. Observances of the various laws of purifications were stopped when Christ died because He eternally purified them with His Blood.

What still remains? Only the ten commandments,

414

which now must be a law of thankfulness for the church.

The Holy Spirit uses the law first as a severe schoolmaster with His whiplashes of the law to bring the convinced sinner to Christ and make him know his misery, obstinacy and helplessness.

But when through this he is taught who has fulfilled the law for him and finds Christ as the end of the law for righteousness, O, then he discovers this same law to be his delight and says, "O how love I Thy law! It is my meditation all the day."

What at first was a burden now becomes a desire and God's law becomes the subject of thankful prayer.

Boys, perhaps you find it troublesome and boring to listen for this length of time. You would rather whisper and play. I know all about it, your undisciplined nature wants to be rid of it. But what if I were to be called to your deathbed tonight, what then? You could rightly say, "Dominie, I am about to die unexpectedly and you never warned me." That would not be good, would it?

I have been told about a woman who had very naughty children. They very seldom attended church services. The minister of that congregation came for house-visitation and asked why she so seldom took her children to church.

"Alas" said the lady, "It is impossible for these children to sit still for two hours. Young, healthy children cannot endure that."

And do you know what the minister said?

"Woman" he said, "You lack reverence for God, I must reprimand you. You are giving your children over to sin and are supporting them in their transgression of God's will and in their lack of esteem for the means of grace. If you say the children cannot endure church services, how shall they endure hell if they should die unconverted? All condemned shall certainly say, 'It is not bearable!' And yet they must bear it eternally. The unbearable will have to be borne there forever."

The Lord had made the minister faithful to his work. Don't give in when it seems you cannot hold out listening to God's Word.

He is calling you through these means and is still allowing it to be said to you, "Call upon me in the day of trouble; I will deliver thee, and thou shalt glorify Me."

May the Lord expose unto you your miserable state with His law and make His commandments the subject of your prayer while you are in the prime of life. May He present that for His Son's Sake.

> Jehovah's perfect law
> Restores the soul again;
> His testimony sure
> Gives wisdom unto men;
> The precepts of the Lord are right,
> And fill the heart with great delight.

(Psalm 19) Psalter 38

Lesson 36

Of the Sacraments

The first question this afternoon is: What means hath God instituted to promote the work of sanctification?

Answer: The word and sacraments.

What are sacraments actually. What meaning do they have?

Answer: Signs and seals of God's grace. Romans 4:11 "And he (Abraham) received the sign of circumcision, a seal of the righteousness of faith."

Hellenbroek starts out by naming two sets of two things each. 1st. Word and sacrament, 2nd, Signs and seals.

I had mentioned in an earlier lesson that there is an audible word and there is a visible word, both are from God.

Before the fall Adam spoke to God, and God spoke to Adam and He confirmed the spoken word with a visible sign: the tree of life. The Lord indicated, "As certainly as you see this tree and obey me so certainly shall you live."

The tree of life was, then, a sign or a seal of the spoken word of God to Adam for his benefit.

But conversely, the Lord said something else which had an exactly opposite meaning; If you disobey Me, you will die.

These words were also sealed with a sign which was the tree of knowledge of good and evil.

Here, too, was an audible Word and a visible Word.

This is the way it was in Paradise and still is today. The Lord continues to give us His spoken and visible word with which He himself directs to attract and instruct His people. His audible Word is that which He causes His prophets, apostles and ministers to preach. His visible Word is the sacraments which are a sign we can see with our eyes.

Were there sacraments during the Old Testament dispensation?

Yes; Hellenbroek indicates to us the two principal sacraments were circumcision and the passover.

He said, the principle ones; were there still more? Yes, there were, besides these two, five events which were to be commemorated because of their special significance, but not on a continuing basis as was true of circumcision and the passover. Who knows which ones they were:

1st. The passing through the Red Sea. That was a sign and seal of God's grace which must never be forgotten, but even so need not ever again to be repeated.

2nd. The manna from heaven. Wasn't that a real sacrament, a sign and seal? It was, but even so, it was a temporary happening and the manna ceased dropping from heaven when the Israelites came into Canaan. They were commanded, though, to commemorate it continually and relate it to their children.

418

3. Then there was the water out of the rock.

4. The looking upon the brazen serpent as to being Christ.

5. The budding staff of Aaron, Psalm 78. All these were important incidents for the Israelites which were to be recounted to their descendants diligently, even though they were not to re-experience them. Circumcision and passover were the only ones to be observed by performance.

Our lesson asks: In whose time was circumcision instituted?

Answer: In Abraham's time.

You are all well aware that Abraham was the son of Terah from the generations of Shem. He lived in Ur of the Chaldees when the Lord called him to go to Canaan. He made a covenant with him and ordered him to circumcise all little boys when they were eight days old. The purpose was that all his descendants would be a separate people from all other peoples of the world.

Now you must pay close attention. What came first with Abraham: the sign or the thing signified?

The thing signified. That is clearly understood. The Lord first made the covenant and afterwards He ordered circumcision as a sign of it. In an outward sense through this sign all the descendants of Abraham were different from the heathen and were set apart as holy. But were all of them partakers of the thing signified? Far from it. Paul said, the elect obtained it and the rest were blinded. Those then who were truly sanctified within possessed the thing signified as well as the sign and were truly a distinctive people. But, because the Lord had special intentions for this people in that the Messiah was to be born out of their descendants, this entire nation had to remain separate by means of an outward sign. That is why the sacrament of circumcision was a continuing sacrament, until the Messiah would come.

And now, the passover. When was that instituted?

Answer: During the time of Moses after the Israelites left Egypt.

Because of the hardness of Pharoah's heart God afflicted the Egyptians with ten plagues. All of you remember these, of course. The last one was the worst, because the oldest child of every household died.

And what were they to do in the land of Goshen?

Answer: During a certain night the Israelites were to kill a one year old male lamb, one without blemish, and strike the blood on the posts of the doorways of their homes. When the angel saw the blood, he knew that an Israelite lived there and so passed by.

That is correct, so it was, but what parts of the door were they to strike with the blood. There are four parts in each door frame.

Answer: On the lintel and on the two side posts.

And why not on the threshold?

Answer: In order that they would not step upon it as they passed through, because the lamb's blood symbolized the blood of Christ.

What further symbolic meaning would there be in this?

Answer: Just as the blood upon the post was a sign that the angel of death would not touch them, but would kill the Egyptians for their own sins; so those for whom Christ shed His blood need not die as would all those who shall be eternally lost because of their own sins.

The slaughtered lamb had to be totally free of any blemishes because it was the symbol of Christ, Who was to be put to death. And of course this passover lasted until the Great Lamb put an end to it with His own sacrifice. Israel held this sacrament every year for ages and the Lord Jesus Himself celebrated it the night prior to His being made captive. It was inevitable; it had to be just that night (that self same night in which the sacrament was established) that He fulfilled the sign by actually offering up Himself as the Lamb of God.

Afterward there was no reason to celebrate the Passover; that which had been a symbol became a reality. The Apostle could now say: "For even Christ our passover is sacrificed for us." I Cor. 5:7.

Which sacraments did the Lord Jesus establish in the place of circumcision and the passover?

Answer: Holy Baptism instead of circumcision and the Lord's Supper instead of Passover.

When did He do this?

Answer: The Lord's Supper on the night He celebrated the last Passover, and Baptism just prior to His ascension to heaven.

What words were used in His doing this?

Answer: He took up the bread and the cup saying, "Do this in remembrance of me."

And what were they in Holy Baptism?

Answer: "Go forth, teaching all nations, baptizing them in the name of the Father, the Son and the Holy Ghost."

Hellenbroek now asks, "With what do we baptize?"

Answer: With water. Now, that is plain enough; but then he follows it with the question: Must this water be mixed with something else?

Answer: No, it must only be pure, unmixed water!

You would say, "That is simple enough; why is he making a special point of this?

Because Roman Catholics mix something with the water.

When I lived in Rotterdam a boy once came to my home and related all that had taken place in his life. Now, they were really pitiful things. His mother died early in life, and when his father remarried the man ceased providing for him. The boy finally left home, knowing he was not welcome anymore. He wandered around from one place to another. After having tried everywhere and failed, he finally, in dire need, went into the Roman Catholics at Maastricht. I was aware that his mother had reared him in the doctrines of scripture while she lived. He had been baptized and had knowledge of the scriptures. With that in mind I asked him, "My boy, how do you reconcile this with your orthodox confession? In the past when a Protestant became a Roman Catholic (according to what I have been told) he had to renounce our confession upon his knees, were you required to do that too?"

"No" said he, "They have discarded that practice, it is not longer required, but it is required to be baptized again." I asked, "And how was that handled?" Then he related further, "First they investigated everything; where I was baptized and to which religion I really belonged. When they were fully informed, they brought me into a dark room, where I was required to kneel. Then a "father" with others like him stood around about me and the father or priest then spoke five Latin words and I had to say some that I did not understand. When that had taken place they poured water over my head and I was baptized. They used the same words we do, "I baptize thee in the name of the Father, the Son and the Holy Ghost." I then asked them why I had been baptized again? Their answer being, "The Protestant baptism is done with too little water, they only sprinkle a few drops on the forehead but the water should flow. Also, there is no sacred spittle put in the baptismal water and for that reason the Protestant baptism has no merit and you have just now been really baptized."

This boy told these things with tears. He could no longer continue with that religion but had to return to the orthodox belief wherein his mother had reared him.

423

The Roman Catholics believe in seven sacraments instead of two, namely; Baptism, Confirmation, The Lord's Supper, Confession, Holy Unction, Priesthood and Marriage. We do not have the time to explain each of these. We shall continue with ours in the Truth and remain with the two sacraments Christ instituted.

Can we prove from God's Word that pure water is sufficient for baptism?

O, yes, we read that John, while at the river, baptized all that came unto him. Now, that river water was not mixed with "holy spittle". And Philip, with the Ethiopian descended into the water alongside which they were riding.

But God's Word teaches baptism by immersion, you might reason, and not that sprinkling is the only way.

In the eastern countries this is possible, but in these cold countries this would be very objectionable, also in respect to modesty.

Would sprinkling be contrary to God's Word?

No, because the New Testament repeatedly speaks of sprinkling. In Hebrews 12:24 it says, "And to the blood of sprinkling, that speaketh better things than that of Abel." Also in the Old Testament in Ezekiel 36:25 - "Then will I sprinkle clean water upon you."

We see then that either a large amount or a small amount of water can be lawfully used.

If you had listened well you could have reasoned: The disciples were commissioned by Jesus to baptize after His death and resurrection. That was a divine mission, but, was John the Baptist's baptism proper prior to Jesus death?

Would he have been sent by God?

Answer: Yes.

Well, well, you appear to have more courage than the Jewish Bible scholars of those days, because when Jesus asked them, "The baptism of John, whence was it? from heaven, or of men?" They answered Jesus, and said, "We cannot tell." But it appears you do know. How do you substantiate your answer?

Answer: John said, "--He that sent me to baptize with water, the same said unto me, etc." John 1:33.

And what others do you have?

Answer: John 1:6, "There was a man sent from God, whose name was John."

These are sufficient proofs but there is still another. According to the sending out of the twelve they were charged to baptize in the Name of the Triune God, but I read in Acts 8:16 that the disciples baptized in the name of the Lord Jesus. Was that proper for them?

It must not have been done as a regular thing, because it is stated often times, "And they were baptized in the name of the Lord." The disciples probably took into account the fact that the Jews did believe in God the Father but not in Jesus the Savior and for that reason expressly baptized in the Name of the Lord Jesus, in order to emphasize that He is true God with the Father.

425

Now there is another question, "May anyone baptize in an emergency?"

Answer: "No, only those who are sent to teach." You would say what a strange question that man asks! The cause for this is to be found in catholicism. They teach, that in time of an emergency, as, suppose a child is about to die, and it is too late to call a clergyman, anyone may baptize.

They contend that it is better a layman baptize than that one die unbaptized. I had been told that as the Egyptian midwives were ordered to drown the Hebrew baby boys, so must the Roman Catholic midwives promise they will baptize babies about to die when there is no time to bring them to the church.

I investigated this at the time and found the civil authorities and the courts of justice consent to the practice of Roman Catholic midwives or doctors baptizing new-born children, when it is evident that the child will not live long. What is their reason for doing this?

Of course it is because they err in the sacrament of Baptism just as badly as in the Lord's Supper. In their catechism book for children they state:

Question 355: Who administers baptism?

Answer: It is usually performed by the priest, but in an emergency it may and must be baptized by anyone.

Question 359: What do we receive in baptism?

Answer: 1st. Forgiveness of original sin and those sins committed before baptism. 2nd. Acquit-

426

tal of all punishment for those sins. 3rd. Sanctifying grace and supernatural assistance to lead a Christian life.

Do you understand why they permit, yes, even command, that anyone baptize a child before it dies? They claim that baptism washes away original sin.

Calvin fought viciously against this in his time too, but in boldness openly dared to dispute their wickedness and wrote: "Christ never commanded that women or all sorts of men should baptize," but gave that command only to those whom He had chosen and sent out as apostles.

But now, if a child had been baptized by a Roman Catholic priest in the name of the Triune God, should their baptism be declared invalid and must that child be baptized again by a lawful minister? There have been differences of opinion about that point since the early centuries after Christ. Calvin in his "Institutes" states regarding that, "Against these absurdities we shall be sufficiently fortified if we reflect that by baptism we were initiated not into the name of any man but into the name of the Father, and the Son, and the Holy Spirit; and therefore that baptism is not of man, but of God, by whomsoever it may be administered."

As early as a synod held in Dordt in 1574, the question was raised, should a child who had been baptized by a midwife or doctor be baptized again in the church?

And the answer was, "Yes, since baptism by a midwife or layman is actually not baptism." It is a great wickedness for anyone who has not a calling fo this to go forth in the Name of the Triune God. The so called, emergency baptism, therefore, is not lawful and a child so baptized must be baptized by one lawfully called.

A sacrament, even though administered by an unlawful minister is, none the less, a sacrament. Baptism in the Roman Catholic church, administered by an acknowledged office bearer and performed in the Name of the Father, the Son and the Holy Ghost, has never been done over by our fathers.

Calvin goes on further to say: "It seems to me to be just the same as found in practical life where a farmer having a flock of sheep sells a few to a broker. When the purchase had been consumated the buyer usually places a mark on each one of the sheep which he has purchased. Now just suppose a naughty boy is present and has exactly the same kind of marker as the buyer and places his mark on various ones, what does the buyer do? He approaches the sheep saying, "This is a good one", but sees a mark on it. This is all right; he doesn't put a second on it, but says to the boy, "Will you please go away, that is my work, keep your hands off, understand?"

In this way (according to Calvin) the Lord shall deal with those who have never been sent out to do this, and yet baptized, preached or administered the Lord's Supper.

Speaking in reverence, he would say, "I shall not

consider these people as heathens by reason of their being baptized by you because they have, none the less, My seal upon their forehead. I shall punish you, however, for your wrong doing. You have performed something which was not yours to do. You have put your hands upon labor to which I call My chosen servants. It is them only I send out to instruct and baptize."

Neither shall these people be lost because they were not baptized by a lawfully called minister but God will deal with such, and not hold them guiltless.

There is another sect among men called the Baptists. These pitiable people contend that only those who are grown up and believe in Christ with full consciousness are permitted to be baptized. They condemn infant baptism. This is another great error, since Paul states plainly that baptism has come in the place of circumcision, wherein all little boys, circumcised when eight days old, without having any consciousness of it, were received into the covenant in an external sense.

For that reason the catechism also states in the 27th Lord's Day:

"Question: Are infants also to be baptized?

Yes, for since they, as well as the adult, are included in the covenant and church of God; and since redemption from sin by the blood of Christ, and the Holy Ghost, the author of faith, is promised to them no less than to the adult; they must therefore by baptism, as a sign of the covenant, be also admitted into the Christian church; and be distinguished from the children of unbelievers as was done in the old covenant or testament by circumcision, instead of which baptism is instituted in the new covenant."

It is plain, then, that a person need only be baptized once. This because baptism is a sacrament (a sign) of being incorporated into the church which can take place but once.

Now I must ask you a question, though. If baptism does not cleanse from original sin (as the Roman Catholics teach) and does not make one a living member of the church, is it at all necessary? Cannot we just as well forego it? It seems to me we need not baptize every child, do we?

Answer: Baptism is to be administered by virtue of Christ's command.

O, but you learned this answer from your lesson; but it is good, because it is the truth. Baptism became necessary through the institution and command of Christ. Just as circumcision became necessary through the institution of God.

Even so, salvation does not depend upon this, because the Lord does not bind His grace to a sacrament. Neither did He do this with circumcision.

Can one of you cite an example from the Bible of someone who was doomed to endless punishment even though baptized?

Answer: Simon the Sorcerer.

Did you hear that? That man was baptized and desired the gift of the Spirit, but it was to his perdition. Peter said to him, "Thy money perish with thee."

Therefore it is also written: "He that believeth and is baptized shall be.... saved, but he who believeth not shall be damned." Mark 16:16. It could be the other way around too, not baptized but yet saved. What example do we have of that?

Answer: The murderer on the cross.

It was not indifference of that man that he was not baptized after his conversion, but it was not possible anymore; time was running out; he began to die on the cross. Despite this he would be with Jesus in Paradise.

These are two proofs that God does not ever commit His grace on the sacraments. The matter rests in His giving of it or withholding of it.

We have discussed briefly together the subject of baptism, but there are a couple of serious questions remaining. The time is about spent now, so, we hope to say something about the proper meaning of baptism next week if the Lord spares us. For instance, how many benefits are sealed in baptism and whether water itself can wash away sins?

Have you ever given thought to the fact, boys and girls, that everyone of you have been baptized because Christ commanded it? Alas, it has become a custom to the majority to baptize their children. They will be called to account for this. Perhaps a few have done it by virtue of Christ's command. Have your father and mother ever spoken to you about the fact that you have the seal of the Triune

God upon your forehead? In one of his books, Rev. Smytegelt says, "If it doesn't shame you to break God's commandments and you continue on in spite of all warnings, come then to the baptismal font where your parents presented you before the Triune God and renounce your baptism in confirmation that you will not have anything to do with Him."

That is the way Rev. Symtegelt put it to his congregation in Middleburg. But I would like to ask this afternoon, "Is there not one among all of you who ever felt what it is to be baptized in the name of the Triune God, and not to know the Lord personally?"

When I bow my knees this evening will it be necessary to say, "Lord, there was not one among all those children that had grief for lack of Thy presence in their hearts?" What a situation that is!

O, I am well aware that without His restraining hand we never tire of living in sin. And even if you had been baptized by the best of ministers and you lived your entire life in church praying and doing good works you would still not receive God's favor because that can be obtained only through the righteousness of Christ. Without that righteousness not one living soul shall obtain, nor want to obtain it. Otherwise the Lord would not receive the glory, and that becomes their highest desire.

But are there not some people living among us that know that salvation cannot be obtained without Christ and yet are strangers to Him? Yes, that can be, but, if they do carry this about by virtue of the work of the Holy Spirit, they will have restless lives. Their pleasure and life in the world will be gone and they will find no city of refuge for their pitiable souls. They come to accept the fact that they mocked the sacrament in the garden of Eden - and it is a wonder that they have not yet gone to the place they deserve.

Each one of you shall go home in company presently and I by myself, but sometime the moment will come that each of us must go to his eternal home all by himself. Our friends will not be allowed to accompany us as they are doing with one another now.

And which shall be your home then? Eternally with Him who said, "In My Father's House are many mansions?" But, if so, then you must also have known in this life how He prepared this house for you. May the Lord make His abode within your heart by His spiritual revelation because by nature we do not want Him there, neither through baptism nor confession.

May He make room where no room exists, and thus sanctify baptism so that it may truly become a sign and seal of grace effectually applied to your soul.

So be it.

Lesson 37

the Sacraments

Continuation of Holy Baptism

Before we pass on to the lesson of the Holy Lord's supper we must discuss some questions about Baptism.

We were taught last week that Baptism is an institution of Christ; May men despise or neglect it?

No, for then they despise God Himself Who has given commandment to use it.

However, it could possibly happen that someone does not despise it and yet neglects it or rather will not submit to it. Under what conditions might this be tolerated?

Well, when men live in times of persecution and there is no opportunity to baptize children and men are forced to omit the Sacrament, would that be considered a sin of despite?

No, because it is omitted of necessity.

Another thing Hellenbroek asks is: What is the significance of immersion or sprinkling with water?

Answer: The washing away of sins by the blood and Spirit of Christ.

If a new-born child dies before it has been baptized it would surely die unsaved, would it not?

No, that is not the thought of Hellenbroek.

New-born children can die without salvation, but it is not because they are unbaptized. If it was so, then it would be necessary to consider that all baptized children will be saved. One as well as the other is contrary to the teaching of God's Word.

All children, who are baptized and receive salvation, are saved out of free grace through the merits of Christ. Contrariwise, all children who have never been baptized and die lost are lost by reason of original sin. The administration of baptism in itself does not save nor does the lack of it condemn.

But what does Hellenbroek mean, then, when he says that the baptism by dipping in or sprinkling signifies the washing away of sin by the blood and Spirit of Christ? We ought first to recite the questions remaining of last week.

Question 6. How many benefits are sealed by baptism?

Answer? Two, justification by the blood of Christ and sanctification by His Spirit.

Question 7. Can water itself wash away sin?

Answer: No. I John 1:7, "The blood of Jesus Christ His Son cleanseth us from all sin."

We found out last week that the Roman Catholics believe that baptism removes original sin, and for that reason their children must be baptized directly after birth and in case of emergency by a lay person.

Naturally, this position is strongly disapproved

by all Protestants. Generally, men confess, as yet, that it is not baptism but grace in Christ that takes away original sin. But even so, there is a great number of deceivers (in the Netherlands) who hold views on baptism different from what God's Word teaches us. We have stated before: Baptism is a sign. The Lord says by this sign, "As surely as the water washes the body of uncleanness, so does the blood of Christ wash the soul of uncleanness."

It is not meant by this that anyone receiving baptism is washed of his sins, no, it is meant as a sign that god also washes away the sins of His people through Christ. Also it is a sign for His people that: As surely as the sign is administered, so surely, do they have a portion in the matter being signified. But this is true only for those who have been made spiritually alive by the Holy Spirit and, therefore, not alone to those who belong to the Israelitish race.

It is too bad that this matter is misrepresented. And because there are men who do this openly from pulpits and in writing books, I want to warn you in a very frank manner. To which teaching am I referring? To the doctrine that Dr. Kuyper has propagated in regard to baptism. Among the many books he has written is one entitled: "Voor de Distel een Mirt". This book deals exclusively with baptism, confession and the Lord's Supper.

He devotes one whole chapter to the three questions asked at baptism and in it uses these exact words: "And you present your child for baptism, not as though it is without Christ but as sanctified in Christ. You are not absolutely sure of this because the Lord did not give a special revelation for that, but you are to consider your little one as such, and because of that and on that basis, you request Christian baptism for this member of Christ's Church."

Continuing on in this chapter to the question whether the parents promise and intend to bring them up properly:

"What can you do to bring up your child and how can you urge them to conversion unless you make *this* your supposition; that your rearing of the child is preceded by God's Grace? Or have you ever given thought to this, that, if your child was still dead in sins and trespasses, you could contribute something with your bringing up of the child?

You can be sure that you could not.

And so there is a firm supposition accompanying the rearing of every baptized child that a hidden and undeveloped grace is sheltered within, and that your bringing up serves very poorly to water that hidden seed in the garden of your child's heart and to remove the weeds that tend to choke out the hidden seed of grace."

Dr. Kuyper speaks very plainly about this in his book entitled "Voor de Distel een Mirt", Chapter 9, page 72. He also leads you to believe that babies should be baptized directly after birth, even the very first Sunday. It is not entirely like the Roman Catholics' practice, but there is not much difference because he says on page 66:

437

"And shall we, then, who possess such a child and such a covenant of peace with God be content to delay the baptism of his baby? -- and then the father oftentimes casts the blame upon the mother by saying, 'Mother wants to be there also when our baby is baptized, so we shall wait until mother can go along'. As if the covenant of God does not always engage the head of the family.

But no genuinely true mother will ever allow, for her own enjoyment, the child of her bosom, to remain unbaptized even for a single week wherein it would be possible for it to die."

This shows how strong Dr. Kuyper was in his belief that baptism should take preeminence immediately after birth.

You shall, if you may become older, come in contact with more of this doctrine. I warn you, boys and girls, do not join with it. The time is much too short for me to refute this ill-founded doctrine.

I related to you an error, and with God's Word as my guide I dare to tell you that nowhere are we taught a "presumptive regeneration" before baptism or in baptism.

Now understand, they are so careful that they use there the word "presumptive". Otherwise they would run into difficulties.

What follows will clarify what I am saying. Just suppose that a father and mother had eight children, all baptized and each had the same good rearing. According to their views respectable people presume that a seed of grace is harbored in

438

their children's soul. If years later when the children are grown, a preacher on family visitation would of course ask these parents how their children are faring. The father says, "Reverend, for the most part it goes well; five of them are married and as you see they are all Christians, attend church faithfully and take the Lord's Supper."

"Yes", says the minister, "I am well aware of that. They are flourishing members of our church. We could certainly wish that all brothers and sisters gave as good an example. But you have at least eight children, do you not? Where are the three others now-a-days?"

Yes---now it finally must be revealed.

"Oh" laments the father, "Reverend, I shall just speak out frankly, they have gone the way of the prodigal son, but have not yet returned. One went to India, the second resides in Amsterdam and the third drifts from one place to another. Those boys live terribly wicked lives. They won't have anything to do with religion."

"Yes, Reverend", added the mother weeping, "I have often said to my husband, if it may just turn out all right with our boys."

What is there for the minister to say?

If his teaching had always been that all baptized children are born again he would in this instance be in difficulty. It would appear that there is such a thing as apostasy of saints and this cannot be the teaching of Christians.

But---they have an answer ready for this too. Do

you know what the minister said? "Come, come, mother, don't give up hope yet. It is true, it appears the boys are far from home, but who knows how soon they will return sorrowfully saying, 'Father, I have sinned against heaven and in thy sight'. We may certainly hope that they have been born of believing parents, baptized and reared in a Christian environment, bearing the seed of the new birth even though this is now smothered under all those sins. If soon they may confess (even if it is on their death beds) Jesus as their Saviour, you shall see that the seed was not entirely choked off--".

This is the way that minister put these people at rest. It appears though, this mother does not trust their religion as much anymore and is always anxious about her children's destiny and says, "But, Reverend, if they continue living this way, no matter how well they are baptized and brought up, if they die in their sins and wickedness, what then?"

"Yes, what then" —answered the minister, "then we can say nothing more than that they were never actually born again. I told you before that we must assume, but can not be sure, that all those that are baptized have the seed of grace in them. In some lives it is apparent that it is not so. Their future life of church attendance, confession and partaking of the Lord's Supper must be an indication whether the baptized are really born again or not."

So much for the example. Do you understand anything of its intent? Try to remember it anyhow, perhaps in later years it will be clear to you. Alas, this doctrine has become accepted at an alarming rate in the last few years, and since there are many who dare to speak and write boldly in favor of it, I dare also to speak out saying, "These people err in two aspects on this matter of baptism. They err in the first place on the necessity of baptism. They err secondly in the efficacy of baptism."

The Word of God teaches us that baptism is necessary only by virtue of Christ's command. In this they go too far. It is true that many among us give too little value to Holy Baptism and baptize merely because it is a custom that we follow. But they err too in the application of the seal, and baptize not only by virtue of Christ's command but go almost as far as to place virtue in the sacrament. God had never assigned this to it.

Last week we spoke of the fact that the Lord never ascribed grace to a sacrament, neither to circumcision, baptism, nor the Lord's Supper. As a sovereign Being He stands above his commands and instituted means. If in truth you are unconverted and remain so, don't let them make you something you are not, children. Don't forsake the truth as so many do in later life. Many forsake the truth for money, or possessions, wife or husband, and pursue the doctrine they think will be most advantageous to themselves.

We shall not go into this any further.

Hellenbroek concludes this lesson with the question: What have the baptized to perform?

Answer: They have to examine whether they

have with their whole heart commended themselves unto the Triune God.

Can we do this by nature?

Answer: No.

Why not?

Answer: Because we are spiritually dead.

Why does Hellenbroek put it in such a way then?

Answer: Because a person is impotent because of his own guilt and the Lord righteously requires of him that which he cannot perform.

Do you hear that boys and girls? Without God it is impossible to inquire after God and yet the Lord can say, "You will not come to me." And do you know what is so perilous? That the devil takes advantage of our impotency in order to say: "You had better give it up, it doesn't help anyway, just get some enjoyment out of life." O, that liar!

Just yesterday I was reading a book written by an English theologian who said, "There was a king who wanted to enlarge his territory through acquisition of the land of another king. He would accomplish this by first doing away with the king of that land. He promised that he would elevate any one of his subjects to the highest office of the land if they would murder that king for him.

When one of the men murdered his enemy and went to the king to obtain his honor as promised, what do you think the king did?

He gave orders to have the man hung from the highest tower in the land saying, "If this rascal dares to murder that other King for a monetary reward, he would dare to do it to me also if someone would pay him to do so."

The theologian went on to say that the devil does this to his subjects too. He promises them much here, but soon he will say, "You knew, of course, that I am a liar, didn't you? Why were you then obedient to me?"

You have been sufficiently warned. May the Lord rescue you while there is still time, and it is my wish and prayer that the significance of baptism may be applied to your soul.

> Mark thou the upright day by day,
> Behold the perfect in his way;
> His journey ends in peace.
> Destroyed at once shall rebels be;
> Cut off from all posterity,
> Their very name shall cease.
>
> -Psalter No. 99:4

Lesson 38

The Lord's Supper

Since we have nothing to review, we shall begin immediately with our lesson on the Lord's Supper.

The first question follows through: Why do we then receive the Lord's Supper often?

Answer: Because it is a sacrament of continual strengthening in faith.

In this lies the actual difference between Holy Baptism and Holy Communion.

Baptism, even as circumcision in the Old Testament, took place but once. But the Lord's Supper, like Passover, must be observed often.

We shall speak briefly now about the institution of the Lord's Supper in its superficial aspects.

What are the external signs in the Lord's Supper?

Answer: Bread and wine.

Why should it be ordinary nutritious bread and not wafers?

Hellenbroek says: They do not fully signify the spiritual nourishment. Wafers are small round pieces of unleavened bread.

What does the bread signify in the Lord's Supper?

Answer: The body of Christ - I. Cor. 11:24, "And when He had given thanks, He brake it and said, Take, eat: this is My Body, which is broken for you: this do in remembrance of Me."

It is for that reason the bread in the administration of the Sacrament is broken, in order to show by a sign that Christ's Body was broken for His own. In like manner, the wine represents Christ's blood and must be poured out in the administration of the Sacrament to signify that Christ's Blood was indeed poured out, too.

The sacrament of the Lord's Supper is, therefore, a clear, certain and sure sign and seal of Christ's suffering and death for His people. The catechism refers to it this way: --"That His body was offered and broken on the cross for me, and His blood shed for me, as certainly as I see with my eyes, the bread of the Lord broken for me, and the cup communicated to me."

At this point I must ask a question. I notice there are far more questions and answers on the Lord's Supper than there is about baptism in the catechism. Would this indicate that the Lord's Supper has much more value as a sacrament than baptism?

Answer: No, both have been instituted by God.

Concentrate on this so you will remember it. One is not lesser than the other, but both are institutions of Christ.

The question is now asked: Is not bread alone sufficient in the Lord's Supper?

Answer: No, Christ says; Matt. 14 "Drink ye all of it."

Does the word "all" mean all of the ministers, or all the lay believers too?

Answer: Yes, I Cor. 11:28, "Let a man examine himself, and so let him eat of this bread and drink of this cup." He speaks of "man" in the universal sense. It means "all believers" and not ministers only.

You would say, "What a strange question! Who would imagine it to be different than that?"

Oh, yes, there are thousands in our country who think other than that about it. The Roman Catholic Church teaches that only the priest may drink the wine and the laymen may not even touch the chalice, it being too holy.

Who knows what else they teach in connection with this matter of the Lord's Supper?

Answer: That the bread being used in the administration of the sacrament actually changes into the body of Christ and the wine into His blood.

Correct, and who knows the word, so difficult to pronounce, which names this teaching?

Answer: Transubstantiation.

Now, who knows the literal meaning of this word?

No one knows? Then I shall tell you. The prefix "trans" means to cross over from one to another. Keep this in mind for a moment, the base word substance means the real or essential part of anything. The two connected together make it clear that the word transubstantiation means cross over from one substance into the other.

In this instance it is this: the one substance (namely the bread) changes into another substance, namely into the body of Christ. Likewise with the wine. The substance wine, changes into the substance blood. They call this "transubstantiation" and this is what Hellenbroek refers to in the question whether the bread and wine undergo a change.

But now he asks another kind of question:

"Is Christ present physically in the signs of this supper?"

He certainly must be alluding to another belief again.

Yes, he has in mind some other error.

What error is that?

Answer: The error of Luther.

You are all aware that the Lord had wanted to use Luther to expose the false beliefs of the Roman Catholic Church and to initiate a reformation especially in Germany and throughout most of Europe.

It was lamentable, despite the exceptional grace and gifts that Luther as child and servant had received, he remained at error in a part of the Holy Communion.

And what was that; did he hold to the opinion of the Roman Catholics, that the bread changed into the body of the Lord and the wine changed into His blood? No, he held no longer to that position. He chose another word, believing no longer in transubstantiation, but consubstantiation.

Now, the prefix "con" denotes "with". Consubstantiation means then, that there is an actual presence of the body and blood of Christ in the Lord's Supper.

Contrary to the Roman Catholic's belief that the bread changed "over" to the true body, he believed that it was present with the bread.

The other prominent reformers, Calvin and Zwingli, were more orthodox in this respect than Luther was. Zwingli tried to come to an agreement with Luther on this point of doctrine once before a large gathering, but Luther remained firm in his error and always said, "The Lord Jesus said literally, 'This is My body'. It is no other way than that Jesus Christ is physically present and with us at each Lord's Supper through means of His every-where present, invisible though real body!"

Since Zwingli would not abandon the truth and Luther would not abandon his erroneous mixture, they, consequently, never came to an agreement on this point.

It is plain, however, that the Lord by the word, "This is My Body", meant, "This signifies My Body and as certainly as I break this bread, so certainly My Body is broken for you."

We reject, therefore, both doctrines, transubstantiation and consubstantiation, as conflicting against sound Truth.

Hellenbroek puts it down with simple words when he asks, "Is Christ's bodily presence in the signs of the supper?"

Answer: No; His human nature is in heaven only.

Is not this bread and wine changed into His flesh and blood?

Answer: No, it remains bread and wine even after the consecration.

How then can Christ say, "This is My Body?"

Do other passages of Scripture speak in this manner?

Yes, often, as appears in I Cor. 10:4. "The Rock was Christ." Now, no one would take this to mean that the rock was truly Christ Himself. Everyone understands Paul to mean here, "The rock signifies Christ."

Can we then not eat and drink Christ Himself?

Answer: Not corporally, but spiritually; to take Him by faith, that is to eat Him spiritually; to become nourished and satisfied spiritually.

Can not Christ be present in the Lord's Supper spiritually, then?

Yes, He certainly can, and His children must experience this often in the emanation or flowing out of His love and favor to their soul.

We have in this way heard about the various errors that exist regarding the Lord's Supper. Now we shall discuss one more aspect of this matter.

When Jesus and His disciples had availed themselves of the Supper, what did they do? In Matt. 26, it says, "And when they had sung an hymn, they went out into the mount of Olives."

Jesus sang a hymn after the sacrament and prior to the bonds and death that He was approaching. That is why we also sing during and after the Supper.

Would this sacrament be for comfort only or

should it be for profit also to the church? Hellenbroek has said, "It is a sacrament which continually strengthens faith." That is why it serves both to profit and to comfort, even though this is not always understood. The disciples would not yet have understood much of what profit there was for them on that first occasion. They had to learn that in retrospect.

It is necessary that I determine whether you understand for whom the Lord's Supper was instituted. Is it for everyone?

Answer: No, only for believers.

But how is that to be understood? Do those who believe with the intellect receive grace by attending the Lord's Supper? No, that is impossible. If that were so, it would be a sign that it has power to give something. That can never be. Faith must have been first granted in the soul for the proper use of the Holy Supper.

But suppose for a moment that it were so, would that faith and the grace received by attendance to the Lord's Supper be increased?

Absolutely not, that is even less possible, because then men would say that the sacrament by itself causes faith and that is erroneous. What does it really do?

The sacrament is for the strengthening of God's people and it was for that purpose the Lord instituted it.

When I eat or drink something does it originate strength? And if I have very little strength, do I at once receive much strength?

No, that is impossible. What is it then? By that food I am adding to the little or great amount of energy that I have. Life is not given by it but is sustained by it.

It is for that reason that Paul says, "For he that eateth and drinketh unworthily, eateth and drinketh damnation to himself." He means to say; The sacrament is not established for those who are not members of the living church.

What profit would anyone, who does not possess grace or faith have of a sign or seal of grace? Who can point out to me a portion of God's Word that says there is profit only for those who believe? No one? Then we shall examine God's Word together and see what it has to say regarding it. Sometimes we can find very instructive observations in God's Word. We read that the daughter of Jairus had died and Jesus had been called to her side. You are all well acquainted with this happening. And when Jesus had brought her back to life, what do we read then? — "He commanded that something should be given her to eat."

Do notice, He didn't say that while she was still dead. He awakened her first and then commanded that food must be given her.

Now, I do not mean that the Lord Jesus was alluding to the Lord's Supper here, O, no, I am using this as an example to show that the dead have no profit of food. I will mention another example.

Paul wrote to the Corinthians, 2 Cor. 3-- "Ye are manifestly declared to be the epistle of Christ ministered by us, written not with ink, but with the

Spirit of the living God; not in tables of stone, but in fleshy tables of the heart."

The living church of God is being portrayed here as a letter; keep this in mind for a moment.

A third example; I pick up a perfectly clean piece of white paper. I write nothing on it; not even one mark. I insert this paper in an envelope, seal it, place a postage stamp on it and to make extra sure I imprint my initials over the edge of the flap in sealing wax. Now I address and mail it. The post office prints their canceling mark on it and carefully deliver it to the proper residence.

Everything turned out as planned. Now, the people to whom this was sent begin to inquisitively open it up, thinking, "What can this be; an important looking letter sealed with wax! There must be something valuable in there."

What a terrible disappointment. There is nothing in there but a piece of clean white paper. Does he still consider this to be a valuable letter? Not anymore. right?

What is it that would actually give it value? Not a neatly written envelope and an impressive looking seal; not correctness in external appearance. No, only the contents. Only a written message would have given the external appearance any value.

The seal on this letter was totally unnecessary because there was nothing in it to be sealed. Do you understand the use of this simile?

A person must be "Christ's written message" inscribed by the Holy Spirit before a seal is proper;

before a sacrament can be truly strenghthening.

But do you know what happens very frequently?

A person is baptized, attends a Christian school, is reared in a Christian manner, makes confession, attends church faithfully, is an honorable citizen; outwardly there is no fault to find in him. A person such as that tends to these thoughts: (and others instruct him in this, too). "It is my duty to partake of the Lord's Supper because I should confess Christ openly and my faith must be strengthened." These pitiable people do as we pointed out in the simile, place a seal on an unwritten letter!

But alas, the truth will be known when death occurs; that it was void of contents; that which had been sealed was not Christ's written message inscribed by the Holy Spirit!

There certainly was a seal of baptism on the forehead but that baptism had never been applied to his soul.

He partook of the Lord's Supper but the faith, intended to be strengthened, was actually not in possession! And what now? Now it will be "For he that eateth and drinketh unworthily, eateth and drinketh damnation to himself." Those seals will make the judgment much heavier.

Boys and girls, I caution you. When you too attend or come to live with the church, but are unconverted and have not been made acquainted with the bloody suffering and death of the Lord Jesus, brought into remembrance and sealed in the administration of the Lord's Supper, do not partake.

But viewing the situation from the other side, should we consider everything coldly? I do not say that. I shall present you with another example:

Two boys sat next to one another in church while the Lord's Supper was being administered. Basically both were unconverted, but there was quite a difference between them. Let's just name them Hank and John.

Hank is very religious and conscientious. He hears the minister's invitation, leaves his place in the pew and joins those at the table.

But John is not so yielding. He really does not want anything to do with religion. He remains in the pew hard and cold, taking nothing of it to himself.

Does John do less wrong in remaining so indifferent toward the service as compared to Hank who goes forward in his unconverted state? No, both are sin in God's sight, the despite as well as the misuse.

What would be far better then? To be exercised under the visible administration of the Holy sacrament thinking, "O, God, I witness the sacrament and see Thy people partaking. I sit here with the sign of baptism upon my forehead but not actually washed of my sins. I merely have a superficial memberhsip in the church. O, that I might have part in it spiritually, too."

That would be a privilege, though one be unconverted, to so witness the administration of the sacrament. The Lord could use this as a means also.

Hellenbroek asks, "What is necessary for

everyone who wants to partake of the Lord's Supper?"

Answer: To examine ones self.

And in what matters must one examine himself?

1. Whether we have a heartfelt sorrow for our sin.
2. Whether we have put our trust in Christ.
3. Whether we express that faith by a holy conduct.

These are three serious matters and in connection with them I shall ask something further:

Who are those invited to the sacrament and who are allowed to come? Or are they one and the same?

No, they are not the same. Only the true, trusting, living members of Christ's body are invited to proclaim His death. But, since even the best minister serving the sacrament is not a discerner of hearts and cannot discern who in the membership make a superficial confession, from those who inwardly bear witness to the faith, therefore, anyone having made public confession and living a life above reproach is permitted to attend.

It is, then, the obligation of a minister and consistory to visit each member of the congregation prior to the Lord's Supper to earnestly question them; also to clearly explain the difference to them in sermons.

There has been much disagreement in this matter. Some English divines held to the opinion for many years that only those who live in spiritual discernment be permitted to the Lord's table and to restrain all others. They were able to maintain this for a certain period of time, but eventually there developed considerable confusion and they saw it was impossible to continue in this.

As long as the world exists the visible church will consist of chaff and wheat. The false church has always existed among the true church and it is impossible for anyone, including ministers, to determine positively who are living members and who are not. The living members only are invited and, in respect to this, everyone is obliged to examine himself (especially in the 3 points Hellenbroek presents above) regarding the relationship between God and his soul.

Further, this examination involves two kinds. One is external and another internal. The external examination concerns a person's abstinence of gross, openly sinful living; which also prohibits him from partaking of the sacraments. The internal examination is a personal matter.

Now Hellenbroek puts this question: "Is it not for children?" "No", says he, "because they cannot examine themselves."

It might be logical to ask, "Cannot children be living members of Christ?" Certainly, that is why it is necessary that we carefully examine this answer together. There are examples in God's Word of persons who feared the Lord while still young; for example, Timothy, Obadiah, Heman and others.

When a child is converted he receives grace and

faith just as surely as does a grown person and he may receive the sacrament for strengthening as well. I do not mean children who have not reached the age of discretion, in other words, infants, but those who can speak with some degree of intelligence.

If a minister notices such a child in his congregation in which it appears something has taken place and of which his thoughts tend to say, "It is very possible the Lord has worked savingly in this child," what should the minister do under such circumstances when speaking to the child? Should he say, "Little boy or girl, you are too young to experience conversion?" That would be foolishness and wickedness too, because the Lord has converted many of His people in their early youth. What then? Would it be more appropriate to say, "Well, my child, you surely have been blest, that you were converted so young. You certainly ought to attend the Lord's Supper?"

Would it be wise to speak in this vein to the child? No, it would show a lack of judgment.

You can see that it is not a simple matter to handle this honorably and just. The most sensible thing for a minister and consistory to do would be to say very little and watch over this child closely, allowing the good work begun within to season, and, trusting the Lord to continue working through. He must not dishearten them in a disparaging or discouraging way but also not immediately beautify with laying on of hands.

This is what Hellenbroek means. When he says that children are not sufficiently capable of examining themselves, he practices exercise of sound judgment.

Of course there can be unusual cases where the Lord glorifies Himself in the knowledge of a child and in such a case the sacrament would not be withheld from such a child. It has happened more than once that the Lord worked in an unusual way in a child and it excelled above many grown ups in spiritual exercise and grace.

But I see the time has gone by and the other catechumens are already waiting to come in.

Boys and girls, meditate upon this serious lesson. In review, I have said; do not attend the Lord's Supper in an unconverted state; but on the other hand, when you sit in church and witness the administration of the sacrament and you say to yourself, "I am unconverted and have no right to it and I will conform to the usual practice and refrain from attending," would not this cold attitude indicate a frightful spiritual state? A state of not being able to receive the holy sacrament? No, that must become a condition you cannot retain because it is a sign that you have no part in the merits of Christ. Hold not a lofty attitude when you abstain from the Lord's Supper having made an orthodox confession, because it should be your greatest grief in prayer to God that you cannot proclaim that you have portion in the death of the Mediator. And may there be among you now, or soon, some for whom this matter is one of close examination. Lay to heart the serious answer of the last of our lesson namely, whether we sincerely repent of our sins. That has serious content! Many people deceive themselves on this particular point.

In some cases, if there had been a change in their lives and they were compelled to forsake certain sins, they think they have genuine sorrow for those sins but it is still far from having sorrow for all their sins. They speak about faith and conversion, breaking with some sins but their heart still cleaves to them. They have not broken with all sins. Why not? Because they never had a heartfelt sorrow for sin as sin.

They chopped the branches because they realized they had damage from them, but the root had never been uncovered, nor lamented.

I do not say that God's people do not sin after their conversion or that they cannot fall into great sins.

Alas yes, the Bible records much of this! This is certain though, every elect sinner, for whom God uncovers his guilt and whom God makes a genuine sinner, shall have heartfelt sorrow for all his sins at the precise moment the blow falls. And he will break with every sin. None are excluded.

Even the most favorite sin becomes an inward loathing. This is true even if he falls into it again later and sometimes living in it for a long period of time.

Many talk about conversion but have never, from

the bottom of their heart, broken with all sin. One of the greatest and deepest of sins is certainly the sin of tolerance of sins, leniency toward sin, first in our heart, then in our home, in the church and finally everywhere. Men tend to leniency in all sin. Just as I have said so often; first it is, give in, then participate and finally conformity to the world. That is the way it goes.

But the Lord is not lenient with sin. He has never been so. The Lord's Supper is a speaking witness of that because the Son of God had to die on account of sin.

He expects, too, that all His sincere people become enemies of sin, not one excepted.

Children, always pay attention whether sin is dealt with correctly in conversation and remember this: if they do not give the genuine account of misery; their account of redemption will not be genuine either. It cannot be any other way.

A sincere soul, who had been made honest by God the Holy Spirit, shall say, "Yes, that is the way I feel the most darling sin must be dealt with and I want that God's justice shall not overlook them.

A definite choice will have to be made. Not to be able to lean on that choice but to learn to know the God of that choice, because He can be the life and breath of a new creature.

May you for the first time or by renewing come into contact with that God. That is the essential fact upon which there can be a heartfelt sorrow for all sin. Only those who do can believe in Christ and

460

that shall surely be revealed in their walk. Depend upon it, that it will be revealed in the fruit and in day by day living!

May the Lord work in and through you and produce within your precious and never dying soul an esteem for the sacrament of the Lord's Supper.

Amid the thronging worshipers
Jehovah will I bless;
Before my brethren, gathered there,
His Name will I confess.
Come, praise Him, ye that fear the Lord,
Ye children of His grace;
With rev'rence sound His glories forth
And bow before His face.

Lesson 39

Of Man's Latter End

Gradually we are nearing the completion of the lessons in our question book. At the beginning we learned of the knowledge concerning God; then the knowledge concerning man and after that the knowledge concerning the Mediator. Now our lesson this afternoon deals·with the latter end of man; not the latter end of an angel or of the Mediator. Was man actually created to have a latter end?

He was created to serve God, to be obedient and finally to live with Him glorifying and praising Him in eternal bliss. But man broke his probation resulting in the threatening sentence being pronounced: "Thou shalt surely die." That is, a threefold death, physical, spiritual, and eternal!

To which death do the questions we have learned refer to? Spiritual, physical or eternal?

Answer: The physical death.

That is clear enough. The first question bears that out: Is man to live forever?

Answer: No, Hebrews 9:27, "It is appointed unto man once to die, and after this the judgment."

Doth every part of man die?

Answer: No, the soul is immortal.

Can this be proven from God's Word, that the soul is immortal?

Answer: Matt. 10:28, "Fear not them which kill the body, but are not able to kill the soul; but rather fear him which is able to destroy both soul and body in hell."

The soul is that part of a person whereby we are able to live and reason; that part which God infused into Adam directly, without use of means, after he had formed his body by use of means. When we speak, then, of physical death, or of man's latter end, or as we usually speak of it, of death, what takes place at that time?

The soul is the life of a person. Without a soul a body is a dead mass, a form which God had made from the earth. "Dust thou art and to dust shalt thou return" speaks God's Word. What takes place when life, that is the soul, departs the body? Is it removed visably or audibly?

No, a person sees nothing. When a kerosene lamp dies out, the light gradually becomes dimmer and dimmer until it is a faint flickering light and then dies out. One can see it but not hear it. It is different with the soul. A person can see a body gradually diminish and life die out, but one cannot hear or see the soul leave the body. Dying itself, comes about in various ways, but it is always visible. The body becomes cold and stiff, movements cease and when the last breath is there, it is announced, "The end is come, death has entered in."

I have seen many people die, but very few in the same manner. I stood at the death bed of a strong intelligent man lately. He was a young man and sick but a short time. He had always been a farmer and enjoyed his work. He employed all his strength with heart and soul in his work involving horses, cows, land and fields. That was his pleasure and his life.

But now he was at the point of death. I was at the bedside where the family was standing, some of them were crying. I said to these people, "Do you see now what takes place when the Lord comes carrying out the punishment of sin? God first took the strength from this man, he had been healthy and strong but suddenly he became weak and was unable to do anything. Then the Lord took away the desire for working; with horses, cows, plows, and sowing. What had taken all his attention means nothing to him anymore.

Then there is the loss of mind. He is no longer rational and says all sorts of strange things.

Now the Lord will come very soon to take the soul away. That is the last. Then it is brought to an end because the body cannot live without the soul."

It was plain to see that this man's life became weaker just as the flame of a candle becomes smaller and finally, when the wick and the wax are consumed, it flickers out.

But death does not always comes as calmly as that.

No, I have experienced seeing it other than that. It happened to a boy who had lived an extraordinary wicked life in the world. He had known how he should live, but he broke all restraints. He suddenly became ill and was to die in the prime of his life. But just prior to dying his conscience struck him fearfully. He pulled the hair from his head and bumped his head against the wall.

464

It was at though he had a vision of the damnation awaiting him and the devil standing at his side to drag him as the prey into it. It was so terrible, hardly anyone dared to remain in the room with him.

Thus it is, that the way it can also go sometimes when an unregenerate person dies. The Lord is sovereign in all things, also in the manner He allows someone to die.

Now Hellenbroek asks: How many places of abode are there for souls after death?

Answer: Only two, hell or heaven. Matt. 7:13, "Wide is the gate and Broad is the way that leadeth unto destruction, and many there be which go in thereat; but strait is the gate, and narrow is the way which leadeth unto life, and few there be that find it."

We shall return to enlarge on this later. Then follows the question: Do souls depart thither immediately after death?

Answer: Yes, as appears in Lazarus and the rich man. Luke 16:22, 23, "The rich man immediately lifted up his eyes in hell, and Lazarus was carried into Abraham's bosom."

The length of time it takes the soul to pass from the body to its predestined eternal home is impossible to determine with certainty.

God's Word does not say anything about it, and the hidden things are for the Lord so we must not involve ourselves with this. The small number of God's children who have been deeply exercised in this mystery say, "It is only a moment." Even

Jesus refrained telling the murderer, merely saying, "Today shalt thou be with Me in Paradise."

Now Hellenbroek puts forth another peculiar question: "Is there no purgatory?" "No", says he. The Spirit instructed John, "Write Blessed are the dead which die in the Lord from henceforth." So, it is without an intervening time of purgatory. And Jesus' word to the murderer was plain in this respect. He said, "Today"; not "After a brief stay in purgatory."

What has this question reference to; do you know who they are who believe in purgatory?

Answer: The Roman Catholics.

Right. These pitiable people believe that there is a vestibule between death and their entrance into heaven. They call this vestibule purgatory. Literally, it means refining or purifying with fire. And do you know who enter there, according to their belief?

They are souls which have received grace and , as such , appointed for heaven, but have not yet made complete reparation for their actual sins. Very wicked people, then, do not enter purgatory but go directly to hell.

But it is, supposedly, a place of purification for the faithful where they must bear their last punishment for sin before they can enter into heaven. If the family of such a deceased send up much prayer and have the priest say the mass for them, the duration of purgatory can be shortened. The more money given by the survivors to "the church" the sooner they can go to heaven.

Of course, it is a frightful mockery. A person reads nothing of this anywhere in God's Word. Yet they think they can prove it from the words of Jesus. When the Lord said, Matt. 12:32 "---but whosoever speaketh against the Holy Ghost, it shall not be forgiven him, neither in this world, neither in the world to come," they interpret it to mean that other sins can be forgiven in purgatory! But the Lord very plainly intended: These sins are not pardonable here on earth and since heaven and hell are beyond the point of forgiveness this blasphemy is never forgiven. Throughtout the entire Word of God it is plain that there are but two ways described. This doctrine of purgatory, along with the entire religion of popery, is an   assault upon the work of the Mediator; as though His work was not complete and a person must suffer punishment to supplement it! It is too wicked to even talk about, because it is a repudiation of God's Gift of His Own Son for the work of redemption.

We shall go a bit further.

We said earlier that all men are subject to a threefold death brought about by the sin in Paradise. They received this in consequence.

But do all people undergo death in the threefold way? No. All undergo spiritual death. Except for the Lord Jesus all people are born Spiritually dead. And almost everyone, elect as well as reprobate, must die the physical death, experiencing the separation of soul and body.

Who are the only ones, as far as we know, who, having received extraordinary grace, are exceptions to this rule? (Enoch and Elijah). God took their soul and body simultaneously into heaven.

It is without saying, that, all the elect are delivered from eternal death. That death no longer has dominion over them.

We would explain it this way then; Spiritual death reigns over all unconverted persons as long as they live. It reigns over the elect till the time they are converted.

Physical death reigns over converted and unconverted alike (except for those mentioned above).

Finally eternal death shall have dominion only over unbelievers, because they shall enter into eternal pain; but the righteous into eternal life.

If physical death has its effect upon all people without exception, would there not be some difference, though, between dying and dying? I would think so! The instruction in God's Word and the catechism states plainly that death for God's people is none other than a departure from this life and a passage to eternal life. When God's people are in the proper spirit, they live as strangers here on earth and sin is a burden to them. When death comes it releases them from this burden and in heaven they will never be able to sin again.

But what about the unconverted?

They find pleasure in sin, vanities and all sorts of worldly amusements. When such a person dies, death disposes him of everything in which he had delight and so, deprives him of his greatest pleasure.

Do you see what a great difference there is between dying and dying? There is not, necessarily, a difference in the death of the body, there being very little difference sometimes. Some unconverted people die sound of mind, calm and without fear. And there are cases where God's Children die with great bodily pain and sometimes bereft of sound minds.

But it is the manner in which they die that makes the difference.

Now I shall ask you something. Pay attention: we were all in accord that an unconverted person by nature finds delight in sin and when death comes he is deprived of that delight. Does this mean there will be sin in hell?

Answer: Yes.

Well, now, if sin is his delight, can he not sin just as much in hell as he did here?

Answer: There is no delight for it then, O, that is the main point. Death does not release him from sin; no, only from the delight of it. Sin will follow eternally.

There will be eternal sinning in hell but never again with delight, always with remorse. Only God's people are released from sin, and, in heaven it is impossible to sin anymore. By grace the desire to sin is taken away from them here in this life.

It is simply one way or the other; death releasing us from sin, or death removing delight in sin, but, in a remorseful abhorrence, sin accompanying us eternally.

It states in the aforementioned text, that the gate is wide and the way broad that leads to destruction and that there are many that go in that way; but contrariwise, few go in at the strait gate. You would think, if that broad way leads to destruction, why do

469

many continue to walk that way? How did they get on that way? Who knows the answer?

Answer: They were born on it.

That is the way it is. The Lord did not create us on a way of destruction, but because of our fall we are all born on that way and we must be placed on the narrow way. It does not say either that a person places himself on that narrow way, but it emphatically states, "Few there be that find it." Would the few who sought it find it by themselves? No, not by themselves. It is recorded in both the Old and New Testaments, "None seek after God;" Psalm 14, and Romans 3, "No, not one." How, then, could those few have found that gate?

The Lord says, "I draw you with cords of love" and, "I lead you in a way you have not known." In that connection, Myseras says, "The soul that seeks God is found of Him."

It is easily understood how they come to that narrow way.

Now, one more thing. It says, "Few". This is consistent with all of God's Word, because it also explains that Christ's Church is a small flock.

But how are we to understand then, what John says, "A great multitude, which no man could number?" Something here appears to be contradictory. It reminds me of a preacher who went on a trip. While he was in a certain place he became involved in a conversation with a man who had approached him even though they were strangers. Toward the end the man asked "You are not a member of the Great Church are you?" "Yes, I am" said the preacher. "I do belong to the Great was about to be buried. Dominie Jansen, who had been one of Barneveld's former pastors, officiated at this funeral. When they arrived at the graveside and Dominie Jansen began to speak, he removed his hat. His opening words were, "People, I noticed something while this funeral procession came along the way to the cemetery."

All the people looked at him in a perplexed sort of way, no doubt thinking, "Dominie, what strange language to be using at a graveside!"

But he proceeded further saying, "Do you know what I saw? A man with a horse and wagon. When he saw us coming he drove his horse and wagon to the side of the road, removed his cap and stood in reverent attitude until we had passed by.

Why did that man do this? It was not without reason, even though he may not have realized why himself.

People, that man did so because the Majesty of God passed by! Death passed by and that speaks of the Majesty of God. The Lord declares therewith this utmost truth, 'I have remained Who I was, God. I have maintained My justice and honor. The soul that sins shall die.'

So, my people, the death of this child is a divine sermon on the Majesty of God!"

The dominie continued with that trend of thought and everyone gave their close attention. He has since passed away and his soul is in heaven.

Boys and girls, always remember to be reverent when someone who has died is being buried. Calmly demount from your bicycle and wait until the body has passed by. Not that one must have reverence for the body as such, but because of God's call spoken to you by it.

We shall close now. May the Lord reveal your spiritual deadness by his vitalizing grace. Then you will not be able to live on in your deadness as we all do in our natural state.

May He bless these truths to your eternal living soul before death comes upon you and it becomes forever too late.

Dust to dust, the mortal dies,
Both the foolish and the wise;
None forever can remain,
Each must leave his hoarded gain.
Yet within their heart they say
That their houses are for aye,
That their dwelling places grand
Shall for generations stand.

Though in life he wealth attained,
Tho' the praise of men he gained
He shall join those gone before,
Where the light shall shine no more.
Crowned with honor tho' he be,
Highly gifted, strong and free
If he be not truly wise,
Man is like the beast that dies.

matter of comprehension. He said, "Behold, I show you a mystery."

Everyone must be raised up. And, what will happen to those on earth who have not yet died when the trumpet shall sound before the judgment? What will happen to them? Will it be necessary for them to first die, too? No, at a certain point of time, in an instant, they shall be changed by Divine power.

What will be the nature of that change? Their mortal bodies shall become immortal. The apostle was steadfast in his belief that this would happen when he said, "For the trumpet **shall** sound; (he was emphasizing the certainty of it) and the dead shall be raised incorruptible and we shall be changed."

What are your thoughts about this? Would the doctrine of resurrection be one of comfort or of terror?

It will be a great comfort to those who have been sanctified by the blood of Christ to know they will soon receive an immortal body with which they can magnify and glorify the Lord in the absence of sin.

O, that incomprehensible resurrection! It is a point of worship and astonishment to the Church. The apostle was so overcome that he called out, "So when this corruptible shall have put on incorruption - then shall be brought to pass the saying that is written, Death is swallowed up in victory. O, death, where is thy sting, O, grave where is thy victory?"

This is the glory the apostles saw in the resurrection; death is swallowed up in victory!

Was there not a reason to be joyful in anticipation

of his presence at the glorious resurrection? And this joy is not exclusive to the people of God in their sojourn here on earth, but it is also shared by the Church triumphant in heaven; the souls of the deceased faithful; those who are now the blessed spirits round about the throne. These have joy too, and do you know why?

Because there exists a certain imperfection prior to the judgment day, that is, before the last resurrection.

Now without a doubt, you are thinking, "But dominie, this is one time you are in error! That is just impossible!"

No, I am not in error. I shall explain it to you.

All elect who had lived and died on earth from Adam on down are now in heaven, perfectly holy and without a body. Heaven for them is being in God's presence. Heaven without God would be no heaven nor would it be a place of bliss. It is not the magnificence of the place that makes it blissful. No, the Psalmist says it this way, "He that is our God is the God of salvation," not, the place is our salvation.

But now to continue — the souls are therefore perfect, God is perfect, the magnificence and holiness is also perfect, and yet with all that perfection there is an imperfection, that is, the souls alone as spirits are awaiting the reunion with their bodies. That is the imperfection in the church triumphant prior to the resurrection. Reverently speaking, the blissful spirits look forward in longing to that great day when the full reunion takes place.

It is not a sinful or impatient yearning they have, but a holy desire; quietly submitting to the will of God as long as He pleases to tarry.

Would not these residents of heaven know when that day shall come?

The Lord Jesus says in Matt. 24:36 "But of that day and hour knoweth no man, no, not angels in heaven, but My Father only."

But even though they do not know when that day will come, they know it certainly will! That was their comfort when they were on earth! The apostle powerfully opposed those who denied the resurrection of the dead! He said, "Now if Christ be preached, that He rose from the dead, how say some among you that there is no resurrection of the dead? He was explaining here that if there was no resurrection of the dead, then is Christ not risen. As a consequence, if Christ be not risen then is your faith and our preaching in vain. What profit is there in my testimony to you if indeed it has not happened? Then we are nothing more than false witnesses, because our preaching did testify of God, that He raised up Christ!

And furthermore, if there is no resurrection, then all the dead are lost. This would include those who are fallen asleep in Christ hoping in the blessed resurrection as Christ was raised up.

And then he concludes by pointing out that if in this short span of life, we only have hoped in Christ, and do not believe that we shall be raised up even as He was, to live with Him eternally, we are all men most miserable!

But now follows his cry of triumph in the abounding

faith of the resurrection, calling out in a way of rejoicing, "But now is Christ risen from the dead." He would say, "I am positive, people, because I saw Him myself. And last of all He was seen of me! He is risen and He is consequently the first fruit of those that are asleep"

The Lord established an order in the resurrection, Christ was the first and then follows those who are Christ's.

And why was it necessary that He be resurrected first? In order that, as all died in the covenant head Adam, they can now also be made alive in their covenant head Christ. "For He must reign till he hath put all enemies under his feet."

Who is the last enemy?

"The last enemy that shall be destroyed is death." (1 Cor. 13).

Paul would say here, "You must understand, Corinthians, if the Lord took the souls only of His elect into heaven, and left their bodies to repose and perish in the earth, then death would retain a great victory." It is true, their souls had been prepared, but, God had created man with a soul and a body. Adam glorified God in his body as well as in his soul. Now, because of sin, we are subjected to a threefold death. The body is subject to physical or natural death. If the body is left to lay in the earth or in the sea and perish, natural death will have kept its prey and Christ will have conquered spiritual and eternal death for the elect in vain. They live spiritually in heaven and eternal death will have no effect upon them, but they are not able to rise above this natural death.

Their bodies are lost to them.

Would then Christ have been a King over all enemies?

I would think not.

That is why death is the last enemy to be conquered. This includes natural death. All the elect will have returned to them a glorified body even as perfect as it was before the fall; but now immortal and incorruptible; unable to sin or to die.

Just as surely as the Head is raised up with a glorified body by the Father, so surely shall the members receive this too. Otherwise how could it become a body, and, how shall they be conformed to the image of His Son? Romans 8. Then, after the great resurrection at the last day, the whole body of Christ shall be perfectly complete.

But on the other hand, the unconverted will also have their bodies restored to them. However, this will not be a reason to rejoice for them. No, to the contrary, it will be a great regret and grief! O, the miserable condemned ones, whose souls are already in hell will wish they never had a body! They will also desire in great despair that they never have it returned to them because that will aggravate their misery. And why? Because then they shall know what it is to the full, to have been a person and to have sinned with every member of the body. Because then, upon recovery of their bodies, each member of the body will be in pain.

Does God's Word indicate that?

Yes, James says that the tongue is a fire, a world of iniquity. With our tongue we curse God our

485

Creator and condemn our neighbor who is made in the image of God.

John says in Rev. 16:10, "And they gnaw their tongues for pain!" Every member of the body which has sinned shall feel punishment. What member is free of that? Think about this; we have sought out vanity with our eyes, have heard it with our ears, spoken it with our mouths, walked in forbidden places with our feet, and done wickedness with our hands, etc. The worst is to carry about a burning conscience, a flame of fire within.

And what kind of situtation will that be? 1st. Never being able to approve that God is fair in punishing this way and 2nd, never able to take over your own guilt and accept the fact that you have deserved this punishment.

If it were possible one would take a respite but there is no opportunity. They will be constantly cursing God and each other, and despairingly cry; "Had I, had I;" but—too late. O, those dreadful words, "Forever too late!"

There will be a clear recollection of all that has taken place in the world. Do not expect the possibility of insanity or numbness. No, each and every sin will be crystal clear in one's remembrance. That is why it will be unbearable, but it will have to be borne eternally.

My poor boys and girls, if I could only make you understand what hell is and how fearful the last resurrection will be for all those who are not reconciled with God!

May you be moved to lamentation and aroused to

jealousy. O, the great difference that will be brought to full revelation in that judgment day! A multitude so large no one can number, standing with glorified bodies on the right hand of the Mediator who in His Holy human nature with the same body is standing in their midst as their oldest Brother. And on the left hand a similar innumerable multitude of hell-deserving rebels who shall hear, "Depart from me, ye cursed, into everlasting fire!"

The first due to free grace and the second caused by their own guilt.

May the Lord warn you and bring you to account in your tender youth. May He set you as a monument of His eternal love.

What a blessed day that will be for God's people when their souls and bodies shall forever be free of wanting to sin, nor will they be able to sin in thought, word or deed. It is no wonder that the apostle was so joyful in prospect of the resurrection!

May the Lord who is bountiful in grace place you, to the glory of His Name, among those to whom He shall say, "Come, ye blessed of My Father, inherit the kingdom prepared for you from the foundation of the world." May He implant within your sighing body of sin and death the need to cry out, "Eternity come quickly, that I may be in your presence." So be it.

> The man that fears the Lord
> God's way shall understand
> His soul shall ever dwell at ease
> His children rule the land.
>
> Psalter No. 62; 1.

Lesson 41

Of the Last Judgment
and Everlasting Life

We shall recite the very last lesson in our catechism book this afternoon.

The Lord in His long suffering has allowed that we began these lessons together and now end them together. It could have been otherwise, one of us could have been removed by death.

Last week we heard something of the lesson on the Resurrection. Our lesson this week begins:

What will follow the resurrection of the body?

Answer: The final judgment.

Will there be a final judgment?

Answer: "Yes, Acts 17:31, God hath appointed a day in which He will judge the world in righteousness by that Man whom He had ordained."

It is peculiar that Hellenbroek would speak of, "The Last Judgment." Would there be other judgments?

Yes, since the fall of man there have been all sorts of judgments; it would take too much time to mention all of them here.

Who can name a few from the Old Testament?

Answer: The flood.

That was a great judgment involving the whole world. It destroyed all living creatures except Noah, his family, the creatures with him in the ark and those that were able to live in water.

This was a universal judgment.

Then there was the overthrow of Sodom & Gomorrah, also no small judgment. That was a local judgment.

Then we have the judgment of Korah, Dathan and Abiram who were carried away alive into hell. This was a personal judgment and an example to all who actually witnessed it and for those who were told about it later.

There were many other judgments we could mention such as the carrying away of the Israelites into Babylon, later on their servitude under the Romans, etc. The Lord often placed judgments upon nations too. There were plagues, famine, wars, etc.

The Lord can place judgments on families too, such as severe sickness, poverty and all sorts of chastisements. I do not say that all sicknesses and poverty are judgments, but the Lord can use them as such. All these judgments have taken place during the world's existence and most of them are temporary; there is an end to them.

But we have been taught of the last or final judgment, after which there shall not follow another.

1. That it will be an actuality, we can read in Acts. 17.

2. The time it will happen is known only to God. No one knows the hour, but it does say there is a day appointed, so, it is a certainty.

3. By whom the judgment will be directed, is the Son of God. "By that man whom He hath ordained; whereof He hath given assurance unto all men, in that He hath raised Him from the dead."

4. Where shall it happen? On earth, in the sea or in the air?

The Lord Jesus speaks of this in Matt. 24:30,

"And then shall appear the sign of the Son of man in heaven; and then shall all the tribes of the earth mourn and they shall see the Son of man coming in the clouds of heaven with power and great glory."

5. Who are the persons to be judged?

The devil and all mankind.

Perhaps you would say, "Must the devil be judged too, has he not already received his punishment?"

Yes, he has for his first sin; having opposed God, wanting to elevate himself above Him, and so fell from Him. For that reason he was actually cast out of heaven and eternally separated from God. There has never been an opportunity for him to repent. He is eternally bound with chains and banished to hell; his own dwelling place.

But do you know what he will be judged for?

1. For deceiving Eve. Sentence was pronounced upon him in Paradise "It shall bruise thy head." This matter will be settled with him at the last judgment day.

2. For attacking Christ during His sojourn upon earth and for his attempt to make Him fall.

3. For his seeking to deceive the elect from Adam and Eve's time on down, as long as the world existed.

He will be held accountable for these three matters in the judgment. God will settle with him then and shall send him to his eternal habitation, a lake of fire.

Can this judgment concerning the devil be proven from God's Word?

Yes, you will remember when Jesus came to the other side of the sea into the country of the Gergesenes he met two persons possessed with devils crying out to Him, "What have we to do with thee, Jesus, thou Son of God? Art Thou come hither to torment us before the time?"

That is what the devils called out from within those people. From that it is plainly evident that they knew exactly what was awaiting him in the great judgment. But they also knew that it was not yet the last day and for that reason they were afraid that Jesus, their Judge, would torture them before the appointed time.

But the Lord does nothing before the appointed time judging devils included. He was revealing there how the devils by their own actions are subject unto Him. They pleaded with Him that He would permit them to enter into the swine. He made manifest there His Divine authority.

Secondly, after the devil, all the people will also be judged. Paul speaks of this in 2 Cor. 5:10 "For we must all appear before the judgment seat of Christ; that everyone may receive the things done in his body, according to that he hath done, whether it be good or bad."

So then, no one will be overlooked. The Son of God will appear visibly in His human nature on the clouds. He will dispatch His innumerable angels, who loudly sounding the trumpet, will gather His elect together.

The Lord speaks personally of this happening. And what did John see in the Divine revelation? He saw the devil, who deceived the people, cast into

491

the lake of fire and brimstone where he will be tormented day and night for ever and ever.

And what else did he see?

A great white throne and Him that sat on it, from whose face the earth and the heaven fled away.

And what followed? Then he saw the dead, small and great standing before God, so, the resurrection was completed, before the judgment was begun. And when all were raised up, a court of Justice was set up and the final judgment began, which would be an eternal pronouncement for every creature.

What marks the opening of the judgment? John tells us plainly, "And the books were opened."

What kind of books would they have been?

Just common books of paper or parchment?

No, the term book is used here in a figurative sense.

1. The book of God's own Word will be opened; the one He Himself had given to His people; the Bible. Many people have mocked with it, and others never give it any consideration, but the Lord will one time give it consideration, you can count on that. Even if we have never asked for it here or taken the time to read it, God will make demands regarding His word and it will not return unto Him void.

2. The book of God's Providence will be opened. showing how He has cared for everyone throughout their entire life and always has done nothing but good for them.

3. The book of God's omniscience, (infinite knowledge) will be opened and, oh, what will then make its appearence! All hidden things will then be

brought to light. Will not then thousands of persons cry out, "Mountains, fall on us, and hills, cover us, from the face of Him, Him who sits upon the throne!" You can be sure that cry will be made when the book of God's omniscience, pertaining to everyone, shall be opened.

4. The book of each one's conscience will also be opened! There shall not even one conscience remain closed that day, even if it had till death been seared shut with a hot iron.

All consciences will then open to an extent never experienced here, and the conscience will have to acquiesce to all that is disclosed from the book of God's omniscience, assent to each and every accusation, and acknowledge all guilt!

The book of the conscience will be a dreadful witness in that day against the wicked; a testifier that every sentence is just.

O, boys and girls, consider all your conscience will have to witness against you in the last judgment.

And even as John said, "And the books were opened" in the plural number, he follows up with, "And another book was opened, which is the book of life", in the singular number. So:

5. The book of eternal election is opened; the book of life of the Lamb! Then the chaff shall be separated from the grain, and the weeds pulled out from among the wheat. On earth everything is grown up together, but at the harvest, that means, at the end of the world, He shall send out the reapers, the angels. They will bind up the weeds into bundles to be burned, but will bring the wheat into

493

God's eternal barn. In nature it is inevitable even with the best farming practices, that there will be a kernal of wheat among the chaff and vice versa.

But that is impossible in the spiritual harvest. Not one elect will stand on the left hand but neither will a condemned person stand on the right hand. Those, whose names are written in the Lamb's Book of life; those, for whom the Lamb made perfect satisfaction, will be placed on the right hand of the Son of God by angels. But those, whose names are not found written in the Lamb's Book of Life will be cast into the lake of fire. Rev. 20.

Furthermore, there shall not be one elect missing, because they all together make up the body of which Christ is the head. There shall not one finger be left behind. Even as a natural body cannot miss a member without disfiguring it and rendering it imperfect, so the body of Christ will not miss even one member. Moreover, there will be nothing defective or missing in its members. Everything will be perfect. He shall present them as a chaste virgin to His Father.

We had mentioned previously that no one knows when the day of judgment shall be. It shall be as related in I Thess. 5:2, " - the day of the Lord so cometh as a thief in the night." It tells us in Matt. 24:14, "And this gospel of the kingdom shall be preached in all the world for a witness unto all nations; and then shall the end come." It says also, that then the falling away shall be at its greatest and there will be all sorts of judgments on the earth.

Would there then be elect still living on earth?

The world will not really perish until the very last one is gathered in, certainly?

That is true, but there will be people, and God's people among them, living on the earth that last day.

It makes a difference whether the elect have been gathered in or have already entered into heaven.

When anyone is converted unto God, the soul is indeed gathered in; grace has been revealed in him, but he still might be required to live 60 or 70 years upon earth before he may enter into heaven.

It does not mention anywhere in God's Word that all the elect must first have entered heaven, and only the reprobates left on the earth, when the world perishes.

No, it does not say that. Only that all the elect shall first be gathered in, and therefore some of them shall be living on the earth.

There will not be anyone, however, living under the seal of election who still needs to be converted.

It is clear that there will still be a portion of the Church Militant upon earth as shown in I Thess 4:16, 17, where Paul speaking about the last judgment, says, "For the Lord Himself shall descend from heaven with a shout, with a voice of the archangel, and with the trump of God; and the dead in Christ shall rise first. Then we which are alive and remain shall be caught up together with them in the clouds, to meet the Lord in the air; and so shall we ever be with the Lord."

Some think, that Paul here thought the coming of Christ on the clouds was so imminent, that he himself would still be living. But it is also possible that he with "we", meant a part of the church of which he also was a member, and so spoke only in the name of the Church Militant.

In either case, it is clear that there shall be children of God living upon earth who will not die but shall be changed in the twinkling of an eye. Symbols of this are given in the great flood when there was a Noah left on earth, and when the Lord oveturned Sodom and Gomorrah, he first led the righteous Lot out of it.

The Apostle also gives here in Thessalonians a sequence of the events. He says, "We which are alive and remain unto the coming of the Lord shall not prevent them which are asleep." The resurrection shall take place first, and after that the judgment and the receiving up into eternal life.

Helenbroek asks in question 10, "What will be pronounced on the righteous? "

Answer: Matt. 25:34, "Come, ye blessed of My Father, inherit the kingdom prepared for you, from the foundation of the world."

What sentence will He pass on the wicked?

Answer: "Depart from me, ye cursed, into everlasting fire, prepared for the devil and his angels." Matt. 25:41.

What will follow the final judgment?

Eternal life or eternal damnation!

O, the unspeakable difference that shall be witnessed at that time. In this world millions of people experience the same lot and portion in life. They are born, eat, drink, work, become sick, have accidents, prosperity, adversity, happiness, sorrow. All these things occur in the lives of both the righteous and the wicked. But then will be seen the great difference between those who served God and those who have not served Him. Persons who were most closely associated here, shall be separated an incomprehensible distance apart from one another! Alas, sometimes here there can arise a great separation between two people, even in the same family.

Have you ever seen a closer relationship than exists between twins? And yet, even though Jacob and Esau were born as twins and reared in the same house, there will be an eternal separation between them. Now this difference involves their souls, but soon in the last judgment it will be visable to the whole world that Jacob shall stand on the right hand and Esau on the left.

Boys and girls, give serious thought to these things. Do you have a converted father or mother (or both) who are carrying you in prayer unto a Triune God?

O, if you, yourself, remain unconverted you shall not stand with your parents on the right hand even though they loved you so much. No more prayers will be made for you there. But, do you know what shall take place? Converted parents shall see their unconverted children and converted children shall see their unconverted parents standing on the left side without the least concern for them, because at one time in their lives they experienced a love for God transcending all else and that love at judgment day shall then be completely perfected. The Lord

Jesus said, "He that loveth father or mother more than me is not worthy of me."

But perhaps you are saying inwardly, "Is not that hard hearted?" No, it is not. They have, through grace, experienced here in time a moment when they were in accord with their own damnation and God's justice in punishing of sin. If they were not able to excuse themselves, would they be able to excuse their dearest relatives on earth? No, they will be able to say, "Amen" upon their sentence without shedding tears.

Through God's grace they have come to love Him above any creature. Every affectionate regard for relatives will fall away on that day.

That day will be a day of finality for every creature from Adam on down to the very last one to be born.

But in contraposition to the indescribable bliss experienced by God's people, will be the indescribable state of those on the left hand!

The bottomless pit shall be opened and the angels as ministerng spirits shall drive them to the place of the damned where there shall be nothing but cursing. God's wrath shall burn eternally there because guilt will always be present. There the. dreadful flames of God's Holy justice will be in constant glowing heat, without ceasing.

God Himself will not be present in that place, nor will His love or favor, or the least bit of His goodness.

The requirements as He had revealed to man in Paradise shall be present there, namely, to obey Him perfectly. This requirement shall remain eternally upon all for whom Chirst had not made the satisfaction.

Why should this requirement continue eternally?

Answer: Because God is also eternal.

It is for that reason, too, that punishment will last eternally, as we have to do with an eternal God.

Would there be stages in this eternal punishment?

Yes, in the main there shall be two stages: they first shall suffer in soul only, but after the resurrection in both soul and body. A person's soul departs to its eternal destiny as soon as it escapes the body. Now, you were taught earlier that the soul is a rational and immortal spirit, through which we live and use reason.

It remains so when it is at its eternal place. So, when the soul of an unconverted person arrives in hell it is immediately aware of it and will have full consciousness of where it is. The soul, the spirit with the faculty of reason, will have to say, "Here I am at a place from which I shall never escape."

The soul will also be perfectly aware that it bore God's image and offended it. It will recall its sinful behavior upon earth. The soul, without the least hope, will have full consciousness and conviction, that these things are true, even though it never realized or believed it in its life time.

In addition, it will anticipate the last day in complete despair, at which time it knows the resurrection will take place. It knows it shall have the return of its body, the body in which it sinned. All of this will burn brightly and clearly in the conscience. It will never be able to say that God is unrighteous, but, also, it will never be able to acknowledge that He deals justly because that would give some relief.

Yet under all this, a person remains a rational creature. You need not think he goes to damnation as a stick or block of wood; no, he remains a rational creature. But, do you know what he will do while aware of all this? He cannot refuse to recognize God for what he is, nor can he accept Him as an actuality; nothing remains but to curse and slander Him. He not only has a desire to sin, but actually does it and that forever.

O, children, reflect upon these three matters:

1st. About the place where all wicked persons shall finally come, and that it will be your place if your are not converted.

2nd. Just consider what your actions will be there, and

3rd. Earnestly think upon the company with which you will be associated; devils, condemned angels, persons of whom you had fear when on earth, wild heathens, murderers, degenerate persons, Christians in name only and strange spirits. These will be your company there. And all of these were once created after God's image!

You will be present at the last judgment with your entire body, the body that you now carefully sustain, wash, clothe and sometimes adorn.

Not one member of your body will be missing and you will know how you used each one. Every thought and desire will be recollected to your unspeakable remorse and despair. Every condemned person and spirit will be incensed with hatred toward God and each other.

Statisticians have calculated that one person dies every second. Think of the significance of that! Without interruption, souls streaming unceasingly through the gates of death to their eternal damnation, and each one then expecting the sound of the last trumpet.

Everyone shall come in possession of his own immaterial and imperishable body, and, similar to the way men rub salt into meat to preserve it from spoil, so, "Everyone shall be salted with fire", (Mark 9:49) so that they never will be able to decompose.

Do you understand, now, something of the solemnity for man to have been born upon this earth? And also, how grossly wrong sin is, contrasted with a Holy God? One must be moved to lamentation and seek God's grace while there is still time.

Many people on earth are sufficient unto themselves. They see their lives are in peril and seek to become saved for their own selfish interests. But God's people have regard for God. They personally become the guilty one; not Adam. It is so necessary that we truly accept the fact that we have terminated our relationship with God (though God has not terminated His relationship with us).

If one may experience through the influence of the Holy Spirit an admission that there is a reason for his lost condition, it must also follow that a possibility to be saved is made known. From the sinner's viewpoint it is an eternally lost cause. But, if the Lord reveals that He has become reconciled to the world of the elect in Christ Jesus from eternity, then such a soul realizes salvation is truly possible.

O, if such a person is given to believe that a perfect reconciliation has taken place for him and he is one of those known of God, who shall stand on the right hand of the King after the last resurrection in the Judgment Day, then that soul is utterly astonished and understands the words spoken, "Death is swallowed up in victory. Death where is thy sting, hell where is thy victory?" He is redeemed from the spiritual and eternal death. Natural death is then only a passage to eternal life.

For God's peoples' sin becomes a damnation on earth and for that reason they heartily desire to be released from its oppressive power. When they are in their place spiritually, they experience no greater sorrow on earth than to find themselves in sin. That is why they look forward with eager desire to the last day of their life. Not because heaven will be a nice place, no, you must not think that heaven is just a blissful situation without having reality. That would be an incorrect representation of it.

Heaven actually exists. When the earth has been purified after the Day of Judgment and the elements have melted in fire, there actually shall be, besides a new heaven, a new earth without sin or imperfections. God's Word says that the new heaven and new earth will be perfect, beautiful and holy, and will be possessed by the Godly as their inheritance.

Glory and bliss will be there because they can then give God the honor which is due Him in pefection and without sin.

O, the transcendent bliss that shall exist there!

John saw not only a new heaven but also a new earth wherein dwelt righteousness.

Everything will be thoroughly pure and clean, sin burned out of it by fire, and the visable consequences of sin wiped out eternally.

The seed sanctified of God shall inherit that blessed earth.

If a child of God receives an impression of this, he is not concerned that he has not many worldly possessions.

God's people may in faith at times catch a glimpse of that last day, after which they shall rule with Christ and shall possess as an inheritance the purified earth. It is inherited because the Son of God is now their oldest Brother from whom they receive salvation as an inheritance.

O, children, we have come to the end of our catechism book. You have turned the last page and so also one day you will turn the last page of your life, whether it be a longer or shorter one.

May God bless the contents of these lessons which you have learned, in beginning or by renewal.

And may He set you as a praise on earth, to continue to magnify His worthy name gloriously. So be it.

> How shall the young direct their way?
> What light shall be their perfect guide?
> Thy Word, O Lord, will safely lead
> If in its wisdom they confide.
>
> Psalter No. 322:1